AF605803

Deleuze, The Dark Precursor

RETHINKING THEORY

Stephen G. Nichols and Victor E. Taylor, *Series Editors*

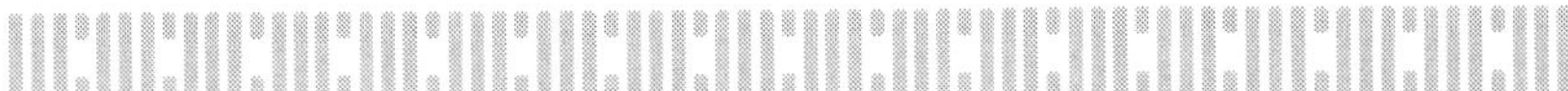

Deleuze, The Dark Precursor

Dialectic, Structure, Being

ELEANOR KAUFMAN

The Johns Hopkins University Press
Baltimore

Printed in the United States of America on acid-free paper
9 8 7 6 5 4 3 2 1

The Johns Hopkins University Press
2715 North Charles Street
Baltimore, Maryland 21218-4363
www.press.jhu.edu

Library of Congress Cataloging-in-Publication Data

Kaufman, Eleanor.
Deleuze, the dark precursor : dialectic, structure, being / Eleanor Kaufman.
pages cm. — (Rethinking theory)
Includes bibliographical references and index.
ISBN 978-1-4214-0589-6 (hdbk. : alk. paper) — ISBN 978-1-4214-0648-0 (electronic) —
ISBN 1-4214-0589-X (hdbk. : alk. paper) — ISBN 1-4214-0648-9 (electronic)
1. Deleuze, Gilles, 1925–1995. 2. Dialectic. 3. Structuralism. 4. Ontology. I. Title.
B2430.D454K38 2012
194—dc23

2011047318

A catalog record for this book is available from the British Library.

Special discounts are available for bulk purchases of this book. For more information, please contact Special Sales at 410-516-6936 or specialsales@press.jhu.edu.

The Johns Hopkins University Press uses environmentally friendly book materials, including recycled text paper that is composed of at least 30 percent post-consumer waste, whenever possible.

To Hank Okazaki,
his family, his friends,
and Ojai

[Guattari] would have to be compared to an ocean, always seeming to be mobile, with constant flashes of light. He can jump from one activity to another, he hardly sleeps, he travels, he doesn't stop. He never *ceases*. He has extraordinary speeds. I would be more like a hill, I move very little, am incapable of doing two projects at once, my ideas are fixed ideas, and my rare movements are interior ones.

— Gilles Deleuze,
Deux régimes de fous, 218

CONTENTS

ACKNOWLEDGMENTS

I would like to thank my editor at the Johns Hopkins University Press, Matt McAdam; my series editor, Victor Taylor; my copy editor, George Roupe; and my research assistants, Michelle Lee and Simchi Cohen. And I would like to acknowledge two decades of institutional support for this project, from the Duke Program in Literature, the Cornell Society for the Humanities, the University of Virginia English Department, and especially the Department of Comparative Literature and Humanities Dean Timothy Stowell at the University of California, Los Angeles. I am also deeply indebted to a Mellon New Directions Fellowship for funding my studies in Medieval philosophy, the results of which appear here for the first time.

It is too much to enumerate the many individuals, including students from four institutions where I taught courses on this material, who gave me guidance and made this project possible, but a good number of them are cited in the extensive footnotes. I will simply mention here my greatest practical-ontological models, my parents, Marvin and Marion Kaufman. And also Cesare Casarino, Brian Selsky, and E.K., the friend who, in the most terrible ordeal, alone discovered the road to Deleuze's philosophy—and guided me onto it.

Earlier versions of the chapters in this book first appeared as noted in the following list.

Chapter One: "Solid Dialectic in Sartre and Deleuze," *Polygraph* 14 (2003): 115–28.

Chapter Two: "Towards a Feminist Philosophy of Mind," in *Deleuze and Feminist Theory*, eds. Ian Buchanan and Claire Colebrook (Edinburgh: Edinburgh University Press, 2000).

Chapter Three: "Klossowski, Deleuze, and Orthodoxy," *Diacritics* 35:1 (2005): 47–59.

Chapter Four: "Deleuze, Klossowski, Cinema, Immobility: A Response to Stephen Arnott," *Film-Philosophy* 5:33 (November 2001), www.film-philosophy.com/vol5-2001/n33kaufman.

Chapter Five: "Betraying Well," *Criticism* 46:4 (2005): 651–59. Also in *Deleuzian Events: Writing History*, ed. Hanjo Berressem and Leyla Haferkamp (Berlin: Lit Verlag, 2009).

Chapter Six: "Lévi-Strauss, Deleuze, and the Joy of Abstraction," *Criticism* 49:4 (Fall 2007): 429–45.

Chapter Seven: "Extreme Formality: Sadism, the Death Instinct, and the World without Others," *Angelaki* 15:1 (April 2010): 77–85. Also with some thematic revision as "Ethics and the World without Others," in *Deleuze and Ethics*, eds. Nathan Jun and Daniel W. Smith (Edinburgh: Edinburgh University Press, 2011).

Chapter Ten: "In the Middle of Things," *Polygraph* 8/9 (1996): 21–25.

Chapter Eleven: "Midnight, or the Inertia of Being," *Parallax* 12:2 (2006): 98–111. Also in *After Blanchot: Literature, Criticism, Philosophy*, eds. Leslie Hill, Brian Nelson, and Dimitris Vardoulakis (Newark: University of Delaware Press, 2005).

Chapter Twelve: "Living Virtually in a Cluttered House," *Angelaki* 7:3 (December 2002), 159–69.

Deleuze, The Dark Precursor

Deleuze's Scholasticism

AGAINST THE TENDENCY to privilege the joint works of Gilles Deleuze and Félix Guattari and questions of becoming and flux, nomadism, deterritorialization, lines of flight, and movements of all sorts so often associated with the name Deleuze, I offer this small study. At its most basic, this study argues for Deleuze as a powerful—perhaps the French twentieth century's most powerful because most unrealized—thinker of *stasis* (which in Greek indicates both a standing still and an internal revolution or disturbance). But beyond that it claims this thought of stasis to be an outgrowth of ontological commitments, often downplayed in the critical literature and arguably by Deleuze himself, that are presented as a question of the genesis of structures, and what is beyond or outside the given structure, yet for that all the more crucial to its operation—essentially the zero or empty point of the structure, to draw on a structuralist vocabulary that Deleuze helps refine. It is the ongoing and implicitly generative role of the empty static point (the third synthesis of time) that this study seeks to consider in all its implications.

It must be emphasized that this is not a project that Deleuze himself takes up in any systematic fashion. Indeed, it is only with hindsight that one perceives a latent systematicity with the force of an epiphany, and chapter 7 on sadism and the world without others is this study's late epiphany, so it might be advised as a starting point for the more thematically or methodologically oriented reader. The other chapters in their fashion engage the implications of this Deleuzian dialectical-ontological stasis structure in other domains or in juxtaposition with other thinkers. In this sense, though I couldn't be more opposed in principle to the idea of "applying Deleuze" (and perpetually caution students, with little success, against such an endeavor), this study, if not exactly an application, might be considered an implication of Deleuze's structural ontology, an implication being that internal domain where the point at which the structure is observable can in no way resemble its larval core, yet is only really perceptible with that framework in mind. This larval core, which is a static and timeless one, is in some sense entirely transcendent, as my discussion of creation in the final section of this introduction outlines, but in another sense it is entirely immanent if not empirical, in a more properly Deleuzian spirit. Yet the terms "immanence" and "transcendence" do not appear with great frequency in this study simply because it seems to me that something else is at stake. The introduction argues against a vitalist reading of Deleuze, insofar as life itself is ultimately a formal—and bifurcated—structure, and it further suggests that much of Deleuze's thought falls into this pattern where the formal structure exists alongside yet distinct from the topos (e.g., life) that is in question. Hence the opposition of immanent and transcendent does not fully capture this structural adjacency. Insistence on absolute immanence cannot fail to call up the specter of a transcendent ontological remainder, and from within the transcendent perspective the field can only be populated with immanent examples, as it is in Scholastic thought, and it is more on this latter side of the equation that I would provocatively locate Deleuze.

The term "Scholasticism" might understandably raise eyebrows—perhaps even more than the terms "dialectic," "structure," and "being"—when associated with the name Deleuze. To be sure, Deleuze is not committed to a transcendental theology in any straightforward sense, nor is he grappling with Aristotle or engaging in disputations. Yet insofar as Deleuze is one of the philosophers in the twentieth-century French tradition most explicitly engaged with ontological questions whose stakes are enormous, and uses a method of strong distinction to outline a rigorous set of concepts, his approach and general topic are in no way diametrically opposed to Scholastic thought. Beyond this general framework, the latter part of this introduction pushes transcendentalizing criticisms of Deleuze made by Slavoj Žižek, Alain Badiou, and Peter Hallward even further, to the point that Deleuze is in fact productively juxtaposed alongside one of his seeming enemies, Aquinas, in a fashion that perhaps exposes a new side to the unsettling radicality, rigor, and potential of his thought. But before getting into these more speculative considerations, I first give a general overview of this book's organization and the way in which it brings the terms in question to bear on one another.

This book is organized around three seemingly non-Deleuzian themes that critically overlap: dialectic, structure, and being. It argues that Deleuze's work is deeply concerned with these questions, even when he advocates for the seemingly opposite poles of univocity, nonsense, and becoming. By reading somewhat against the grain to see a Deleuze who gives new resonance to these themes, especially as they are thought in combination, I hope to reveal the mechanism behind Deleuze's celebrated introduction of new conceptual building blocks to a series of domains that extend beyond philosophy, specifically here feminist theory, film, American studies, anthropology, and architecture. The readings that follow dwell in similar fashion on that term that the field in question would seem to have critically transcended: the mind, the still or *tableau vivant*, a strain of American literature fundamentally concerned with thought and stasis, the notion of structure itself, and baroque space. Moreover, this book positions Deleuze's work in relation to other French philosophers of his generation such as Jean-Paul Sartre, Pierre Klossowski, Georges Bataille, Alain Badiou, Claude Lévi-Strauss, and Maurice Blanchot. It follows Žižek's *Organs without Bodies: Deleuze and Consequences* in that it situates Deleuze's "early" work, above all *The Logic of Sense* from 1969, but also *Difference and Repetition* from 1968, at the heart of his oeuvre.[1] And it seeks, somewhat more than Žižek, to link this work to the slightly later collaboration with Guattari in *Anti-Oedipus* and *A Thousand Plateaus*, though ultimately it shares the standpoint that there is a fundamental difference between the single-authored and the joint works in terms of the ontological questions they propose, and especially the way they are posed. This is not to say that the joint works don't pursue the same concerns by other means, and indeed some of my examples will take this up; nonetheless, there is a fierce if not disturbing structural-ontological persistence that permeates the earlier single-authored work, and my use of Deleuze's relatively undeveloped term "dark precursor" is meant to designate this. Deleuze is not simply the positive friend of philosophy and of the concept (though he is also those things, as they are presented in the late *What Is Philosophy?*), but he is unsparing to the point of perversity in terms of thinking the quasi-sadistic force of structures and forms. In this regard, as I will suggest in chapter 7, Deleuze is not far from the Lacan of "Kant with Sade" and seminar 7, *The Ethics of Psychoanalysis*, and it is not surprising that Lacan was so drawn to *The Logic of Sense*. Not only did Deleuze make a choice not to affiliate with Lacan, but he also chose to let this darker and more exacting side of his thought transform into the no less exacting and perverse (but less explicitly ontological) *Anti-Oedipus*. Of course, May '68 intervened, with its attendant libidinal economic syntheses of Freud and Marx, *Anti-Oedipus* along with Jean-François Lyotard's *Libidinal Economy* being foundational texts.

One of the goals of this study is thus to develop the implications of this "dark ontology" that Deleuze himself chose not to undertake. Although it may at times appear this way, it is not the case such a development simply dwells on a negative or diabolical underside to Deleuze's earlier work. Quite the contrary. Instead it alights on those states—stuckness, disembodiment, isolation, the world as perceived by the immobile underclass—that we would generally rather not dwell on and argues that looking at these things in an unflinching fashion may in fact allow the discernment of more positive and in any case less pathologizing modes of perception. In a strange way this project would align itself with certain strands of utopian Marxism, which are in no small way its inspiration. However, its focus is perhaps arrested at an early stage in such a panoramic undertaking. That is, rather than looking to a beyond, it tries to examine why certain situations of extreme exploitation, illness, and alienation may not be as uniformly negative as they may appear from the outside. And that is because these states approach pure being, if one might call it that, in a less mediated way than is normally the case. This is the perception that Deleuze's work helps facilitate. Though he and Guattari took this elsewhere in the *Capitalism and Schizophrenia* volumes, it seems that a dwelling on these difficult states is also to a certain extent a residence outside of capital (even while existing otherwise in the heart of it), and there is no small utopian potential in mining any portion of that. A distinguished scholar once remarked upon reading an earlier version of chapter 8 on American literature that "this is nothing but an apology for the contemplative life." Such a pronouncement is in many ways correct, because it seems that those facing the most difficult circumstances are in fact forced to engage the toughest ontological questions in unmediated fashion. This work is an exploration of the form such questions take in Deleuze and elsewhere.

This unorthodox reading at once puts Deleuze in dialogue with important contemporaries and extends his thought beyond the three categories it is usually grouped around (the philosophical Deleuze, the Deleuze of the art and cinema books, and the collaborative writings with Guattari). Part 1 gives careful consideration to Deleuze's repeated defense of univocity, or the idea that being is said in only one sense. It claims, above all in conjunction with Deleuze's long-standing engagement with the philosopher, novelist, and painter Klossowski, that there is often a dualism or hidden dialectic that escapes from the univocity under consideration. I begin in the first chapter by going back to Sartre and arguing that Deleuze and Sartre share a Platonic model of absolute separation, of difference of kind rather than degree. The next chapter extends these questions into that of the mind-body dualism and looks at productive possibilities within feminist thought for separating mind and body and not renouncing mind as retrograde and masculinist. The third chapter situates Deleuze with respect to Klossowski and Bataille, locating Klossowski's work between Bataille's model of transgressive dualism and Deleuzian univocity. I thereby map the work of these three thinkers onto the Scholastic terms of univocity (Deleuze), equivocity (Bataille), and analogy (Klossowski), but I also suggest that there is more proximity between Deleuze's univocity and Klossowski's analogy than Deleuze might concede. Chapter 4 explores the differences between Deleuzian and Klossowskian models of disjunction in the cinematic register, above all in Raúl Ruiz's film adaptations of Klossowski's fiction. I explore the importance of immobility for Klossowski and conclude that the immobilized poses—or *tableaux vivants*—that Klossowski frequently depicts allow Deleuze's meditations on movement and immobility to be thought in a new register.

Part 2 extends the case for an underlying Deleuzian dialectic by linking the thought of the dialectic to a certain formalism or, more precisely, to an interest in "structure," in his work from the 1960s. Chapter 5 considers the controversial monographs on Deleuze by Žižek and Badiou, which both assert after a fashion that there is an underlying dualism in Deleuze's work. Rather than arguing that Deleuze resorts to a notion of quasi-Hegelian mediation (Žižek) or a false notion of the One (Badiou), I locate a compatibility between a Spinozist Deleuze and a structure-oriented Deleuze by focusing on Deleuze's *The Logic of Sense*, *Difference and Repetition*, and some of his essays from the same period. Chapter 6 takes up Deleuze's discussion of Lévi-Strauss in "How Do We Recognize Structuralism?," arguably one of the most important theorizations of structuralism ever written. Whereas Lévi-Strauss is always hesitant to isolate form from content, Deleuze insists there is a joy in the recognition of the form, or structure, apart from its content. I suggest that this emphasis or nonemphasis on the joy inherent in abstraction is one of the few discernible markers of the break between structuralism and poststructuralism. Thus I argue for a reconsideration of the way this break is narrated in light of Deleuze's surprisingly positive discussions of Lévi-Strauss and also of Sartrean seriality.

Chapter 7 examines a series of striking convergences in a number of disparate texts Deleuze wrote or published around 1967. It seeks to map out a structure that traverses "Coldness and Cruelty," "Michael Tournier and the World without Others" (subsequently published as an appendix to *The Logic of Sense*), and parts of *Difference and Repetition*. This structure is essentially the realm Deleuze describes in his analysis of Tournier's rewriting of *Robinson Crusoe*, a state that Robinson enters into on the desert island, which is an elemental state beyond the "structure-Other," one that has no need for a human other. Thus Deleuze uses structure to go beyond structure, and in this fashion, and in his ecstatic description of Robinson's blending with the island in order to "consecrate" it, Deleuze comes closer than in virtually any other of his writings to describing a state of pure being. Yet I argue that this state is structurally similar not only to Deleuze's discussion of sadism (in contradistinction to masochism) in "Coldness and Cruelty" but also to what Deleuze culls from his more positive reading of Freud's death drive in *Difference and Repetition*, and furthermore to the notion of the "third synthesis of time" as it is outlined in the same work and to which concept I return later in this introduction.

Chapter 7 thereby articulates the logical argument of this book at its most explicit. It attempts to delineate a structure that inheres in Deleuze's magisterial work from the late 1960s and serves as the hidden kernel of his ontology. This structure is simultaneously that of sadism (not masochism), the world without others (not the structure-Other), the Freudian death instinct (not the Freudian unconscious), and the third synthesis of time (not the Aion of *The Logic of Sense*). These works share a dark and anethical vision and a high formalism that might appear anathema to the reception of Deleuze, inflected through the joint work with Guattari, as a purely positive thinker. However, part 3 of this study focuses on the forms such a dark ontology might actually take and suggests they might in fact hold out another sort of positivity, one that is not dissociable from the so-called negative states at issue in the concluding section's examples.

If parts 1 and 2 outline the workings of a particular Deleuzian valence of dialectic and of structure, then part 3 attempts to situate the way these valences *appear*, or perhaps one could say, using Deleuzian terminology, actualize. If the movement from the virtual to the actual would fall for Deleuze under the domain of "static genesis," then in part 3 by contrast I examine how dialectic and structure serve as points of genesis for something at once static and full of ontological plenitude because of that very stasis. In this fashion, part 3 explores extreme states of stasis that, not unlike the one Tournier's Robinson inhabits, would seem to be overwhelmingly negative yet in fact allow being to emerge in a fashion that escapes the mediation of the tyrannical Other.

There is unquestionably a tension in Deleuze's work between a repeated celebration of movement and a gesture to something else, the latter sometimes articulated as the recognition that movement can happen "*sur place*" (on the spot). This gesture is most pronounced in Deleuze's writings on American literature of the nineteenth and twentieth centuries, which is my focus in chapters 8 and 9. Chapter 8 explores the dialectic of movement and stasis in "road trip" novels by Jack Kerouac, Vladimir Nabokov, and Paul Auster. I suggest that these literary works broach the vexed possibility of whether thought and movement can coexist insofar as they squarely pose the question—one that Deleuze at points comes close to articulating—of whether being and stasis can similarly coexist. In this fashion, Deleuze's fascination for American literature exposes an orientation toward an even more profound state of inertia than Deleuze explicitly embraces. Chapter 9 addresses the singular text that formulates these questions in the strongest possible fashion, not only for Deleuze but for many of his French and European contemporaries. This is Herman Melville's "Bartleby, the Scrivener," and the chapter examines Deleuze's essay "Bartleby; or, The Formula" and responses to this essay by Jacques Rancière and Giorgio Agamben. The repetitive passion for the dialectic of the "or" in all of these essays is taken as a symptom of an impasse between a glorification of American movement and an attraction to theories of *désoeuvrement*, or unworking. Chapter 11 makes the most pointed claim for the force of *désoeuvrement*, which is here discussed through close readings of Blanchot's fiction. It calls for an ontology of inertia above and beyond Deleuze's more overt emphasis on movement and becoming and looks at the parallels and divergences between his work and that of Blanchot. While Blanchot sometimes heralds the elusiveness of temporality, that things are always just past or forever to come, there are other moments in which Blanchot imagines a more weighty state of being stuck in the present. I contend that the former logic of a past-future temporality is an essentially Deleuzian one but that the later realm of radical stuckness overturns and revalues Deleuze's seeming rejection of being and presentness. The short chapter that precedes the discussion of Blanchot, chapter 10, is an interlude that attempts to translate this latent Deleuzian ontology into the perception of space, specifically small-town midwestern space. The concluding chapter is a meditation on what the ontology of inertia would look like and takes as its guiding example that of a child who imagines that the ceilings of a cluttered house are vast open floor spaces. Alongside Deleuze's analyses of baroque architecture in his book on Leibniz, I draw on the French phenomenological tradition to propose a virtual space of perception that favors a dwelling in being over a movement of becoming.

In this fashion, I show how three terms that are generally considered antithetical to Deleuze's philosophy—dialectic, structure, and being—open up a secret underside to Deleuze's oeuvre, all the more so when read in the context of Deleuze's contemporaries who employ these terms more openly and favorably. Each part opens with a short preface that goes into more detail about its chapters than is provided in this brief overview, and I refer the reader to those prefaces for a more detailed outline of this book's contents.

For the remainder of this introduction, perhaps in the fashion of Deleuze's appendixes to *The Logic of Sense* that overlap significantly with the thirty-four short series contained in the body of the text yet also go into uncharted domains, I would like to put forward in far stronger terms, and in dialogue with some of the key texts in the staggering critical literature on Deleuze, the argument that Deleuze not only has certain affinities with Scholasticism but that his affinities with Aquinas in particular touch on some of the critical claims, made by other means, of this study as a whole.

It is of course often noted, by Deleuze himself and by commentators, the importance of John Duns Scotus (1265/66–1308) for Deleuze's thought, above all for Deleuze's admittedly idiosyncratic deployment of the concepts of *univocity* (the idea that being is said in one sense) and *haecceity* (thisness, individuating difference as opposed to *differentia* or specific difference). How this reading of Scotus came about and in what circumstances is not entirely clear.[2] As has often been noted with respect to Deleuze (and not generally as a criticism, which it is also not intended to be here), his "borrowings" often so little resemble the original that they tell us more about Deleuze's own system than the thinker he is explicating. Such a claim is particularly resonant in the case of Scotus, for Deleuze takes "univocity" from Scotus without situating this term within the "logic" (the grounding in Aristotle's *Categories*, Porphyry's commentaries, the *Sentences* of Peter Lombard, etc.) that were a foundation for Medieval thought, or in Scholastic debates about nominalism and universalism, or in discussions of God and the persons of the trinity, with only slight mention of the question of divine names.[3] Deleuze's Scotus is virtually unrecognizable as that portrayed by major contemporary Scotus commentators such as Richard Cross and Giorgio Pini, or even as that of Étienne Gilson, who might properly have influenced Deleuze.[4] Again, this is not said by way of critique but simply to buttress my reading of Deleuze alongside Aquinas in what follows. If Deleuze himself engages Scotus somewhat fleetingly[5] and from a somewhat eccentric perspective, then the mere fact that Deleuze engages Aquinas even less and in a couple of instances is expressly hostile to Aquinas[6] is in no way a sufficient ground for considering the juxtaposition of Deleuze and Aquinas as some kind of outlandish enterprise. While Scotus's work represents a significant break with Aquinas, if not more precisely Henry of Ghent, on questions of logic, it is not altogether clear that such a hard and fast break takes place in the realm of metaphysics.

Most of the extant commentaries on Deleuze's relation to the philosophical tradition tend, understandably, to focus on those thinkers that Deleuze explicitly cites as having influence on him, and it should be noted that such a method of being attentive to what a thinker actually says he is doing has recently been given brilliant psychoanalytically inflected approbation by Adrian Johnston in his work on Žižek.[7] Nevertheless, I will risk incurring the disapprobation of Deleuze's more faithful readers and commentators by suggesting that in certain respects Deleuze may have important affinities with Aquinas that perhaps help open his work to a different framework of dialectic, structure, and being.[8]

What is at stake in linking Deleuze to a notoriously methodological, theological, and seemingly doctrinaire thinker such as Aquinas? Apart from the idea that both oeuvres mark exceptionally creative moments in the history of philosophy (this claim has certainly been made repeatedly for Deleuze, and it is also something of a truism that Aquinas himself invents some of the best objections to his propositions, per the format of the *Summa Theologica*, whereby each question begins with an objection to it that in the end is refuted—clearly different from Deleuze's style but not unlike his insistence on emphasizing problems and the way a question is posed), and apart from the specific topoi—creation, genesis, and eternity—that I turn to at the end of this introduction, another reason for thinking Deleuze alongside Aquinas is the high realism of both bodies of work.

There has for years been somewhat of a polarized tendency in studies of Deleuze to focus either on the joint works with Guattari or on Deleuze's earlier, more strictly philosophical single-authored work, or alternatively on the works on cinema and painting. As is taken up in chapter 5, Žižek and Badiou both express a strong adherence to the "philosophical" early Deleuze at the expense of the more generally popular Deleuze as coauthor with Guattari of *Anti-Oedipus*; *A Thousand Plateaus*; *Kafka: Toward a Minor Literature*; and *What Is Philosophy?*[9] Badiou claims that all of Deleuze's work can be reduced to a few oft-repeated concepts that are entirely present in Deleuze's work from the 1960s (including *Nietzsche and Philosophy*; *Expressionism in Philosophy: Spinoza*; *Bergsonism*; *Difference and Repetition*; and *The Logic of Sense*, but not *Anti-Oedipus* from 1972 and *A Thousand Plateaus* from 1980, the latter both coauthored with Guattari). Žižek specifically states that Deleuze's major work is *The Logic of Sense* and the work that must be bracketed is *Anti-Oedipus*, in that the latter gives itself over to the pernicious anything-goes model of Deleuzian commentary that favors flux, forces, movement, radicality, and speed—but with no underlying order.[10] While I am following Badiou and Žižek in also attending to the more strictly philosophical part of Deleuze's corpus, I do give some consideration to the jointly written works, the cinema books, and works such as the book on Leibniz and the writings of Melville that came later. It is undeniable that questions of dialectic, structure, and being are less explicit in the joint-authored and later works, but it is not clear that these questions are therefore less relevant to the reader of those works, even if they were, perhaps at that time of writing, to those works' authors.

In an earlier oral version of chapter 7 presented at an annual Deleuze studies conference, which outlined as indicated the striking proximity between four concepts that Deleuze elaborated around the year 1967—the world without others, the particular characteristics of sadism (as opposed to masochism), the death drive, and the third synthesis of time—my position on this underlying "dark precursor" structure in Deleuze's thought, especially the elevation of sadism over masochism in its relevance to the core of Deleuze's thought, generated quite expectedly some protest and heated discussion. Less expected was the seemingly incongruous set of comments that indeed these overlapping sets of terms that I was attending to in work from the 1960s certainly extended throughout Deleuze's entire oeuvre. I make overtures to such a claim here, and I do think there is important scholarship that moves in that direction,[11] but I am also agnostic about the applicability of the approach I am outlining to every dimension of Deleuze's oeuvre. Such a totalizing idea is certainly interesting, but there is no need for the stakes of this project to be overarching in this fashion. If I can convince the perhaps skeptical reader that questions of eternity, stasis, and the work of Aquinas are even somewhat relevant to Deleuze, perhaps primarily to Deleuze's pre-1972 thought, that will be interesting enough.

The stakes of this book are dual, and their two poles do not necessarily come out at once or in equal balance at all points. On the one hand, this study attempts to give a voice to states of being and spaces that are frequently pathologized or not considered worthy of consideration (extreme stuckness and inertia, simple objects of daily life, the child's perspective and the hoarder's perspective, and flat, provincial middle-American landscape—all examples from part 3) and suggests the usefulness of thinking these states alongside Deleuze, at times taking them further than he does. This rigorous and serious treatment of "minor states,"[12] or at least there is the hope it will be deemed so, is a resoundingly feminist and object-oriented approach to Deleuze, though generally not one presented in the language of those discourses. This approach is particularly resonant in part 3 (on being) and partially so in part 1 (on dialectic). I will note that chapter 10, "In the Middle of Things," was written considerably prior to the final two chapters it prefaces ("Midnight, or the Inertia of Being" and "Living Virtually in a Cluttered House") and contains in nascent and less developed form some of their materials. It is included because there are ontological intensities that a younger self can remember and express with far more clarity and simplicity than an older one, and it seems that younger self captured in many ways the essence of this work's devotion to the minor, before even (I believe) having encountered some of the work of Alphonso Lingis that is roughly in this genre. This reflective interlude is also all the more poignant now in that most of the small-town midwestern sites evoked no longer exist, or exist in the same fashion, including the city of Joplin.

The other stake, which is elaborated in the rest of this introduction, is more of a provocation and more counteractive (or in good Deleuzian terminology, counteractualizing). In other words, in attempting to pin Deleuze to an underlying structural ontology that he surely would have resisted, I am not, as outlined above, necessarily claiming that this strong reading holds equally for all of Deleuze's writings. Thus I am not claiming that those studies that place Deleuze's work under the heading of a certain hermeticism, vitalism, virtuality, or negative theology are wrong tout court. There are many things about such approaches, and I will highlight a few of them below, that are particularly insightful and useful—and in many respects entirely in keeping with this study's very different logical orientation. But the countervalent terms of dialectic and structure are indeed and emphatically meant to stand in contradistinction to any notion of a mystical, otherworldly, negative Deleuze whose whole oeuvre can be reduced to a "Platonism of the virtual."[13] In what remains, I briefly outline a salient example from each of these four headings—hermeticism, vitalism, the virtual, and negative theology—and suggest its connection to the terms of this study, but with the caveat that these headings do not go far enough toward a positive elaboration (Deleuze is, after all, an eminently positive thinker), and it is indeed toward the latter that the recourse to Scholastic thought is most valuable.

There has been an impressive strain of recent work linking Deleuze to the esoteric and hermetic traditions, as well as to a Jungian model of the unconscious. Particularly notable in this regard are journal issues of *SubStance* and *Collapse* devoted to Deleuze that highlight this dimension of his work, as well as Joshua Delpech-Ramey's *The Hermetic Deleuze: Philosophy and Spiritual Ordeal* and Christian Kerslake's *Deleuze and the Unconscious*.[14] The title of chapter 7 is based on Deleuze's refrain in *Difference and Repetition* of "the formless as the product of the most extreme formality."[15] If these hermetically oriented studies tend to focus on the generative power of the formless as such, then this study looks at the formal logic of causation of the formless, in the hope that it will give us new insights toward its generative powers.[16] It is not exactly at odds with the scholarship mentioned above but rather draws out a different part of the equation. This is perhaps best illustrated by one of Deleuze's earliest writings, one he later excised from his bibliography, which was the introduction he wrote to Johann Malfatti von Monteregio's book *Mathesis; or, Studies on the Anarchy and Hierarchy of Knowledge* and is available in English in the *Collapse* volume mentioned above. It is of course tempting to speculate why Deleuze regarded this early writing unfavorably. Was it because of its latent humanism, vitalism, if not Hegelianism and strange theologizing (and written after all at a very young age, twenty-one), because it nonetheless captures some important thematics that Deleuze would later develop, such as a gesture to objects as "outside of us"?[17] Or, as Robin Mackay notes in his editor's introduction, does it serve as a prolegomena to Deleuze's notion of a "phosphorescence of objects" to be developed in the 1967 essay "Michel Tournier and the World without Others" (discussed in chapter 7)?[18] In short, we see a sort of object-oriented ontology (OOO) avant la lettre, though one might argue, as I do in chapter 1, that in fact Deleuze and Sartre share a penchant for thinking the thingness of objects,[19] and his earliest writings reflect Deleuze at his most overtly, if not actually, Sartrean.

I have not made the effort here to enter into more extended dialogue with the rich domain of OOO and the umbrella category of speculative realism under which it falls, for the simple reason that most of the material in this book was drafted either before I knew of the existence of these emergent bodies of thought or before they had actually emerged. There is much work being and to be done on the intersections of the work of Deleuze, Badiou, and Quentin Meillassoux, and Ray Brassier's excellent and difficult essay on the third synthesis of time in *Nihil Unbound* is perhaps the mediating link between my treatment of this material in chapter 7 and Meillassoux's *After Finitude*.[20] The major difference between OOO, as it is currently instantiated in the disparate foursome of Graham Harman, Levi Bryant, Ian Bogost, and Timothy Morton, and the approach taken here — and this is exemplary of the tenor of my critiques in this whole section — is that for OOO, virtually anything can be an object: a text, an iPad, the National Organization for Women (these are actual examples used on the relevant OOO blogs),[21] whereas to think according to the parameters of Scholastic thought, an entity, generally a living one, must be categorized according to a Porphyrian tree of alternating branches (notably similar to Deleuze's method of Platonic dialectic discussed in chapter 1) and then according to its genus and species and specific difference or *differentia*. Now Deleuze avowedly focuses more on *haecceity*, or individuating difference (how you get from a species to an individual versus how you get from a genus to a species, *haecceity* versus *differentia*), yet he nonetheless and at times in spite of himself produces a hierarchical and divisive structuring system not unlike the Porphyrian tree. The end result may be a certain empty square, as he outlines it in his important essay "How Do We Recognize Structuralism?" discussed in chapter 6, but it matters how that square or formless entity was arrived at, for if one can outline with precision how it was generated, then the gambit is that being attuned to the at times stultifying and quasi-Scholastic method of Deleuzian structure and genesis itself opens new domains of perception.

Deleuze writes provocatively in "Mathesis, Science, and Philosophy": "And the key notion of mathesis—not at all mystical—is that individuality never separates itself from the universal, that between the living and life one finds the same relation as between life as species, and divinity."[22] If one parses the above phrase, as Deleuze does a bit later in the same essay,[23] we have "living" being related to "universal" life as the species is related to divinity. Not only does this introduce the important question of the realm of the divine (which I suggest is not unlike Deleuze's third synthesis of time, though one might also wonder if this is precisely an aspect of the "Mathesis" essay that was later unsatisfying to Deleuze), but more immediately it introduces a major crack into life itself (not unlike the workings of the crack, or "*la fêlure*," that Deleuze analyzes so beautifully in his essays on Fitzgerald, Zola, and Lowry in *The Logic of Sense*),[24] for life is divided between the living on the one hand and life as an ordering principle on the other, where the latter is entirely distinct from human life per se. This division is not without its affinities to Giorgio Agamben's celebrated distinctions between *zoê* and *bios*, or naked life versus life in its fullness,[25] but here it is more nearly a distinction between the living creature and life in its most universal sense, which is paradoxically not aliveness as such but rather a structural category. That is, one can see in this very early essay the germ of the type of structural-ontological (if not dialectical) thought that is a mark of Deleuze's work from the 1960s.

Rather than align Deleuze with an easy vitalism or engagement with the question of life—and Deleuze's last work, "Immanence: A Life," certainly gives an opening of sorts for such claims—it is imperative to see the way in which "life" is always cut in two, cracked, by a line of division, or an "engine of difference."[26] Keith Ansell Pearson's *Germinal Life* importantly emphasizes the strong ontological and nonorganic component to Deleuze's concept of life. As he writes, "Although the notion of nonorganic life is not found in either *Difference and Repetition* or *The Logic of Sense*, it could be argued that these books are devoted to nothing other than a thinking with and beyond the organism."[27] Eugene Thacker's *After Life* links this twofold division of creaturely life versus structural life (what he sees as the bifurcation between living and "Life") explicitly to an Aristotelian and Scholastic lineage. He analyzes in precise detail the way in which, both for Aristotle and for the Scholastic thinkers who followed him, there is difficulty in classifying the classificatory structure as such. That is, if the Aristotelian *psuchē* (sometimes rendered as "soul," from Aristotle's *De Anima*) can be classified into intellective, sensitive, and nutritive elements, which could all be said to be forms of the living, what about the *psuchē* itself and its complex tripartite (if not proto-Trinitarian) structure? Is it also living, or is it more of a logical if not ontological structure apart from the living that is nonetheless necessary for an understanding of Life? One might say, perhaps reductively, that Deleuzian univocity—following Scotus but extending the thought of the Subtle Doctor to comprehend a Spinozist realm of substance, modes, and attributes—provides a way of thinking through this problem, of locating difference within individuating difference in such a way that every entity, whether a distinct life form or a structure, falls under the same immanent rubric such that divisive or hierarchical distinctions become irrelevant.[28] However, it is the claim of this study, above all of part 1, that a mode of nonunivocal divisive distinction is intrinsic to Deleuzian ontology and, moreover, that the formal separation discussed above between living and form-of-life resurfaces in a range of Deleuzian guises.

Instances of this structural split that is necessary for the elaboration of Deleuze's thought include the formation of disjunctive syntheses, divergent series, the second-order incorporeal, and the difference between the name of the thing and what the name of the thing is called, just to take several important examples from *The Logic of Sense*. Jameson refers to this as a latent dualism, and Badiou and John Milbank see it as the failure of the professed univocity at the hands of the equivocal, all of which is taken up in what follows. Unlike most Deleuze scholars, I am not fundamentally at odds with these readings. However, I would insist that Deleuze's is no ordinary dualist dualism. It is more nearly a dualist monism, because it is a structural dualism and a hierarchicizing procedure used at the service of an undermining of dualism, which debatably might then form a non-Hegelian higher unity, or univocity. Yet for my part—and this is above all at issue in the book's more meditative final section on "being"—I wish to dwell more squarely on the often static building blocks of the Deleuzian conceptual apparatus, for example the inorganic Life as an abstract entity that grounds the living, the point of immobility that grounds becoming, or the counter-intuitive static part of the genesis of the actual from the virtual—in short, a bevy of stuck, dead, eternal, dual structures that are more nearly categories rather than concepts.[29] It is my contention, and I attempt to illustrate this in part 3, that when seriously examined and not dismissingly passed over, these entities seemingly negative in connotation are in fact potentially positive both in terms of distinction and in terms of generative power.

I cannot here do justice to the rich work that explores this generative power by linking Deleuze's thought to intricate issues in biology and the life sciences; to mathematics, cybernetics, and neuroscience; or to thinkers such as Saint-Hilaire, Simondon, Bateson, von Uexküll, and Whitehead.[30] To risk a severe reduction, many of these approaches seek to level customary barriers (between organic and inorganic, and between persons as distinct from things, forces, processes of individuation, and networks), which, to be sure, Deleuze's, and especially Deleuze and Guattari's, work indeed achieves. However, it is more in the spirit of holding fast to the importance of the distinction outlined above between the living and Life, and to the structure itself of Deleuzian distinction that I proceed, for the contention is that attending to this mode of *static difference* brings us closest to a new form of minor ontology that admittedly in the end may not be entirely Deleuze's but at the very least is something Deleuze's work opens onto.

It might be objected that what I am gesturing to as the "structure itself" and as static difference is none other than what Deleuze characterizes as the virtual (the virtual being a major focus of the works cited in the note to the preceding paragraph), and this would not be wrong. The last chapter of this study explicitly addresses the generative force of the virtual. Yet on the whole I have avoided this term, to some extent because there has already been a great deal of excellent scholarship on this topic,[31] but more importantly because the very multidimensionality of the term and the difficulty of defining it (not unlike trying to define the body without organs, but with even greater stakes)[32] lends itself, I think, to sophisticated attacks by thinkers such as Badiou, who as noted above seizes on Deleuze's "Platonism of the virtual," and by Peter Hallward, whose critique I turn to presently. Unlike many of Deleuze's staunchest defenders, I think there is merit in these critiques, and my approach is not to deny the criticisms but to push them to the next level. That is, if we really consider the Deleuzian virtual, do we not see something more akin to an Aristotelian if not Scholastic system of ontological classification and parsing? This, at least, is the claim of the first two parts, though it is acknowledged that this method is also quite Platonic. Rather than denying the objection that Deleuze erects quasi-transcendental categories that bring down his system in the end—the implication of Badiou's attack that his is a Platonism of the virtual (though Badiou of course is eminently partial to Plato, so even this assertion is not without its complications of nuance) or Hallward's criticism that Deleuze's thought is prone to these pitfalls and not grounded in the world—by contrast I am suggesting that we linger precisely on those transcendental categories and use the fully transcendentalizing theological language that Deleuze is generally evoked in the same breath with only as insult as in fact a *positive* point of reference, just as Freud purportedly turned the pejorative assertion of psychoanalysis as a Jewish science into a badge of honor.[33]

Thus, instead of the virtual, I take up in the remainder of this introduction another concept from *Difference and Repetition* that is more limited in its employment but not without affinities to the seeming "otherworldly" domain of the virtual. This is the third synthesis of time, introduced in the second chapter of *Difference and Repetition*, as an outgrowth of the first synthesis of habit and the second synthesis of memory. The three syntheses of time will be discussed further in chapter 7, but at this juncture I would simply marshal the third synthesis of time and its relation to Scholastic conceptions of eternity to defend Deleuze against critiques that his project is transcendentalizing and otherworldly by actually affirming some of the claims made by way of attack on Deleuze, but taking those claims in a different direction. Badiou calls Deleuze an aristocratic thinker, and Žižek focuses on what he calls the "sterile Sense-Event" of *The Logic of Sense* as opposed to the flux and flow of *Anti-Oedipus*, both of which are taken up in chapter 5, but here I turn to Hallward's particularly insightful and damning critique in *Out of This World: Deleuze and the Philosophy of Creation* that elaborates on the virtual, immobilized, nonproductive aspect of Deleuze's notion of creation, which Hallward considers in rigorous detail but in the end pejoratively. Albeit routinely dismissed and severely criticized by most Deleuze scholars, Hallward's critical, or quasi-critical, analysis is one of the most important to have emerged in years, and one that must be engaged.[34] Žižek, Badiou, and Hallward each in his way recognizes cracks in Deleuzian univocity along with a certain strain of rarefied transcendentalizing that is hard to know what to do with, especially for a thinker so widely "applied" and lauded for the immanent materialism of his thought.

My claim is that this "inapplicability" of Deleuze's thought, what Hallward critiques resoundingly as being "out of this world" and not adequate for proper political change or transformation, is precisely what makes it worth grappling with and trying to deform or transform. Such a claim accords with Hallward's in certain points, yet it dwells more squarely and *positively* on those moments where Hallward takes most issue with Deleuze, particularly insofar as Hallward links Deleuze to a variant of negative theology. Deleuze writes in *Expressionism in Philosophy* that "it was without doubt Scotus who pursued farther than any other [Medieval philosopher] the enterprise of a positive theology,"[35] but I turn to Aquinas to help bolster the positive enterprise and retrieve Deleuzian univocity from an easy alignment with negative theology, in part by insisting that Deleuzian univocity, like the univocity of its Medieval predecessor, is not as pure as it appears. Hallward effectively demonstrates that if you take Deleuze's Spinozist-Nietzschean-Bergsonian penchant for univocity (not something I would connect so squarely with Scotus all said and done, as Scotus in earlier works also advocates equivocity in logic and analogy in metaphysics)[36] to its limit, you get into a register that stops you in your tracks, a radical stasis outside of movement and time (hence "out of this world"). Yet Hallward in turn stops with this, without considering the seeming paradox that such a stasis might itself entail a generative dimension. In short, dwelling in a positive fashion on those places where Deleuze gets deliberately or involuntarily stuck is the driving methodology of this study. But rather than simply enacting this methodology, I here attempt, albeit fleetingly, to account for it through recourse to Aquinas.

It is precisely on the question of univocity that Deleuze makes his brief but very stringent attacks on Aquinas. As Deleuze glosses it in a 1974 course lecture, which is cited at length in chapter 3, univocity is the idea that "being . . . is said in one and the same sense of everything of which it is said," and a term that Deleuze will go on to link very squarely to Spinoza. Univocity is here opposed to equivocity, which is the idea of being said in different senses, for example that God is named differently from the flea; but as Deleuze points out, if you insist that God is *not* rather than that God is a like a flea, then you get into a potential heresy. As he puts it rather scathingly, the term that won out historically, which is associated with Aquinas, is the damnably, for Deleuze, lukewarm idea of analogy, that the Creator and the creation are not of the same stuff but that there is an analogical relation, a divine trace as Aquinas calls it, between them.[37]

Deleuze, then, condemns Aquinas on the grounds of a certain style of moderation or mediation, both in the course lecture on Scholastic thought and in moments cited above in *Difference and Repetition* and in *Expressionism in Philosophy*. Insofar as Thomist analogy serves as a mediating category, Deleuze is understandably dismissive of it, as he is in similar strong fashion of the Hegelian dialectic. Nevertheless, Deleuze's repeated emphasis on difference in kind (as opposed to difference of degree) and a penchant for hierarchical dualisms of terminology in his work (virtual/actual, differen*t*iation/differen*c*iation, intensive/extensive, to take examples from *Difference and Repetition*) make him not incompatible with Thomist thought, which is, after all, wonderfully complex precisely in its notion of difference.

John Milbank has developed some of these links between Deleuze and Thomism, insofar as he argues, both in his earlier "The Soul of Reciprocity, Part Two" and in the more recent *Monstrosity of Christ*, that Deleuze does not really escape analogy.[38] Badiou makes the same point in different language in *The Clamor of Being*, that in order to think the bifurcation between the name of the thing and what name of the thing is called, there is something else—a two or a dualism—beyond univocity that creeps in. I take up these lines of argumentation in chapters 3 and 5, respectively, and while I do not disagree with them, I here focus on a problematic that is closer to what Deleuze does in fact claim to be doing, and that regards his description of the third synthesis of time in *Difference and Repetition*. This is a concept that in chapter 7 is linked to other Deleuzian concepts from the same period such as the world without others, the death instinct, and the structural reading of sadism—not masochism—in "Coldness and Cruelty." Insofar as I claim in that chapter and chapter 6 that these literally "empty structures" serve as a "dark precursor" and hidden kernel to Deleuze's oeuvre (and perhaps also come to bear on concepts from the joint work such as the plane of consistency, even the body without organs, and also perhaps the crystal-image of time or the noosign of differentiation from the cinema books, though I do not develop these lines of thought), such a claim is in many ways resonant with Hallward's detailed analysis in *Out of This World* of the way in which such concepts are at the ontological core of Deleuze's notion of creation. In this regard, the third synthesis of time is a concept that would appear to succumb to Hallward's attack insofar as it bears the strong mark of the atemporal and the eternal.

Chapter 7 goes into greater detail about the differences, as Deleuze outlines them in the "Repetition for Itself" chapter of *Difference and Repetition*, between the first synthesis of habit and the second synthesis of memory, but of import here is that the third synthesis is strikingly pure, empty, and static in Deleuze's characterization: "[T]ime out of joint means demented time or time . . . freed from the events which made up its content, its relation to movement overturned; in short, time presenting itself as an empty and pure form. . . . The [third] synthesis [of time] is necessarily static, since time is no longer subordinated to movement; time is the most radical form of change, but the form of change does not change."[39] At issue is a conception of time that is essentially motionless, a pure order of time, where succession from past to future is no longer operative. Yet, in Deleuze's complex hierarchy—and his works especially from this period are full of hierarchical structures—the third synthesis of time is clearly the superior and favored one. As discussed in chapter 1 with respect to the incorporeal, it is not the first order but the last order that is almost always the favored one for Deleuze, not the first-order corporeal but the second-order incorporeal, not so much the first and second syntheses of time but rather the third.[40]

When we probe what Deleuze means by the seemingly paradoxical statement that "time is the most radical form of change, but the form of change does not change," Aquinas's notions of eternity and of creation are remarkably apposite, although for Aquinas these domains are exclusive to the realm of God. For Aquinas, eternity also entails an overcoming of both movement and time, which are connected. In the *Summa Theologica*, Aquinas answers, in defense of Boethius:

> For since succession occurs in every movement, and one part comes after another, the fact that we reckon before and after in movement, makes us apprehend time, which is nothing else but the measure of before and after in movement. Now in a thing bereft of movement, which is always the same, there is no before or after. As therefore the idea of time consists in the numbering of before and after in movement; so likewise in the apprehension of the uniformity of what is outside of movement, consists the idea of eternity. Further, those things are said to be measured by time which have a beginning and an end in time, because in everything which is moved there is a beginning, and there is an end. But as whatever is wholly immutable can have no succession, so it has no beginning, and no end.[41]

It would seem that Aquinas's immutable, immobile, successionless eternity would go hand in hand with Hallward's contention in *Out of This World*, which again is not a positive one, that Deleuze's whole philosophy of creation rests on a fundamentally theological framework. Hallward's detailed close reading of Deleuze essentially takes Deleuzian univocity back to its theological or quasi-theological foundation and then reapplies it to Deleuze's oeuvre as a whole. However, that foundation is a very different one than the Thomist one I am proposing, because, in insisting with Deleuze on univocity, Hallward is on the one hand driven toward a mystical reading of Deleuze whereby God and the creature are one, and on the other toward a transcendentalizing and no less mystical reading whereby the Creator and the creation are necessarily purely separate and one cannot know God in any absolute fashion.

Such a doubleness comes out in the following passage from *Out of This World* with its recourse to the negative theology of Eckhart, and this is also where creation comes in to resolve all dilemmas:

> Deleuze takes us back in this way to the central theophanic conviction —that only God is capable of affirming God, only God is capable of

> thinking the idea of God, only God can think with an infinite power of thought. We express God by allowing God to work (think, create, act . . .) through us, or as Eckhart puts it, "I never see God except in that in which God sees Himself." De-theologise the terms and the logic stays much the same: only being can affirm itself. Only affirmation itself can affirm a power of infinite affirmation.[42]

Hallward thus presents a recursive "theophanic" model whereby the act of creation, even in its distance from God, nonetheless affirms itself through itself and thus unites with the mind of God. For Hallward, this is the way of getting around what I discuss, especially in chapter 1, as the problem of nonmediation in Deleuze's thought. Hallward gets around this by first emphasizing the Deleuzian disavowal of relation, something that my reading also emphasizes, and then by announcing that it is the power of creation that enables such a vision of difference:

> Most commentary on Deleuze has tended to assume that what he's proposing is a relational account of being as difference. There might seem to be a fair amount of evidence for such a reading. Doesn't he privilege multiplicity over unity? Doesn't he denounce every recourse to a transcendent principle of individuation? Doesn't he emphasise the way becomings take place "in the middle," in a "between"? Doesn't he privilege *et* [and] over *est* [is] — the serial syntheses of the "AND AND AND" over any definitive determination of what is? Doesn't he provide an account of the generation of ideas and problems in terms of the "differential relations" modeled on the infinitesimal relations of calculus (dx/dy)?
>
> The answer is of course yes, he does all these things — but he does them, nevertheless, in such a way as to ensure the exclusive primacy of non-relational difference, a notion of strictly intra-elemental rather than inter-elemental difference. From start to finish, Deleuze's concern is always with a logic of difference whereby, before it differs with other anything [*sic*] external to itself, a differing "differs with itself first, immediately," on account of the internal and self-differing power that makes it what it is. We know that what animates such a force is a power of unconditional, self-affirming creation.[43]

I concur with Hallward's pointed assessment of the "primacy of non-relational difference" over the various "multiplicity" readings, an assessment which is for the most part also in keeping with the readings of Badiou and Žižek. Yet I part ways with Hallward when he reaches the conclusion that this bifurcation in Deleuze's thought can be explained by a recourse to creation as animating principle of this thought. What instead, to my mind, is needed is a more structural and analogical account of this seeming impasse, rather than a mystifying one, and it is such a model that Aquinas provides.

Aquinas insists on the disjunction between God and creature, on the disjunction between eternity and temporality, yet to think that disjuncture necessitates a structural or dialectical model (his term being "analogy") for perceiving it. Although such a necessity exists for Aquinas strictly within the theological sphere, the model it produces provides more of a groundwork for thinking outside the theological dimension insofar as this structural-dialectical framework—as opposed to the univocal Spinozist-Scotist model Deleuze draws on—admits more readily of the possibility of an outside and thus frees us from the interminable recursion of Hallward's vision of Deleuzian creation, which is irrevocably stuck by the very dint of its continual movement. By focusing instead on the point where the movement stops, where the absolute difference inheres, and thus regarding the disjunction structurally rather than through the lens of creation, I hope after a different fashion to suggest more properly "creative" ways of thinking ontology.

Such a structural model allows for a reversal that in turns helps distinguish Deleuze from a purely theological model of creation. Albeit presented with even greater nuance and lucidity, Aquinas's description of eternity is a nearly perfect parallel to Deleuze's third synthesis of time except for one key aspect, which is the idea of eternity's immutability. At the heart of *Difference and Repetition* and *The Logic of Sense* is the Nietzschean idea of the eternal return of the Same, but always with a difference. Although Deleuze does not exactly develop this implication, it seems to me that the third synthesis of time harbors a generative potential, perhaps not unlike the communication between incorporeal effects described in *The Logic of Sense*, and that will be discussed in chapter 1.

To speak of generative potential means insisting on the important difference between creation and genesis. If creation always refers back to the Creator and does not escape the theophanic framework Hallward so meticulously affixes to Deleuze, then "genesis," in being about process or structure more than beginning or end product, is a useful term for escaping the impasse into which Hallward places Deleuze's oeuvre. To argue that Deleuze's thought is all about creation in the loose sense of, say, philosophy being the creation of concepts, or the artist creating a work of art, is to miss the strong impersonal and non-human-oriented dimension of Deleuze's thought. Hallward certainly does not fall into this trap, but the current secular usage of the term "creation" does, and Hallward is quite right to point out that a theological and basically Scholastic notion of creation is in fact much closer to Deleuze's project. It is certainly more apposite to appeal to a theological model, according to which the process of creation does not originate in a strictly human source (which it certainly does not do for Deleuze), than to a secular model. But crucially, insofar as Deleuze embraces creation, it is bound up with his notion of both static and dynamic genesis, and it is the claim here that a rigorous investigation of the static realm with its theological counterparts allows for the subsequent possibility of bringing this divine sphere squarely into the world.[44]

In other words, the highest plane for Deleuze, as with Aquinas, is linked to an intemporal form of stasis. Whereas for Aquinas, this is the realm of God as Creator and first mover, for Deleuze this is a second- or third-order realm. And this is the critical difference: Deleuze's most rarefied pronouncements may resemble a theological domain—and these are the bold stakes of Hallward's thesis—yet the directionality is different. Whereas Aquinas's model is top-down, Deleuze's is bottom-up, and it is never clear how high it can go. It is never clear what can be generated in strange and perhaps monstrous creation from the third order of time or, as discussed in part 1, from Deleuze's desubjectified incorporeal states of affairs.

In *Summa contra Gentiles*, Aquinas writes: "God's action, which is without pre-existing matter and is called creation, is neither a motion nor a change, properly speaking."[45] At the end of the chapter, he continues: "[I]f creation preceded its product, as do motion or change, then some subject would have to be prior to it; and this is contrary to the nature of creation. Creation, therefore, is neither a motion nor a change."[46] Whereas the "before" of God's creation is not only immobile but subjectless for Aquinas, it is the "after" of Deleuzian genesis that is properly desubjectified in its space of higher immobility (an example discussed in chapter 7 is the "world without others"). In Thomist creation, at issue is a type of static genesis in which something comes from nothing but not in a way that is univocal. As

Aquinas writes in chapter 19 of the same section of *Summa contra Gentiles*, "But between being and non-being, which are as it were the extremes of creation, no mean can possibly exist. Therefore, in creation there is no succession."[47] Despite the idea of analogy so importantly linked to Thomas, we also see, in the elaboration of creation, the idea of a differential that cannot be broached, and indeed Aquinas goes on to note the way in which "substance is not susceptible of degrees."[48] This is the nonunivocist side that Deleuze shares with Aquinas, the emphasis on difference of kind and the rejection of categories of mediation, and this will be discussed in part 1 under the rubric of dialectic (clearly a non-Hegelian variant that rejects mediation).

This process of creation has a remarkable similarity to Deleuze's notion of static genesis, one of the types of genesis outlined in *The Logic of Sense* and *Difference and Repetition*. In *Difference and Repetition*, Deleuze writes:

> It is sufficient to understand that the genesis takes place in time not between one actual term, however small, and another actual term, but between the virtual and its actualization — in other words, it goes from the structure to its incarnation, from the conditions of a problem to the cases of solution, from the differential elements and their ideal connections to actual terms and diverse real relations which constitute at each moment the actuality of time. This is a genesis without dynamism, evolving necessarily in the element of a supra-historicity, a *static-genesis*.[49]

One of the difficulties of Deleuze's model, something that distinguishes him from Aquinas, is that the directionality of genesis is ultimately variable. On the one hand, as described in the passage above, static genesis goes from the structure to its incarnation, from the virtual to the actual. Hallward thus concludes that any form of actualization in the world is confined to these static structures outside of history that stop "real politics."[50] Yet this only accounts for one Deleuzian directionality. Harder to grasp is the simultaneous movement from the more worldly to the otherworldly (the structure-Other to the world without others, discussed in chapter 7; the corporeal to the incorporeal, discussed in chapter 1). Is this the same movement? Or, to put it differently, is the *static genesis* the same as the seeming *arrestation in stasis* (the incorporeal, the third synthesis of time)? My contention is that the latter actually opens onto a barely thinkable realm that may have unexplored potential. An attempt at exploring such potential is made throughout but especially in chapter 2 and all of part 3.

This book's final section, then, argues that Deleuze's notion of becoming is bound up with this second-order stasis of being (as opposed to Aquinas's first-order divine stasis). Aquinas writes in *Summa contra Gentiles* that "[God] is immobile, as we proved in Book I of this work. It therefore remains that creation is instantaneous. Thus, a thing simultaneously is being created and is created, even as a thing at the same moment is being illuminated and is illuminated."[51] Or in the reply to an objection in the *Summa*, he writes: "In things which are made without movement, to become and to be already made are simultaneous."[52] This brings us directly to *The Logic of Sense* and to Aquinas's once again remarkable proximity to the Deleuzian motif of Lewis Carroll's Alice, who is simultaneously becoming bigger and smaller. These are the opening lines of *The Logic of Sense*:

> *Alice* and *Through the Looking-Glass* involve a category of very special things: events, pure events. When I say "Alice becomes larger," I mean that she becomes larger than she was. By the same token, however, she becomes smaller than she is now. Certainly, she is not bigger and smaller at the same time. She is larger now; she was smaller before. But it is at the same moment that one becomes larger than one was and smaller than one becomes. This is the simultaneity of a becoming whose characteristic is to elude the present.[53]

This passage suggests that it is not only the third synthesis of time from *Difference and Repetition* that can be compared with the Thomist model but also the logic of being, becoming, and event from *The Logic of Sense*. Chapter 11 argues that Blanchot's fiction at once describes a temporality of the Aion, such as the one presented above using the example of Alice, and arrests that becoming so that it no longer eludes the present but resides squarely within it. In this fashion it returns becoming to being in reverse fashion from Aquinas's theological model. This is the space that Deleuze gestures to but does not quite arrive at, and this book's final section attempts to envision, alongside Blanchot and certain examples from American literature and landscape, several possibilities for thinking such an arrival. To reiterate, I am not claiming that the parallels between Deleuze and Aquinas are perfect, or that Deleuze's model is theological through and through, but that the heuristic of such an unlikely comparison actually helps defend Deleuze against concerns that his too-close association with univocity, mysticism, vitalism, and the virtual opens his work to. Thus the theological model — the assertion of Deleuze's Scholasticism — helps to articulate more precisely the ontological import of Deleuze's project but also where his ontology departs from a theological domain. For if God is the terrain where these other forms of logic and temporality can be accessed, as is done in such extraordinary fashion in Scholastic thought, then Deleuze, contra Hallward, actually provides the structure for bringing this material down into this world, because he shows that in fact anything at all, especially something like a rock or a larval subject, may be just as capable, if not more so, of the same types of static — and even dynamic — geneses.

PART ONE

Dialectic

The four chapters in part 1 consider Deleuze as an unlikely thinker of the dialectic. They follow from a minor strain of Deleuze scholarship that looks beyond Deleuze's avowed renunciation of the dialectic and instead probes another, perhaps less Hegelian mode of dialectic that persists in Deleuze. In this fashion, I am attempting to think Deleuze's penchant, at least in the period before his joint writings with Guattari, for a logic of form and division that not only has pronounced affinities with Scholastic thought but also corresponds to a certain "valence" of the dialectic. This valence of dialectic takes its model in Plato's dialectic of division and is developed by an extended juxtaposition of Deleuze's early theory of temporality alongside that of the early Sartre, where there exists a surprising affinity in both thinkers' consideration of what happens when a solid object is cut or bent.

The second, third, and fourth chapters each consider the work of Pierre Klossowski in order to highlight, in the fashion of the Sartre example, the more predictable affinity between Deleuze and his fellow philosopher (and novelist and painter) Klossowski. But they go on to suggest that Klossowski in fact espouses a more radical form of dialectic or disjunctive synthesis, one that draws on the force of the disjointed mental state that often accompanies physical hardship and recuperates a Thomist model of analogy, something as outlined in the introduction that Deleuze overtly rejects yet flirts with in his early work and his writings on Klossowski. Nonetheless, a convergence emerges from these readings, whereby Sartre, Klossowski, and Deleuze are shown to champion a similar structure, or logic of form, which will be the subject of part 2. Part 1 concludes with a reflection on the importance of the *tableau vivant*, and immobility more generally, in Klossowski's fiction and Deleuze's writings on cinema. This anticipates the sustained discussion of the ontology of immobility in part 3.

CHAPTER ONE

Solid Dialectic in Sartre and Deleuze

NOT ONLY IS THERE a common persistence of the dialectic in the philosophy of Jean-Paul Sartre and Gilles Deleuze, but linked to this there is a persistence of the solid object that cuts to the very heart of a theory of temporality. Lurking on the horizon of smooth space is the equally intricate concept of solid time. Here, solid time is used in two related senses. First, it indicates a theory of temporality that is not fluid or continuous but rather makes concrete distinctions between past and present and between present and future. Second, it refers to the exemplary function of solid objects in illustrating the dialectical possibilities of time; rather than flowing like a river, time is malleable in the form of a solid object—it may be bent like a nail or cut like a piece of fruit. Solid, then, refers both to solid distinctions and to the literal solid objects that are used to make such distinctions. It is my contention that solid objects provide the framework for a phenomenology of time that goes beyond the customary limitations of the human and the corporeal.

Though Sartre discusses temporality at length in *Being and Nothingness*, it is fundamentally a time that is perceptible from the standpoint of a human consciousness located within a human body. Yet submerged within this eminently humanist enterprise is a counterrealm of "incorporeal transformations," to draw on a concept from Deleuze's *The Logic of Sense*. What links Sartre's incorporeal to that of Deleuze is that both depend in their very form on a logic of complete separation. Such a juxtaposition of Sartre and Deleuze seems, particularly from a Deleuzian perspective, somewhat counterintuitive. Insofar as Sartre is often regarded as an unreconstructed humanist from the vantage point of a slightly later moment in French philosophy (the moment of Deleuze, Foucault, Derrida, etc.), it might be asked very justly what Sartre has to offer the so-called poststructuralist turn toward the inhuman, where, among other things, the inhuman signals the question of what it might mean to regard the human from the perspective of the inanimate object.

The superlative model for this attention to the gaze of the inhuman is Jacques Lacan's anecdote of the sardine can in *The Four Fundamental Concepts of Psychoanalysis*. Lacan illustrates how the inanimate object, in this case a sardine can, repositions the human viewer in an unsettling fashion through its capacity to stare back. He tells a lengthy story about being a young intellectual "slumming" on a fishing boat in Brittany. A fisherman named Petit-Jean, spying a sardine can floating in the water (the fishermen helped supply the canning industry), accosts Lacan: "*You see that can? Do you see it? Well, it doesn't see you!*" Lacan analyzes the encounter as follows: "To begin with, if what Petit-Jean said to me, namely, that the can did not see me, had any meaning, it was because in a sense, it was looking at me, all the same. It was looking at me at the level of the point of light, the point at which everything that looks at me is situated — and I am not speaking metaphorically."[1] One thing that Sartre and Deleuze have in common is that they are not metaphorical thinkers. They are thinkers of difference and disjunction rather than similarity. Given this common focus on disjunction, Sartre provides the examples and Deleuze the tools to conceptualize how we might think the sardine can looking, though not so much at the level of the point of light as Lacan suggests, but at the level of the opaque solid object.

Although Sartre would not grant a solid object the capacity to stare back, he defines it so forcefully in opposition to the human that a new objectival dimension is paradoxically opened up. Sartre frequently refers to a realm of solid, opaque objects — chairs, tables, and inkwells crop up a lot — as a backdrop for the human viewer. In *Being and Nothingness*, he poses a radical disjunction between the affect of a person and the objects that surround the person:

> The dog-eared book with the well-read pages is not by itself a book of which Pierre has turned the pages, of which he no longer turns the pages. If we consider it as the present, transcendent motivation of my perception or even as the synthetic flux, regulated by my sensible impressions, then it is merely a volume with turned down, worn pages; it can refer only to itself or to present objects, to the lamp which illuminates it, to the table which holds it.[2]

This example from the early part of *Being and Nothingness* illustrates Sartrean method at its most extreme. Although Sartre qualifies statements such as this, especially at later points where he introduces the complexity of the body and the gaze in their relation to others,[3] his whole philosophy nevertheless rests on a series of absolute separations. The dog-eared book is not tinged with human affect, does not harbor a trace of Pierre's person, his self-consciousness, or of its proper history of production — "it can refer only to itself or present objects." In *Sartre: The Origins of a Style*, Fredric Jameson highlights the fundamental opposition between things and consciousness that underlies Sartre's work, noting that "this particular work turns out to depend constantly and insistently on such an opposition."[4] Such an opposition might be expanded to include, at different junctures of Sartre's oeuvre, oppositions between ego and consciousness,[5] self and other, and in particular between human and object. To be sure, there is a relation between the two terms of each opposition, a relation that, as many of Sartre's critics have noted, is hard to define because it seems to be constantly shifting.

Rather than adding one more voice in an attempt to delineate what the relations between opposing terms might entail, my aim is to focus instead on the opposition itself, on the flickering moments of boldly defined opposition that populate Sartre's philosophy and literature. Furthermore, there exists an odd copresence of extreme opposition with moments where the opposition is entirely undone, especially if Sartre's fiction is read alongside his philosophy. In *Being and Nothingness* — that work where objects are so carefully set apart from the human — one finds the following sentence that leaps out in the middle of Sartre's famous discussion of the caress: "In my desiring perception, I discover something like a *flesh* of objects."[6] "A *flesh* of objects" is a notion that anticipates Maurice Merleau-Ponty's concept of flesh in *The Visible and the Invisible* (where the corporeal and the incorporeal coexist in such a way that one cannot be isolated from the other), yet it is a notion that seems very un-Sartrean.[7] In a similar fashion, Sartre's fiction, especially the early short stories collected in *The Wall*, are replete with flying statues, obsequious Turkish delight candies, wooden benches that register a death about to happen, and forks with evil intentions: in short, a world poised on the disintegration of a rigid boundary between the object and the human.[8] Yet, as Jameson suggests with respect to *The Wall*, the opening up of the human/object distinction only serves to underscore the very separation it would seem to undermine:

> So here the extreme humanization of things is the one formulation of them which will not falsify them: we know that they are not human, that they are the absolutely non-human, and the terms are sufficiently exaggerated for us to make no mistake about it. If all language is an assumption of objects, if all language is a kind of humanization, then the only safe formulation is one that pushes the humanization to absurd lengths, that labels and announces itself so blatantly a falsification that it can do no harm, and that behind it, behind this terrifying suddenly human mask, the inhuman being of things makes its presence felt. It is obvious that this literary solution, and the problem to which it was a response, are both dependent on the radical split of the world into two parts: only in a world where things were so divorced from consciousness and from its language would it be necessary for them to leap into their opposite to be presented.[9]

Sartre's great originality—in contrast to the more nuanced phenomenological writings of Simone de Beauvoir and Merleau-Ponty—is an almost vulgar penchant for defining two terms in the most extreme form of opposition. While Merleau-Ponty uses concepts such as flesh and even perception (not unrelated, despite Merleau-Ponty's protestations, to what Bergson does with matter and memory)[10] to gesture to the mutual embeddedness, the intertwining of things that would appear to be separate, Sartre gives a radical separation to things that would appear to be interconnected. How can we even conceive of going into the absent Pierre's room and entirely dissociating Pierre's objects from his person? Such a thought process goes against the very fiber of a contemporary theoretical discourse that seeks to make alignments, chart interconnectedness, note the persistent traces of memory or history or what have you. Yet this is precisely what Sartre is suggesting at this juncture of his argument. The question, then, is what new perception is opened when we take Pierre's room and posit that, rather than his objects bearing the haunting traces of his person, the two are in some sense entirely distinct?

Such a disjunctive logic is precisely what Deleuze employs in *Difference and Repetition* and *The Logic of Sense* when he emphasizes the need to make differences of kind rather than differences of degree. Using the model of division from Plato's *Sophist* (where everything is posed in terms of a twofold distinction, and once a choice is made a new opposition presents itself, thus forming a lineage of the terms chosen), Deleuze is careful to note that it is a specific type of dialectic that is at issue here — one where there is no mediating term, where it is not so much the distinction at issue but the lineage that issues from the distinction. The following commentary on Plato in *Difference and Repetition* also appears nearly verbatim in *The Logic of Sense*:

> For example, we divide art into arts of production and arts of acquisition: but then why is fishing among the arts of acquisition? What is missing here is mediation — that is, the identity of a concept capable of serving as middle term. . . . Division is not the inverse of a "generalization"; it is not a determination of species. It is in no way a method of determining species, but one of selection. It is not a question of dividing a determinate genus into definite species, but of dividing a confused species into pure lines of descent, or of selecting a pure line from material which is not. . . . Difference is not between species, between two determinations of a genus, but entirely on one side, within the chosen line of descent: there are no longer contraries, within a single genus, but pure and impure, good and bad, authentic and inauthentic, in a mixture which gives rise to a large species. Pure difference, the pure concept of difference, not difference mediated within the concept in general, in the genus and the species.[11]

Although I would argue, in continuing the case for Deleuze's often disavowed Scholasticism, that the *differentiae* that enable the predication of species from genus have more in common with Deleuze's notion of "pure difference" (*haecceity*) than Deleuze would allow, what is significant here is precisely the series of differences rather than the specifics of the difference itself, the lineage of the line of descent rather than the third term that mediates between the first two — though, again, I do not agree that the *differentia* or "specific difference" is simply a mediating predicable, but that is another argument. As Deleuze writes of the dialectic in *The Logic of Sense*, "The Platonic project comes to light only when we turn back to the method of division, for this method is not just one dialectical procedure among others. It assembles the whole power of the dialectic in order to combine with it another power, and represents thus the entire system."[12] The Platonic method of division here emerges as an ultimate expression of the dialectic. It is precisely such a strong notion of difference, so strong that its status as dialectic is in fact called into question (is it still dialectic when the possibility of mediation is put into radical abeyance?)[13] that is the crucial link between Deleuze and Sartre. Though their respective philosophies differ markedly in content—Sartre's humanism versus Deleuze's antihumanism is but one striking distinction—these philosophies share a law of form,[14] a similar method (even a similar ethics) of radical differentiation.

This similar formal penchant for pure differentiation in Deleuze and Sartre is at certain moments marked by a convergence of content. The domain of temporality is such a point of convergence. Although they employ different terms and examples in their respective discussions of temporality, both Sartre and Deleuze draw on a fundamentally dualistic notion of time, and indeed a strange resonance inheres between Sartre's *Being and Nothingness* and *The Logic of Sense*. Moreover, both thinkers appeal to the nether realm of solid objects—and as we shall see, solid vegetables—in elaborating a philosophy of temporality.

One of the finest illustrations of Sartrean temporality is the example in *Being and Nothingness* of two nails that appear identical. However, one is newly made and the other was once bent but has been straightened. Though similar in appearance, upon hammering, one goes straight into the wall and the other becomes bent the way it had been before. Thus it would seem that the two nails react differently because of their different pasts. However, Sartre judges this example (given by one Chevallier) to be in bad faith and argues against the idea of the present being determined by its past. He writes that

> to offer as proof of this permanence of the past the remanence of magnetization in a piece of soft iron is not to prove anything worthwhile. Here we are with a phenomenon which outlives its cause, not with a subsistence of the cause qua cause *in the past state*. For a long time after the stone which pierced the water has fallen into the bottom of the sea, concentric waves still pass over its surface; here nobody makes an appeal to some sort of action by the past to explain this phenomenon; the mechanism of it is almost visible.[15]

On the one hand, the very framework for Sartre's argument comes from a marked anthropocentrism, for he argues that there is no violence in the phenomenon of an object both possessing and possessed by its past — as if there were no violent history of the canning process that produced the sardine can — and suggests by implication that this investigation of material objects may serve as a groundwork for approaching the more complex question of the "past of *living beings*."[16] On the other hand, though devaluing the object used as an example, Sartre's writing is nevertheless haunted by solid objects, and not infrequently solid objects such as the nail that are acted on violently — cut, hammered, or bent.

Jameson notes, in his study of Sartre, the odd violence of Sartre's verbs:

> [V]erbs of unusual violence, especially in the philosophic works where milder ones might have been used, keep things moving explosively forward: such verbs as "die," "surge," "seize," "invade," and so on. But such verbs have ambiguous effects: they do keep things going but at the same time they separate the new thing bursting into being somewhat irrevocably from all that has preceded it, as if it had been separated by the enormous gap of one of those instants.[17]

Sartre's solid objects, like his verbs, are surrounded by a syntax of violence, and they thereby undergird a logic of irrevocable separation. Though the objects are used as limit examples to distinguish them from the human, and also perhaps to gesture to a better and nonviolent realm in which human interactions will take place, they are conjured with such force and such relish that it is hard not to read a bit against the grain, to read in Sartre a fervor for the very realm of the inanimate that he is constantly setting off against the human.

What is noteworthy here is the *form* through which Sartre's temporal reflections are introduced, the violent exemplarity of inanimate objects that serve as a prolegomena to a study of human temporality. Although Sartre uses the objects in question primarily as a means of accessing the radical disjunction between past and present, it is hard to read these passages without considering the vivid specificity of the examples. Are the exuberant, and often exuberantly violent, actions performed on solid objects (along with the verbs used to describe them) perhaps a signal of something else? If so, this something else is not simply that the object substitutes for some underlying violence actually directed toward the human or reflects its own production by the human hands. Rather, it is the object itself that points to a mode of perception that is beyond the limitations of the human, in spite of the fact that Sartre would claim to use the object only to anthropocentric ends.

In *The Logic of Sense*, Deleuze employs a notion of solid time that is strikingly similar in form to that of Sartre, though without Sartre's anthropocentrism. Like Sartre, Deleuze envisions two distinct notions of time, writing that

> time must be grasped twice, in two complementary though mutually exclusive fashions. First, it must be grasped entirely as the living present in bodies which act and are acted upon [this would correspond to the notion of a purely present temporality, which Deleuze calls "Chronos"]. Second, it must be grasped entirely as an entity infinitely divisible into past and future, and into the incorporeal effects which result from bodies, their actions and their passions [what Deleuze terms "Aion"]. Only the present exists in time and gathers together or absorbs the past and future. But only the past and future inhere in time and divide each present infinitely. These are not three successive dimensions, but two simultaneous readings of time.[18]

While Chronos and Aion are on one level entirely distinct, they both reflect a copresence of present in past and future. In the present-centered Chronos, there is a live present of past and future. In the past- and future-centered Aion, there is a constant parceling and dividing of the present.[19] Thus, Chronos and Aion are always inextricably bound up with each other yet defined according to two separate rubrics. This is not unlike the separation of the in-itself and the for-itself in Sartre's *Being and Nothingness*. While the for-itself is defined in terms of its being haunted by the in-itself (what Sartre terms "facticity"),[20] it is nonetheless present as a separate register. What is more difficult to ascertain is if or how Deleuze's Chronos/Aion distinction maps onto Sartre's in-itself/for-itself distinction. The complexities of this mapping come to the foreground when the disjunctive logic of both thinkers is illustrated by the example of the cut.

Just after the passage cited above, Deleuze goes on to quote the brilliant study by the early twentieth-century French philosopher Émile Bréhier, *La Théorie des incorporels dans l'ancien stoïcisme*:

> When the scalpel cuts through the flesh, the first body produces upon the second not a new property but a new attribute, that of being cut. The attribute does not designate any real *quality* . . . , it is, in fact, neither active nor passive, for passivity would presuppose a corporeal nature which undergoes an action [not unlike Sartre's discussion of the nail]. . . . [The Stoics distinguished] radically two planes of being, something that no one had done before them: on the one hand, real and profound being, force; on the other, the plane of facts, which frolic on the surface of being, and constitute an endless multiplicity of incorporeal beings.[21]

In this quotation Bréhier locates in the Stoics the distinction of being cut from the attribute of cutting. The one supposes a "corporeal nature," the other a more counterintuitive "incorporeal being." This in turn maps onto the division between Chronos as purely present and Aion as locus of past and future and of incorporeal events. For Deleuze, the incorporeal inheres in the past and future (Aion) and in the transformative possibilities of each. The incorporeal inheres in the verb, in the *attribute* of being bent or being cut, and not in the physical present of the cut itself. According to this system of mapping, Deleuze's Aion corresponds to Sartre's for-itself and Deleuze's Chronos to Sartre's in-itself (Sartre writes following the example of the nail that "these observations enable us to refuse *a priori* to grant a past to the in-itself").[22] However, Sartre not only links the in-itself to the past a few pages later,[23] but in the example of the nails, the present appears imbued with the incorporeal, insofar as it marks the present sameness of the two nails as opposed to their past-laden material histories where one is bent and the other straight. I argue, particularly in part 3, for the importance of attending to the potential of the incorporeal or virtual present where the present's force of inertia has the potential to arrest movement and being in a fashion that is provocative for thought. Yet at this juncture of attempting to coimplicate Sartre and Deleuze, suffice it to say that the mapping of Aion/Chronos onto for-itself/in-itself could work both ways, thus highlighting how Sartrean and Deleuzian temporalities are both marked by a structure of division that seems eminently reversible. When we move to the examples of Klossowski (in the remaining chapters of part 1) and Blanchot (in part 3), the reversibility will no longer be thinkable in the same fashion.

Such a reversibility even at the heart of what would seem to be irreversible is epitomized by the figure of the cut, which serves as a limit case in approaching a phenomenology of the inhuman. Deleuze, following Bréhier, makes a distinction between being cut and the attribute of being cut, the latter *not* being coterminous with the cut body. This second incorporeal cutting might be seen as reversible in that the cut is not irreparable. Yet when Sartre speaks of the cut, it is with the strikingly liminal vegetable example of cutting fruit. In positing that it is nothingness itself that separates human consciousness from a consciousness of its past ("it is necessary then that conscious being constitute itself in relation to its past as separated from this past by a nothingness"), he argues that "neither has there been an abrupt interpolation of an opaque element to separate prior from subsequent in the way that a knife blade cuts a piece of fruit in two."[24] By distinguishing nothingness from this opaque element that separates, he implies that a fruit cut by a knife has a simple temporality that is not infused with the nothingness of the more complex human temporality. What, however, if we were to take Sartre's example of the fruit and give it a Deleuzian twist by suggesting that the act of cutting also carries its incorporeal transformation such that on some level the cutness of the fruit is an attribute and not a corporeal state? This allows for a multiple set of associations. It suggests that what the human perceives as a radical transformation in the state of an object (the fruit being cut, the nail being bent) but also perceives as a nonthreatening form of violence (it is after all, an inanimate object or vegetable being cut and not a human) is doubly wrong.

On the one hand, we might say that the perceived radical transformation is but part of a series of incorporeal transformations. In this sense, Sartre's two examples are somewhat at odds, for the fruit example implies an irreparable corporeal transformation, whereas the nail example argues that there is no substantial difference in the nails' two histories. The nail, then, has undergone an incorporeal transformation and the fruit a corporeal one. But what makes the fruit's cutting corporeal and the nail's bending incorporeal? Does the fruit—or the human, for that matter—not harbor the same incorporeal potential? It seems that the underlying issue here is that all objects harbor both corporeal and incorporeal attributes, and it may be a matter of perception as to which takes place at a given moment. (Perhaps from the fruit's perspective there is an incorporeal and not a corporeal transformation.)

On a second level, every act of cutting is an act of violence, whether it is on a human or on a fruit; we are always being cut, but what we have in the cutting of the fruit or the bending of the nail is an encounter with the limits of human perception, the fact of our inability to understand the temporality of the nail or the fruit in anything but our terms. As Derrida has noted in his interview "Eating Well" and as Deleuze notes in a later discussion of *Alice in Wonderland* in *The Logic of Sense*, one is always doing violence to both the inanimate and the animate other, and the question is how to do it ethically. Deleuze writes:

> To eat and to be eaten — this is the operational model of bodies, the type of their mixture in depth, their action and passion, and the way in which they coexist within one another. To speak, though, is the movement of surface, and of ideational attributes or incorporeal events. What is more serious: to speak of food or to eat words? In her alimentary obsessions, Alice is overwhelmed by nightmares of absorbing and being absorbed. She finds that the poems she hears recited are about edible fish. If we then speak of food, how can we avoid speaking in front of the one who is to be served as food? . . . How can we avoid eating the pudding to which we have been *presented*?[25]

This is the eerie interpellation of Lacan's sardine can, which looks at him all the same. It is the nightmare of the edible fish looking back from its state as an inanimate object, confronting the human perceiver both with the violence he or she would rather not take note of and with the fact that this violence, this cutting, has its own nonviolent quality as a verb, as an attribute, as an incorporeal event that operates, if it is perceived at all, at the limits of human perception.

The very notion of cutting, whether as entity or as attribute, implies an object that is amenable to cutting. Although a fruit is all the more liminal in that it is largely liquid, it is nonetheless solid enough to be the object of a cut. But what about a substance so liquid as to be uncuttable? On the one hand, such a substance resists the temporal permutations of the object that is fundamentally altered by a cut at a certain point in time, taking on, as it were, the attributes of the incorporeal. On the other hand, is a dialectics of liquid even possible in the fashion of a solid dialectics? Does not liquid always defy the method of division and separation that seems so basic to Sartre and Deleuze? This opens at once a number of lines of inquiry that might be summarized as follows: what is the place of the nonsolid in Sartre and Deleuze, and how is it both figured and gendered?

It should be noted that both Deleuze and Sartre are famously associated with the nonsolid. Among other things, there is Sartre's discussion of slime at the end of *Being and Nothingness* and Deleuze and Guattari's discussion of holey space at the end of "Treatise on Nomadology." Yet the nonsolid is in both texts a vague and uncharacteristic middle category.[26] According to Sartre, "[T]he slimy reveals itself as essentially ambiguous because its fluidity exits in slow motion; there is a sticky thickness in its liquidity; it represents in itself a dawning triumph of the solid over the liquid, that is, a tendency of the indifferent in-itself, which is represented by the pure solid, to fix the liquidity, to absorb the for-itself which ought to dissolve it."[27] Slime incarnates the reversal of the directionality Sartre has been at pains to set up throughout *Being and Nothingness*, in which the for-itself is defined in its active relation to the more passive in-itself. Here, slime designates the "revenge of the in-itself," which, by this definition, is also the revenge of the solid.[28] Paradoxically, this revenge has been acted out all along in *Being and Nothingness* (not to mention the rest of Sartre's oeuvre) in the very materiality of the solid object examples he returns to again and again. As much as his work is known for slime, viscosity, nausea, and the like, it is also and more flagrantly a veritable catalog of chairs, tables, inkwells, pens, and paper cutters (objects that are interestingly visible from the writer's desk).[29] These solid objects are put in the ambiguous position of the in-itself, at once the debased term of the dualism and that which ultimately and actively haunts the seemingly more intricate for-itself. They are also the necessary counterpart to the privileged term they are defined against, here the human. They are at once what makes the human human and the marker of the nonhuman persistence that haunts. The oppositional solid, then, is absolutely necessary to Sartrean phenomenology, whereas the in-between register of slime is more nearly a middle term used to illustrate the solid and liquid in relation. Although the synthetic moment of relationality or "situation" is an important term for Sartre, my contention is that it is nonetheless subsumed by the more pervasive Sartrean methodology of extreme opposition.

Holey space serves much the same role for Deleuze and Guattari, coming in at the end of "Treatise on Nomadology—the War Machine" as the happy intermediary between the striated and the smooth. Deleuze and Guattari locate the metallurgists or smiths in an intermediate position between the sedentary peoples and the privileged nomads:

> Smiths are not nomadic among the nomads and sedentary among the sedentaries, nor half-nomadic among the nomads, half-sedentary among sedentaries. Their relation to others results from their internal itinerancy, from their vague essence, and not the reverse. It is in their specificity, it is by virtue of their itinerancy, by virtue of their inventing a holey space, that they necessarily communicate with the sedentaries and with the nomads. . . . They are in themselves double: a hybrid, an alloy, a twin formation. . . . This hybrid metallurgist, a weapon- and toolmaker, communicates with the sedentaries and with the nomads at the same time. Holey space itself communicates with smooth space and striated space.[30]

Again, this middle ground of the holey could be read as the hybrid intermediary between the smooth and the striated or the nomad and the sedentary. For that matter, I would contend that it is more the hallmark of the collaborative works—there is even less space for middle ground or mediation in Deleuze's single-authored works. And despite the favorable description the smith as inventor of holey space receives, it is only insofar as the hybrid quality of the smith and the holey itself approaches the smooth and the nomadic that these terms take on a positive valence. It is ultimately on one side of the line of division that they fall, and their mediating function—like Sartre's slime—is if anything more nearly the exception that proves the rule of nonmediation.[31]

It is precisely in the realm of nonmediation that I would locate the embedded feminist potential of this work. It is certainly not an easy task to redeem what would seem to be the relentless masculinist point of view of these writers, especially Sartre.[32] It might seem that, by elevating the solid object as the marker of radical separation underlying the work of Sartre and Deleuze, there is an unquestionable privileging of masculinist categories. Nonetheless, it is not so much solids that are gendered masculine as it is slime and holes that are gendered feminine, once again especially in Sartre.[33] Important work, notably by Luce Irigaray, has been done in defense of the often debased and feminized concept of the fluid.[34] Yet what has not been systematically undertaken is a feminist defense of the solid. One approach to such a project would entail a bracketing of the middle ground in favor of more extreme polarities, whether they be an affirmation of so-called essentialist categories, a claim of absolute difference, or even a direct reclaiming of attributes associated with the masculine, such as the solid and the mind. An example of the feminist potential of Deleuzian difference will be taken up in the next chapter, as we shift our focus to Deleuze and Klossowski. If Sartre and Deleuze do not provide the content for imagining a future project oriented toward the solid feminine, they do suggest a form, and as we shall see, the Deleuze-Klossowski conjunction brings that content and form closer together.

CHAPTER TWO

Toward a Feminist Philosophy of Mind

ONE OF DELEUZE'S PHILOSOPHICAL achievements is that he renders the classic mind-body dualism both more complex and ultimately beside the point. He does this by showing over and again how the body and the mind are inseparably linked to each other, how they are part of the same assemblage that is to be regarded in terms of what it can do rather than what it is or is not. It follows, then, that to link Deleuze to a concrete distinction between the mind and the body is treading on risky ground. In the same fashion, feminist readings of Deleuze by Rosi Braidotti and Elizabeth Grosz underscore the difficulty of the mind-body distinction and suggest a form of "thinking through the body" as a way to get beyond this dualism. What I propose is an extension of these analyses that builds on their insights yet returns to the unwanted mind-body split to suggest that there are perhaps some things — and things pertinent to both Deleuze and feminism — that a mind in disjunction from its body can still do. Indeed, in certain (and often extreme) cases there is a lived necessity of maintaining such disjunctions. Drawing on the work of Braidotti and Grosz, I outline a parallel but reconfigured framework that puts greater emphasis on the world of the spirit and the mind. Using Deleuze's studies of Spinoza and Pierre Klossowski's study of Nietzsche, I then suggest ways in which the mind's potential for exceeding the body and maintaining the dualism allows access to new states of health and exuberance.

In the essay "Toward a New Nomadism: Feminist Deleuzian Tracks; or, Metaphysics and Metabolism," Braidotti maps the work of a series of feminist thinkers of sexual difference — including Luce Irigaray, Monique Wittig, Judith Butler, and Donna Haraway — onto such Deleuze and Guattarian concepts as the rhizome, the body without organs, becoming-woman and becoming-minoritarian, and nomadic thinking.[1] Without rehearsing the various linkages Braidotti proposes or attempting an overall synthesis on the same scale, I wish instead to highlight those specific points in Braidotti's text where she discusses the mind-body relationship and the relationship of embodiment to thinking.[2]

Initially, Braidotti casts feminist theory as working to overcome a history of female disembodiment:

> [F]eminist theory . . . expresses women's . . . structural need to posit themselves as female subjects, that is to say, not as disembodied entities, but rather as corporeal and consequently sexed beings. Following Adrienne Rich I believe that the redefinition of the female subject starts with the revaluation of the bodily roots of subjectivity and the rejection of the traditional vision of the knowing subject as universal, neutral, and consequently gender-free. This "positional" or situated way of seeing the subject is based on the understanding that the most important location or situation is the rooting of the subject into the spatial frame of the body.[3]

This passage begins by locating a fundamental disjunction between "female subjects" and "disembodied entities." While these disembodied entities have historically fallen on the side of the "universal, neutral, and consequently gender-free" masculine subject, the question at hand is whether there is anything in these disembodied entities that is redemptive for feminism. Moreover, could the very disjunction female subject/disembodied entity be in itself a productive contradiction?

Braidotti concludes this passage with a call for a "rooting of the subject into the spatial frame of the body." While such a rooting is a necessary corrective to a long-standing disdain for the body, it also seems that more than one such rooting is possible. An alternate perspective would be to situate the subject along the lines of tension between the body and the mind. Indeed, later moments of Braidotti's text provide the seeds for such an alternate form of embodiment, one where the body does not simply correspond to the physical frame of the person. Rather, the body is itself a complex interaction of forces, not all of them clearly readable as either physical or human. It is in articulating such a notion of the body a few pages later that Braidotti has recourse to Deleuze. I quote at length:

> The embodiment of the subject is for Deleuze a form of bodily materiality, but not of the natural biological kind. He rather takes the body as the complex interplay of highly constructed social and symbolic forces. The body is not an essence, let alone a biological substance. It is a play of forces, a surface of intensities: pure simulacra without originals. Deleuze is therefore of great help to feminists because he deessentializes the body, sexuality, and sexed identities. The embodied subject is a term in a process of intersecting forces (affects), spatiotemporal variables that are characterized by their mobility, changeability, and transitory nature.[4]

In thinking the body as an interplay of forces,[5] Braidotti uses Deleuze to portray a body that is populated with things and flows and movements that would belie any static or absolute essence (I argue in subsequent chapters for the force of the static essence). Furthermore, such a fluid conception of the body reinforces the now standard and certainly somewhat simplified critique of the Cartesian system of the mind-body dualism or split. Such a critique would run as follows: if the body really were a complex system of forces, not a distinct entity in itself but rather a system of overlapping and changing boundaries, how can there be some kind of pure and absolute boundary between it and the mind? Braidotti presents precisely this argument when she writes: "Clearly for feminist corporeal materialism, the body is not a fixed essence, a natural given. . . . [T]he 'body' as theoretical *topos* is an attempt to overcome the classical mind-body dualism of Cartesian origins, in order to think anew about the structure of the thinking subject. The body is then an interface, a threshold, a field of intersecting material and symbolic forces."[6] According to such an analysis, the body is used as a philosophical tool to disrupt the mind-body dualism.

In *Feminism and Geography*, Gillian Rose helpfully explicates this use of the body as an anti-Cartesian tool when, after reviewing several feminist theories of space, she concludes: "This sense of space offered by these feminists dissolves the split between the mind and the body by thinking through the body, their bodies."[7] What Rose puts forth is a bodily appropriation of a mental capacity—thought. Thus thought is not just the purview of the mind but is also integrated into the fiber of the body, and in this fashion both mind and body partake of the same mechanism. In other words, thought is not thought without the body to "plunge" into. This expression is taken from the opening lines of Deleuze's chapter "Cinema, Body and Brain, Thought" in *Cinema 2*. Here, Deleuze presents a slightly different version of thinking through the body, one in which thought, in order to reach its unthought, must delve into the body. Deleuze writes that "the body is no longer the obstacle that separates thought from itself, that which it has to overcome to reach thinking. It is on the contrary that which it plunges into or must plunge into, in order to reach the unthought."[8] The apparent ease with which the body can be "thought through" or "plunged into" is striking. At issue is how mind-body relations might work differently in those cases where the body actively resists integration with the mind or vice versa. Furthermore, could something interesting be said to happen when, to reverse Deleuze's formulation, thought also reaches itself by working through the body as obstacle? That is, could thought work both through and against the body in ways that are not exclusively masculinist or retrograde?

Apprehending such a potentially antagonistic working of thought or mind *against* the body entails looking at thought for what it can do. Deleuze's entire oeuvre might be considered as a manual for precisely this, for articulating what it is that philosophy as thought does. It is in this sense, then, that while not drawing necessarily Deleuzian conclusions, my line of inquiry strives to work within a Deleuzian framework of conceptualizing that which is potentially new about thought.

Braidotti describes the newness that Deleuze brings to thought when she writes that "thinking is for Deleuze not the expression of in-depth interiority, or the enactment of transcendental models; it is a way of establishing connections among a multiplicity of impersonal forces."[9] Furthermore, "[T]hinking for Deleuze is instead life lived at the highest possible power—thinking is about finding new images. Thinking is about change and transformation."[10] In holding to the spirit, if not the letter, of a Deleuzian quest for thinking as newness, I use Deleuze to elaborate what I would term a new form of disembodied thought. In the same chapter of *Cinema 2*, Deleuze compares "cinema of the brain" to "cinema of the body" and distinguishes them in terms of attitude and geste: "There is as much thought in the body as there is shock and violence in the brain. There is an equal amount of feeling in both of them. The brain gives orders to the body which is just an outgrowth of it, but the body also gives orders to the brain which is just a part of it: in both cases, these will not be the same bodily attitudes nor the same cerebral gest[e]."[11] While the brain and body are presented as parallel and equal, they are nonetheless marked by an important differential. This differential occurs on the level of "bodily attitude" and "cerebral gest[e]," which, according to Deleuze, are not the same. To push this line of reasoning further, what if we were to magnify the differential between bodily attitude and cerebral geste so that the space in between becomes a radically disembodied and incorporeal one? (The disjunction of bodily attitude and cerebral geste in Klossowski is taken up in chapter 4.) And if this is done, how could that space be used productively and strategically?

It is here that Elizabeth Grosz's account of Deleuze with respect to the mind, the body, and the incorporeal is of particular importance. Like Braidotti, Grosz provides a series of frameworks for a new conjunction of Deleuze and feminism, drawing on such feminist theorists as Alice Jardine, Irigaray, and Braidotti and on such Deleuzian concepts as rhizomatics, the body without organs, and becoming-woman.[12] Like Braidotti, Grosz articulates the conjunction of Deleuze and feminism along the axis of the mind-body duality and, more specifically, the displacement of this axis by a foregrounding of the body. Grosz first poses her argument for Deleuzian embodiment as a series of rhetorical questions at the beginning of her chapter on Deleuze in *Volatile Bodies: Toward a Corporeal Feminism*. This series of questions echoes many of Braidotti's formulations, discussed above:

> Can accounts of subjectivity and the psychical interior be adequately explained in terms of the body? Can depths, the interior, the subjective, and the private instead be seen in terms of surfaces, bodies, and material relations? Can the mind/body dualism be overcome using the concepts associated with the devalued term of the binary pair of mind and body, that is, are the body and corporeality the (disavowed) grounds and terms on which the opposition is erected and made possible? What happens to conceptual frameworks if the body stands in place of the mind or displaces it from its privileged position defining humanity against its various others?[13]

Like Braidotti and Rose, Grosz claims the body as the unacknowledged framework for the mind-body duality. By supplanting the mind, the body allows feminist access to a new space that is neither masculinist nor humanist. Such a new space has indeed been charted by such thinkers as Grosz and Braidotti and has opened the way for still different approaches. One such approach is also neither masculinist nor humanist, though in privileging a certain concept of the mind it might appear to be precisely that which a corporeal feminism is defined against. Yet, just in the way the body has been reclaimed as a site of feminist practice, so too does the realm of the mind contain the same, albeit difficult, potential. In charting out a Deleuzian-feminist space of corporeality, Grosz simultaneously provides the navigational tools for a feminist inquiry into the incorporeal.[14]

In the same fashion as Braidotti, Grosz gives a new definition of the body, which surpasses the restricted physical space of the person. However, Grosz goes beyond Braidotti in inscribing the incorporeal into this new definition of the body. Following from Deleuze and Guattari, Grosz specifies how such seemingly disembodied notions as the incorporeal, the nonhuman, and the inanimate can help form a new definition and practice of the body:

> [Deleuze and Guattari's] notion of the body as a discontinuous, nontotalizable series of processes, organs, flows, energies, corporeal substances and incorporeal events, speeds and durations, may be of great value to feminists attempting to reconceive bodies outside the binary oppositions imposed on the body by the mind/body, nature/culture, subject/object and interior/exterior oppositions. They provide an altogether different way of understanding the body in its connections with other bodies, both human and nonhuman, animate and inanimate, linking organs and biological processes to material objects and social practices while refusing to subordinate the body to a unity or a homogeneity of the kind provided by the body's subordination to consciousness or to biological organization.[15]

If the body combines "corporeal substances and incorporeal events," it seems that the act of thinking, or an act of mind, would also be just such an incorporeal event in conjunction with a corporeal substance.

Where exactly lies the disjunction between mind and matter, thought and body? In his study of Bergson, Deleuze links the coincidence of mind and matter to a form of virtual perception. Explicating Bergson, he writes,

"We perceive things where they are, perception puts us at once into matter, is impersonal, and coincides with the perceived object. . . . There cannot be a difference in kind, but only a difference in degree between the faculty of the brain and the function of the core, between the perception of matter and matter itself."[16] This is a curious reference, as Deleuze goes on to champion the Bergson who insists on difference of kind over difference of degree. Yet, just as Deleuze finds elements of degree over kind in Bergson, so too Deleuze does not always pursue to its conclusions the logic of difference in kind and pure difference that he puts forward in his work from the 1960s. The question of difference of degree in Deleuze is considered further in what follows, but first it is useful to examine how the coincidence of thought with matter might as readily fall under the domain of the incorporeal as the corporeal.

Such a vision of mind as orchestrating a mind-body conjunction is perhaps closest in the philosophical tradition to Spinoza's view of mind as the idea of the body. By this account, the mind and body are inextricably linked, yet the mind as idea also exceeds the boundaries of a single physical body and takes in or intersects other conjunctures of minds and bodies.[17] Deleuze glosses this helpfully in *Expressionism in Philosophy*, where he writes that "the soul, insofar as it is the idea of an existing body, is itself composed of a great number of ideas which correspond to the body's component parts, and which are extrinsically distinct from one another. The faculties, furthermore, which the soul possesses insofar as it is the idea of an existing body, are genuine extensive parts, which cease to belong to the soul once the body itself ceases to exist."[18] On this account, the intricacy of the soul or mind is fundamentally dependent on the body's existence. If the body is no longer living, the mind is no longer the idea of the body. Yet, as Genevieve Lloyd underscores in her reading of *Spinoza*, there is a fundamental ambivalence in the final section of the *Ethics* over this question, where Spinoza at once suggests that "the mind can only imagine anything, or remember what is past, while the body endures" (part 5, prop. 21) and that "the human mind cannot be absolutely destroyed with the body, but there remains of it something which is eternal" (part 5, prop. 23). While Lloyd does not view this conflict over whether the mind outlives the body or coincides with it as a contradiction—but argues instead that "the mind resorts to the 'fiction' of eternity as a state to be attained"[19]

—I think that Spinoza's philosophy of mind is useful precisely because it enables the mind to simultaneously inhabit seemingly contradictory states.[20] That is, the mind is interwoven into the very fiber of the body and at the same time seeks to outlive or transcend the body, here in the form of taking on a quality of eternity, not unlike eternity as Deleuze takes it up in *Difference and Repetition* and at other points in *Expressionism in Philosophy*, as discussed in the introduction. It is this oscillation or dialectic between mind as idea of body (mind as mind-body) and mind as exceeding body (mind as not mind-body) that is at the heart of the philosophy of mind at issue here.

This disjunctive dialectic between mind as coincident with body and mind as somehow apart from it contains a potential energy that, if capitalized on, might have useful practical consequences. Not least of these consequences is a revaluation of the complexity of mind in feminist thought. It seems fair to state that in contemporary feminist philosophical discourse, it is still the body and not the mind that holds sway.[21] While the body has been studied with all its attendant complexities, the mind is skirted around with much more caution, and for good reason. Yet it seems that we have arrived at a time and a place in feminist thinking where to move forward might just mean to welcome back the mind (albeit hesitantly) into the registers of acceptable discourse. These registers would not be the old ones where the mind signaled a cultivated humanism, but rather ones where, according to the logic of oscillation outlined above, thought is mobilized both to heighten the mind-body conjunction and to dismantle it. Grosz expresses this twofold dynamic with respect to the body when she discusses Deleuze and Guattari's antihuman and elemental approach to the body:

> Deleuze and Guattari produce a radical antihumanism that renders animals, nature, atoms, even quasars as modes of radical alterity. . . . Deleuze and Guattari imply a clear movement toward imperceptibility that is in many ways similar to the quest of physics for the microscopic structures of matter, the smallest component, the most elementary particle. If it remains materialist at this level, it is a materialism that is far beyond or different from the body, or bodies: their work is like an acidic dissolution of the body, and the subject along with it.[22]

Grosz highlights the way in which the body is not to be thought of as coincident with the human, or with a particular human being. Rather, it is to be considered on a level that is much more elemental (or even molecular, to use Deleuze and Guattari's terminology). When one breaks the body down into its affective components, or its components of movement and work, what results is a body that is no longer a body strictly speaking, and a subject that is no longer a subject. If this is the case for the body, then couldn't this same elemental reading be applied to the mind? It would then follow that the mind would similarly not coincide with the human, nor with the subject. Rather, it too would be a space of dissolution and materialism conceived otherwise. Indeed, an illustration of this is Spinoza's notion of the mind that miraculously outlives the body, taking on, as it were, the materialism not only of the mind-body nexus but of the eternity existing above and beyond that nexus. Whether this eternity actually exists or not is, as Lloyd argues, somewhat beside the point.[23] What matters is that the potential or possibility for the mind to outlive or be radically separate from the body incites the mind to new levels of exuberance.[24]

By way of conclusion, I would like to illustrate this logic of the mind as both coextensive with and excessive of the body with reference to two quite different concrete situations. The first directly entails a woman-focused approach to the mind-body assemblage that can be found in various self-defense and martial arts programs designed for women. In this context, the attention paid to mental preparation is particularly striking. What is emphasized over and again is that self-defense is never merely a matter of executing physical skills but more importantly a matter of combining those skills with mental concentration and awareness. Clearly, the mental and the physical are entirely bound up with each other, and this is nowhere more true than in the emphasis placed on the voice and its crucial function in linking and enhancing the mind-body conjunction. Indeed, much time is devoted to noncontact self-defense in which the voice (which utters a few select words), in combination with a strong neutral or ready stance, is the sole instrument employed on the would-be assailant. Such a defensive strategy illustrates the way in which mind and body come together as both voice and stance and also as the potential for the unleashing of further—and primarily physical—energy. But here mind and body are conjoined under the auspices of a mental energy that is one of collecting, focusing, and concentrating. So far, this example attests to the way in which both mind and body think each other and are ultimately not entirely distinct, what we might term a difference of degree.

There is, however, a second order of defense, which mobilizes a more radical separation of mind and body, a veritable difference of kind that comes to the forefront in the remainder of Deleuze's reading of Bergson. This is a defense called upon when the first order defense and other physical resistance has failed and an attack may be already in progress. At this stage what is called for is a momentary but necessary disengagement of mind and body in which the body plays at capitulation and the mental awareness moves away from what is happening to the body and instead focuses on the surprise reversal that is about to be unfurled in the form of a full-body throwing off of the attacker. The execution of this powerful technique rests fundamentally on the disentangling of mind and body so that the mind can function as the strategizing spectator to the body's disempowerment. That this moment of mind-body separation may last only a few seconds in no way minimizes its role as a crucial catalyst for the force that is to be unleashed. In this fashion, martial arts and self-defense techniques employ, at different moments and sometimes in conjunction, both mind-body fusion and mind-body separation, and both at the service of women's empowerment. Furthermore, these two formations are at once contradictory and complementary, and in this sense they reflect a dialectical form of logic, one that does not collapse oppositions but allows them to constructively coexist side by side.

A second example concerns the relation of mind to body as inflected by bodily sickness. In certain cases of illness, the double process outlined above—that of the mind orchestrating a coterminous relation between body and mind and secondly a break or cracking between the very same mind and body—might be said to reach its epitome. Nowhere is this process better explicated than in Pierre Klossowski's monumental study of Nietzsche, *Nietzsche and the Vicious Circle*, which takes Nietzsche's physical suffering (his migraines) as the central barometer for reading Nietzsche's work—here, quite literally his corpus, or body of thought. Klossowski gives particular attention to the multiple letters Nietzsche wrote between 1877 and 1881 describing his condition, and this powerful analysis perfectly illustrates the dialectic of mind-body conjuncture and disjuncture with respect to sickness.

First, we see the dissolution of the mind-body boundary, this time in the form of the ravaged body's threat to dissolve both itself and the mind that supports it. Klossowski describes how this threatened dissolution is experienced by the mind:

> The agonizing migraines, which Nietzsche experienced periodically as *an aggression that suspended his thought*, were not an external aggression; the root of the evil was in himself, in his own organism: his own physical self was *attacking* in order to *defend* itself against a dissolution. But *what* was being threatened with dissolution? Nietzsche's own brain. Whenever his migraines subsided, Nietzsche would put his state of respite in the service of this dissolution. For the dissolution was judged to be such only by the brain, for whom the physical self and the moral self apparently coincide. But the body provided the perspective of *active forces* which (as organic and therefore subordinate functions) expressed a will to break with this servitude. But they could do so only if this will passed *through the brain*. The brain, on the other hand, could experience this will only as its own subordination to these dissolving forces: it was threatened with the impossibility of *thinking*.[25]

Already the dynamic between body and mind is one of contradiction and paradox, and this at a stage where the body and mind are largely dissolved into one entity of pain. The attack of the body is so strong that it threatens to dissolve the very distinction between mental and physical. Yet this threat of dissolution is perceived as such by the mind, is experienced only by passing through the mind, and is registered as an attack on the mind. Though the mind and body approach a state of total collapse into one another, the mind remains separate from the body in that it perceives this impending dissolution as an attack on itself. In this fashion, we have a dissolution of the mind-body split from the direction of the mind. However, rather than the mind instigating this dissolution (as in the previous example), this dissolution actively presses against the mind. Moreover, this pressing against the mind is experienced as an aggression, an aggression of the body on the mind, but one that simultaneously prevents the mind's dissolution. Of particular note in this passage is the language of attack and aggression, or what Deleuze discusses as active and reactive forces.[26] Rather than signaling an undesirable dualism, these forces produce a dialectical tension that has surprising results.

Klossowski goes on to describe the counterintuitive outcome of the mind's encounter with the threat of mind-body dissolution: pleasure, lucidity, and joy. Through a process of the mind's experiencing the potential of mind-body dissolution in its fullest thought-shattering intensity, a strange reversal occurs where new and voluptuous thoughts are actually produced: "Physical suffering would be livable only insofar as it was closely connected to joy, insofar as it developed a voluptuous lucidity: either it would extinguish all possible thought, or it would reach the delirium of thought."[27] As Klossowski elaborates, this potential thought-delirium is achieved through an act of mind that entails a "spiritualizing" mechanism in which the mind not only experiences the threat of dissolution but responds to this threat by revoking it, a revocation that allows the mind access to still-higher realms of lucidity and joy.[28]

Yet the condition of possibility for this separation of mind and body is none other than an extreme coincidence of mind and body, here in the form of bodily sickness, that makes these two entities virtually indistinguishable:

> There seems to be a strict correlation between the phenomenon of pain, which is experienced by the organism as the aggression of an invading external power, and the biological process that leads to the formation of the brain. The brain, which concentrates all the reflexes on fighting the aggression, is able to represent the *inflicted* pain as degrees of excitations oscillating between pain and pleasure. The brain can have representations only if it meticulously spiritualizes the elementary excitations into the *danger* of pain or the *good fortune* of pleasure — a discharge that may or may not result in further excitations.[29]

There are at least two things here that are of crucial importance for this transformation of pain into something other. First is the necessity of "meticulous spiritualization." This spiritualization entails the mind perceiving the dissolving pain as simultaneously dissolving and enhancing. In other words, the mind produces a distance, if only a minute one, between itself as coming into imminent dissolution and its unique excitement at this impending prospect. It is this excitement, distilled and magnified, that leads to the possibility of unparalleled joy. Second, it is important to underscore the phenomenon of oscillation, here described as an oscillation between pain and pleasure. Previously such an oscillation has been described as the dialectic between the two processes of mind-body conjuncture and mind-body disjuncture. Insofar as pain might corresponded to the former and pleasure to the latter (as in the example of sickness, but not in the self-defense strategies), then we are dealing with oscillations of a similar order.

Finally, just as the disjunction between mind and body was a brief but crucial one in the self-defense example above, so too is the short durational quality of the sickness-induced suspension of mind and body emphasized in Klossowski. Such brevity also heightens the experience of confronting and surpassing mind-body boundaries.[30] In the passage that follows, Klossowski describes the relapse as the shortening of duration combined with the heightening of boundary consciousness:

> Convalescence was the signal of a new offensive of the "body" — this rethought body — against the "*thinking Nietzsche self*." This in turn paved the way for a new relapse. For Nietzsche, each of these relapses, up until the final relapse, heralded a new inquiry and a new investment in the world of the impulses, and in each case he paid the price of an ever-worsening illness. In each case the body liberated itself a little more from its own agent, and in each case *this agent* was weakened a little more. Little by little, the *brain* was forced to approach the *boundaries* that separated it from these somatic forces, in that the reawakening of the self in the brain was brought about *ever more slowly*. And even when it occurred, it was these same forces that seized hold of the functional mechanism. The self was broken down into a *lucidity that was more vast but more brief*.[31]

According to this analysis, the brevity of the mind-body separation is directly proportional to the intensity of the lucidity it brings about. Furthermore, as the separation shortens and the lucidity increases, the boundary between mind and body is approached. One might picture a hyperbola that comes ever closer to the axis it approaches without ever coinciding with it. Such is the experience of mind-body separation at its highest, where the very boundary necessary for the experience of separation is simultaneously at its most tenuous yet still distinct from a complete dissolution. It is this state of disjunctive equilibrium, momentarily balanced yet about to explode, that, when mobilized, represents one of the most extraordinary states of being.[32] Such a state is in many respects not far from a body-centered exploration of mind-body boundaries. Yet it seems that a body-oriented focus works best in the realm of the positive, while a mind-centered one helps precisely at that point—and perhaps it is the briefest of points—where the body is besieged by or under threat of great pain.

CHAPTER THREE

Klossowski and Orthodoxy

IN A FASHION NOT UNLIKE what we have seen with the mind-body disjunction, Klossowski's oeuvre is also a preeminent illustration of what divides univocity and equivocity, and in this fashion serves as one of the twentieth century's most instructive models for thinking the complexity of the dialectic. As discussed in the introduction, univocity and equivocity are significant both in their roots in Scholastic philosophy, as the idea that being is expressed in either one or several senses, and as belonging to a long-standing framework that helps demarcate the differences, nuanced yet significant, among members of the extraordinary generation of French intellectuals of which Klossowski and Deleuze were a part. These terms, apart from their theological and philosophical import, serve as a heuristic for renarrating points of filiation and divergence between Bataille, Klossowski, and Deleuze, above all with respect to dialectical thought. They also bring us back to Sartre and forward to Badiou to frame the series. I approach this in segmented fashion, first opposing Bataille's dialectic of transgression to Klossowski's more univocal method of disjunctive synthesis before returning to Deleuze.

When juxtaposed with Deleuze's Spinozist affirmation of univocity, however, Klossowski would seem to be more on the side of the equivocal. Whereas Deleuze criticizes the realm between the univocal and the equivocal as the lukewarm space of the analogical, my contention is that this middle realm allows for a space of movement and reversal that escapes the pitfalls Deleuze locates in the dialectic, and it does so without a strict adherence to Spinozist univocity. Whereas Bataille and Deleuze remain closer to Klossowski in the tenor of their thought, I nonetheless suggest in conclusion that Sartre and Badiou are actually closer to Klossowski on a formal level, in that each poses a similarly analogical challenge to the thought of the dialectic.

For many reasons Bataille and Klossowski can be paired together. They were contemporaries, both born around the turn of the twentieth century, both writing in a variety of literary and philosophical genres, including pornographic or semipornographic fiction, and working outside the academy. Both wrote studies of Nietzsche and Sade, and both developed radical economic treatises. They were friends and fellow members in the late 1930s of the College of Sociology, which was modeled after a secret society, the members taking great interest in such topics as sacrifice and headlessness. Bataille and Klossowski wrote about each other. Both were at different points obsessed with Roman Catholicism, both at different points prepared to enter monastic orders, both in different fashions fell away. As might easily be imagined, their fiction is an outrageous mixture of the sacred and the profane, including sexual encounters and other desecrations staged at church alters and the like. Both work in that realm where pornography and theology come together. Yet while the more familiar Bataille uses pornography toward transgressive aims, the lesser-known Klossowski uses a more nuanced and interesting mechanism of boredom to elaborate an intrinsically disjunctive structure.

Even boredom, for Bataille, partakes of the transgressive. In his novella *The Story of the Eye*, the narrator describes offhandedly how he and his companion Simone have just found their friend Marcelle's body. She has hung herself. The narrator and Simone take the body down and have sex for the first time next to it. Then the narrator describes the boredom that ensues even in the face of death:

> We were perfectly calm, all three of us, and that was the most hopeless part of it. Any boredom in the world is linked, for me, to that moment and, above all, to an obstacle as ridiculous as death. But that won't prevent me from thinking back to that time with no revulsion and even with a sense of complicity. Basically, the lack of excitement made everything far more absurd, and thus Marcelle was closer to me dead than in her lifetime, inasmuch as absurd existence, so I imagine, has all the prerogatives.[1]

This is actually an unusually meditative moment in Bataille's story of murder, priests, bullfights, and constant sex.[2] Here his narrator links boredom to death, and to a reflection on the absurd boundary between life and death. But by commenting on boredom in this specific situation, that of two young people discovering their friend's dead body, the text enacts anything but boredom. Whether one finds it shocking or humorous, the disjunction between the situation and the understated commentary produces a strong effect of something jarring, of something that must be noticed, of something flagrantly perverse. I would categorize this type of jarring dynamic, where the commentary is an understatement of the event, as a transgressive disjunction: the two aspects — the event and its narration — do not go together.

Klossowski, on the other hand, employs another form of disjunction, one that Deleuze refers to as "the disjunctive synthesis." In this form of disjunction, the two terms in question are not restrictive, exclusive, or at odds with each other — a sort of noncontradictory contradiction as it were. Such is the fashion in which Klossowski combines a pornographic narrative and a theological discourse in his trilogy *The Laws of Hospitality*. In the first volume, *Roberte Ce Soir*, the central character, Roberte (modeled very strikingly after Klossowski's wife, Denise Marie Roberte Morin-Sinclaire), is a staunch atheist and inspectress of censorship. She is agitating to have the works of her husband, Octave, banned. Octave, an aging professor of Scholastic philosophy, is an ardent Catholic and author of erotic fiction based on the works of the Marquis de Sade. When Roberte finds herself thinking about the pornographic writings in question, her thoughts materialize and accost her. Their aim is to replace the disjunction of impure thoughts and a pure body with the preferable disjunction of pure thoughts and an impure body. While accosting Roberte, a fantastical Hunchback gives the following speech (mixed with a description of his physical actions):

> "Whether it is conceived in itself or not, there is no being rid of it, it returns constantly of its own accord, and if there is something that determines that existence be existence, in that something you have its essence." (*Words which, coming from inside her skirt, Roberte only confusedly makes out, for to dodge the blow that landed on his neck, the Hunchback has burrowed his face between Roberte's thighs and it is with his nose pressed to the Inspectress' underpanties he continues*): "But from the moment it is this which allows or does not allow existence, which allows or does not allow naming, would one have the right to name it censorship as if there had always been censorship? For the fact one can no longer name it God can hardly be otherwise explained than by something in existence which henceforth forbids that it

> be named God." . . . Roberte strikes a second blow, which is deadened by her own skirt which she raises to discover him again: it is with a strange smile that the Hunchback gazes at her, her arm lifted high, fingers shining on the leather handle of the crop brandished above the rich braids of hair that frame a face gone scarlet, dilated nostrils fluttering from indignation, when, upon the point of striking a third time, Roberte feels her wrist seized.[3]

What we see in this passage is an oddly verbose and idiosyncratic description of Roberte's attack by the Hunchback, itself interwoven with a convoluted speech that ranges from a brief discussion of existence and essence in Scholastic philosophy to the question of censorship and finally to the question of God's existence. Arguing that both the thing censored and God must exist in order for their existence to be then so fervently denied, the Hunchback simultaneously speaks from underneath Roberte's skirt. As with much of Klossowski's fiction, characters refer to questions in Scholastic thought (here the disjunction between essence and existence, and the question of divine names, the latter being the rubric under which discussions of univocity, equivocity, and analogy are often presented) at the same time as they perform unusual erotic acts. While we see the disjunction between sex and philosophy as in Bataille, here it is not bound up with death so as to render it transgressive, but rather bound up with God so as to render it erudite, or even boring. In this case, boring is not so much the uninteresting as it is the smoothing over, the making uniform and nonshocking of an otherwise flagrant disjunction. Boring is here the marker of a constancy of form and content, of descriptive language and what it describes, though this does not mean, as is addressed in what follows, that the disjunct terms are collapsed or entirely integrated. Whereas for Bataille there is disjunction between the description and the thing described, Klossowski makes the pornographic of a piece with Scholastic philosophy, detailing both in a florid and arcane language that in its overbearing quality serves to undermine even further any distinction of pornographic content and philosophic form.

It is to describe this nontransgressive linking of pornography and theology that Deleuze, in "Klossowski or Bodies-Language," coins the term "pornology," in conjunction with an elaboration of the concept of "disjunctive synthesis." I quote at length:

> Theology is now the science of nonexisting entities, the manner in which these entities, divine or anti-divine, Christ or Antichrist, animate language and make for it this glorious body which is divided into disjunctions. Nietzsche's prediction about the link between God and grammar has been realized; but this time it is a recognized link, willed, acted out, mimed, "hesitated," developed in all the senses of disjunction, and placed in the service of the Antichrist, Dionysus crucified. If perversion is the force proper to the body, equivocity is that of theology; they are reflected in one another. If one is the pantomime par excellence, the other is reasoning par excellence. . . . It is this that accounts for the astonishing character of Klossowski's oeuvre: the unity of theology and pornography in this very particular sense. It must be called a superior pornology. It is his own way of going beyond metaphysics: mimetic argumentation and syllogistic pantomime, dilemma in the body and disjunction in the syllogism. The rapes of Roberte punctuate reasoning and alternatives; inversely, syllogism and dilemmas are reflected in the postures and the ambiguities of the body.[4]

There are two movements at work in Deleuze's presentation of Klossowski. The first and predominant one is the emphasis on disjunction, even dualism, that informs nearly every sentence in the passage above: Christ and Antichrist, God and grammar, equivocity and perversion, theology and pornography. Indeed, it is more nearly a series of dualisms, for if equivocity and later "the ambiguities of the body" fall each to its own side of the disjunction in question, they redouble this division by in turn serving as markers for an ongoing dualism. For example, Klossowski returns repeatedly to the question of the ambiguities of the body, to what he denotes as "solecism." This is a term that Klossowski links to Quintillian's *Institutio Oratoria* and glosses as follows: "[S]ome think there is solecism in gesture too, whenever by a nod of the head or a movement of the hand one utters the opposite of what the voice is saying."[5] Thus, we might find a small gesture of beckoning that occurs alongside an otherwise hostile stance. In Klossowski's fiction, this gesture is always made with the hands, which are the primary erotic locus (as opposed to the genitalia in Bataille). Klossowskian perversion is the disjunction between the positioning of the hands and the stance of the rest of the body, often envisioned in the form of *tableaux vivants*, the subject of the next chapter. This is dramatized in his description in *The Revocation of the Edict of Nantes* of the imaginary painter Tonnerre's *Belle Versaillaise*, where "with one of her sparkling hands, the palm pressed against this leech's face, she is still fending off but provoking his attempts to fasten on by giving him a foretaste of her satiny skin; meanwhile, leaning an elbow on the arm of the easy chair, she lets her right hand hang, idle."[6] Thus, if solecism refers to the body working in two directions that oppose each other, then equivocity, insofar as it marks the seemingly more disembodied realm of reasoning, refers to the Scholastic debates about the question of "being" being said in one or more than one sense, as in the perceived split outlined in the introduction between Aquinas's model of analogy and Scotus's more univocal propensities. Like the solecism, equivocity signals that there is more than one thing going on, often exactly two things, even within a body—or a philosophical construct such as being—that might generally be counted as one. Deleuze clearly emphasizes this dualism in his reading of Klossowski and does so in a strikingly favorable fashion that would seem to align his thought quite seamlessly with Klossowski's.[7]

Yet Deleuze's own work, his proper thought, if it can be called that, simultaneously shuns the dualistic and the dialectic in favor of a more Spinozist notion of the One. This is the second movement barely discernible in the passage above, and one that I will elaborate in what follows. Despite Deleuze's impressive catalog of the disjunctions in Klossowski's work, his strongest pronouncement comes at the moment he departs from the list of dualisms in order to emphasize the underlying univocity: "It is this that accounts for the astonishing character of Klossowski's oeuvre: the unity of theology and pornography in this very particular sense. It must be called a superior pornology." What for Deleuze is astonishing in Klossowski is not the disjunctions per se but their particular unity, a unity marked by the neologism "pornology" and the laudatory term "superior." It is not difficult, then, to demarcate the differential between Bataille's transgressive disjunction, which remains on the side of the dialectic, and Deleuze's nondialectical disjunction, which favors univocity. What is more challenging is situating Klossowski's position, which falls in between; it is at once explicitly preoccupied with the set of Bataillean dualisms circulating around the discrepancy between the sacred and the profane, yet flattens them in a nonjarring, neutral fashion that gives them an ultimate unity and would seem quite proximate to Deleuzian univocity.

In the spirit of situating Klossowskian disjunction midway between that of Bataille and that of Deleuze, I turn to one of Deleuze's course lectures from 1973–74, which performs a similar overview and mapping of Scholastic philosophy, situating the analogical as the middle term between the equivocal and the univocal. Deleuze begins the seminar—part of a larger rubric focused on some of the material informing his capitalism and schizophrenia project with Guattari and thus not specifically on Scholasticism—with the injunction "I must pass by a kind of terminological detour." He then goes on to devote the rest of the session to delineating the differences between the equivocal, the univocal, and the analogical, and I dwell at length on his mapping of Scholastic thought. Deleuze defines equivocity as follows:

> Those who were called the partisans of equivocity, no matter who they were, argued a very simple thing: that the different senses of the word "being" were without common measure and that, in all rigor—and what is interesting in theology are always the limit points at which heresy peeks out. . . . Well then, the heretical point of equivocity is that those who said that being is said in several senses, and that these different senses have no common measure, understood that at the limit they would have preferred to say: "God is not," rather than to say "He is" to the extent that "He is" was a utterance which was said of the table or the chair. Or else He is in such an equivocal manner, such a different manner, without common measure with the being of the chair, with the being of man, etc . . . that, all things considered, it's much better to say: He is not, which means: He is superior to being. But if they had a sense of wordplay this became very dangerous, it sufficed that they insist only a little on "God is not." If they were discreet they said "God is superior to being," but if they said "God is not," that could turn out badly. Broadly speaking they were partisans of what is called the equivocity of being.[8]

On the one hand, this passage captures the jarring aspect in the examples from Bataille presented at the outset: in Bataille's fiction, the event and its narration are quite strikingly "without common measure"; to the contrary, in Klossowski's fiction the pornographic content and the philosophical discussion are, in true Sadean fashion, of the commonest measure. In this regard, Klossowski might seem at some remove from Deleuze's sense of equivocity. On the other hand, if we turn to one of Klossowski's lesser-known and more impenetrable works, *La Monnaie vivante* (Living currency), this question of being without common measure turns out to be at the heart of the matter at hand.

Klossowski's essay-length book *La Monnaie vivante* is one in a series of works in the wake of May '68 that articulate a theory of libidinal economy through a synthesis of key Freudian and Marxian themes. In this work from 1970, which coincides with Lacan's seminar 17 *L'Envers de la psychoanalyse* (*The Other Side of Psychoanalysis*) and anticipates Deleuze and Guattari's *Anti-Oedipus* and Lyotard's *Libidinal Economy*, Klossowski postulates that industrial production is in no way distinct from the voluptuous pulsions of bodies.[9] In presenting this claim, the details of which I will leave aside,[10] Klossowski distinguishes between the phantasm and the simulacrum. While the simulacrum serves as an approximation or mode of equivalence in an exchange economy, the phantasm is that which is outside equivalence: "In order for there to be simulacra, there must be an irreversible ground, this reality being inseparable from the phantasm that dictates the reality of perverse behavior. Sade affirms that the phantasm acting in the organism and its reflexes remains ineradicable; Fourier contests this: the phantasm is reproducible inasmuch as it is a simulacrum."[11] The split that Klossowski situates between Sade and Fourier is precisely the fracture that lies at the heart of his own oeuvre. On the one hand, *La Monnaie vivante* falls more to the side of Sade in its affirmation that the phantasm is fundamentally outside a system of equivalences (and similarly, in the language of equivocity—which is not that of equivalence—the phantasm and the simulacrum are not said in the same sense). Yet, on the other hand, there is also the sense, following Fourier, in which the simulacrum is indistinguishable from the phantasm. This would amount to the idea, generally contested in Klossowski's version of libidinal economy, that, inasmuch as the simulacrum serves to express Platonic original form, and this simulacral quest for the original or the individual—which is also the hidden drive of the mercantile economy—is itself inseparable from that original, the counting as the thing cannot be demarcated from the thing. This later formulation, postulated but never entirely affirmed by Klossowski, would fall more squarely in the camp of the univocal than the equivocal.

Deleuze continues his seminar with a useful distinction between the univocity and the equivocity of being:

> Then there were those who were partisans of the Univocity of being. They risked even more because what does this mean, univocity, in opposition to the equivocity of being? And all the treatises of the Middle Ages are filled with long chapters on the univocity or equivocity of being, it's very interesting. But those who said that being is univocal, supposing that they had done so and were not immediately burned, what did that mean? That meant: being has only one sense and is said in one and the same sense of everything of which it is said. Here one feels that if the equivocists already had such a possible sin in themselves, the univocists were thinkers who told us: of everything which is, being is said in one and the same sense — of a chair, of an animal, of a man or of God. Yet again, I'm simplifying everything because perhaps they didn't dare go that far, perhaps there's only a single thinker who would have gone that far, perhaps none, but in the end there is this idea.[12]

This single unnamed thinker might seem to be at a far remove from the theatricality of Klossowski's disjunctions, which maintain a manic energy of oscillation, especially in the fictional works, between the mind and the body, between the simple substances and the composite ones, and between the frenetic pornographic narrative and the endlessly arcane phrasings of the philosophical disquisition. Yet one might argue that Spinoza's excessive focus on the shortcomings of the prophets in *A Theologico-Political Treatise* has its own form of hilarious mania ("as I have said, the prophets were endowed with unusually vivid imaginations, and not with unusually perfect minds")[13] and that, when all is said and done, there are many traces of a Spinozist univocity to be found in Klossowski's oeuvre. An example of the latter is Klossowski's *Baphomet*, where the "pure breaths" — one in the form of the spirit of Saint Teresa — "insufflate" the body of a dead boy page.[14] Here, the breath, the boy, and Saint Teresa, in their almost absurd inseparability, serve as a marvelously literal illustration of the Spinozist notion of the mind as an idea of the body: the simple pure breath both encompasses and is delimited by what these (dead) bodies can do.

It is the aim of these brief examples to indicate the way in which Klossowski's oeuvre falls, once again, in the middle, at times on the side of equivocity, at times more aligned with the univocal counterpart. But it is not my point thereby to suggest that Klossowski is hard to pin down or that his work collapses the distinction between that of Bataille and Deleuze or between the equivocal and the univocal. Klossowski's vacillation is unsettling (perhaps this is why his work is on the order of an acquired taste, or so often goes unread); indeed, it maintains unfalteringly the distinction between terms, even when it would seem to fall to one side or the other. It is in this maintaining of distinction that Klossowski's work bears an orthodoxy at odds with the touted slippage and multiplicity of the poststructuralist moment, even though "slippery" and "multiple" might seem to be terms that epitomize the Klossowskian terrain.

Deleuze's seminar on Scholastic philosophy groups such orthodoxy rather disparagingly under the Thomist banner of the analogical:

> And then inevitably there are those who were between the two, between the univocists and the equivocists. Those who are between the two are always those who establish what we call orthodoxy. These people said that being is not univocal because it's scandal; to claim that being is said in one and the same sense of God and of the flea is a terrible thing, we must burn people like that; and then those who say "being is said in several senses which have no common measure," we no longer know where we are with them: there is no order anymore, there's no longer anything. Thus these third people said: being is neither equivocal nor univocal, it's analogical. Here we can say the name, the one who elaborated a theory of analogy on the basis of Aristotle, Saint Thomas, and historically he won. Being which is analogical meant: yes, being is said in several senses of that of which it is said. Only these senses are not without common measure: these senses are governed by relations of analogy.[15]

For Deleuze, the orthodox is akin to the damned position of the lukewarm, being neither hot nor cold, univocal nor equivocal, but trying to smooth things over by having it both ways. Such is clearly the tenor of Deleuze's pronouncements in this seminar, which echo and develop similar arguments in *Difference and Repetition*. But being in the middle, at least in a geographical if not a philosophical sense, is, as we will see, something Deleuze defends with great eloquence in "On the Superiority of Anglo-American Literature" or, as we have seen, extols in his meditations with

Guattari on metallurgy (a practice suspended in an oddly utopian fashion between the sedentary and the nomadic) in *A Thousand Plateaus*.[16] In this regard, it is not so much the middle position of the analogical—between the equivocal and the univocal—that is at issue as much as the way it aligns with a notion of category rather than concept.

Deleuze elaborates the distinction between categories and concepts with the example of the lion:

> Why categories and not concepts? What difference is there between the concept of causality or quantity and the concept of lion? . . . [O]ne calls categories the concepts which are said of every possible object of experience. Lion is not a category because you cannot say "lion" of every possible object of experience. On the other hand, every possible object of experience has a cause and is itself cause of other things. There, that clarifies everything. The categories, thus defined, are strictly inseparable from an analogical conception; one calls categories the concepts which are said of every possible object of experience, or what amounts strictly to the same thing: the different senses of the word "being." And the categories in Aristotle are presented as the different senses of the word "being," exactly as in Kant the categories are defined as the concepts which are said of every possible object of experience. Therefore there's no question of a thought proceeding by categories if it does not have, as background, the idea that being is analogical, which is to say that being is said of what is in an analogical manner.[17]

As opposed to concepts, categories are both too universal (said of every possible object of experience) and too differential (equivalent to being as it is said in several senses as opposed to the one sense of the Spinozist univocal, which Deleuze goes on to elaborate and champion). Lion, on the other hand, belongs to the realm of the concept in its singular specificity. It is striking, as an aside, that Barthes in "Myth Today" keeps returning to a phrase from his old Latin textbook that states, "[M]y name is lion," and he highlights this phrase's function of demonstrating grammatical exemplarity rather than portraying any individual lion or the singularity of lion-ness, giving Barthes's lion an analogical aura that contrasts with Deleuze's more conceptual lion.[18]

In any case, Deleuze's problem with the analogical categories seems to be one of stasis. They are too fixed at both ends of the spectrum, in their universality in the big picture and in their minute differences in the small one, so that each is ultimately an immobile reflection of the other; analogy is thus mired in a representational logic. Deleuze elaborates this attack on analogy in the concluding pages of *Difference and Repetition*:

> In effect, the genus *in relation to its species* is univocal, while Being *in relation to the genera or categories themselves* is equivocal. The analogy of being implies both these two aspects at once: one by which being is distributed in determinable forms which necessarily distinguish and vary the sense; the other by which being so distributed is necessarily repartitioned among well-determined beings, each endowed with a unique sense. What is missed at the two extremities is the collective sense of being (*être*) and the play of individuating difference in being (*étant*).[19]

Once again, the analogical model is stuck in a static generality at the one end and a static specificity at the other, rather than a more uniform model of "individuating differences," which is for Deleuze the breakthrough inaugurated with Duns Scotus and culminating in Spinoza: "This program is expounded and demonstrated with genius from the beginning of the *Ethics*: we are told that the attributes are irreducible to genera or categories because while they are formally distinct they all remain equal and ontologically one, and introduce no division into the substance which is said or expressed through them in a single and same sense."[20] What this critique of analogy assumes rather contentiously is that analogy is itself static, that it can only speak or signify in a single and univocal fashion. In a footnote to his essay "The Soul of Reciprocity Part Two," John Milbank counters Deleuze's position against analogy on exactly these grounds, that Deleuze falsely accuses analogy of being univocal and thus partaking of the absolutizing synthesis of the (Hegelian) dialectic. Milbank cites Deleuze's conclusion to *Difference and Repetition*: "Univocity signifies that being itself is univocal, while that of which it is said is equivocal; precisely the opposite of analogy."[21] Milbank retorts: "Of course, precisely not. Analogy speaks analogously of the analogical and so truly does escape dialectic. Whereas, if one says that the equivocal univocally is, then a dialectic after all ensues: being is also equivocal, differences are a veil for the same sameness."[22]

Insofar as Milbank can be categorized as a proponent of radical orthodoxy, and this orthodoxy translates into a model of "analogy speak[ing] analogously of the analogical," I would like to propose that a similar structure is at the heart of Klossowski's radical orthodoxy, which, while sharing many affinities with Deleuzian thought, differs specifically in its relation to the possibilities it affirms for the analogical above and beyond the univocal. Whether one labels this, with Milbank, an escape from dialectics or, with Deleuze, a superior dialectic (not unlike his characterization of Klossowski's "superior pornology"), what is crucial is maintaining the possibility of "speak[ing] analogously." This is dramatized in absolutely literal fashion by the speech of the simple substances, cited above, that attack Roberte. They might be said to be fighting against the Deleuzian assertion that "[u]nivocity signifies that being itself is univocal, while that of which it is said is equivocal" (that is, the person is univocal, while its thoughts and gestures are equivocal) by asserting that being is equivocal (the difference between simple and composite substances), while that of which it is said is univocal (these substances can materialize or change shape into their opposite but remain one substance). In short, where one would think there is one thing (one person, one form of speaking), there are in fact two, and where one would think there are two (bodies and language, that of which being is said), their boundary is dissolved and they are shown to have the potential of metamorphosis into one.

I would contend, following Milbank, that Klossowski is not dialectical in the fashion of Bataille. But neither does he smooth over Bataillean transgression with a simple univocity; rather, he explores a mobile and chiasmic mode of analogy. Instead of the transgressive per se, in Klossowski there is always a movement of reversal at stake, where the oscillating form this reversal takes surpasses the perversion of the content. The Hunchback and Guardsman do not rape Roberte in *Roberte Ce Soir* for the transgressive potential of the act alone or with the exclusive aim of proving a philosophical point. Rather they attack her to demonstrate that she entertains a disjunction between, on the one hand, her actions on the censorship committee and, on the other, her personal fantasies, and that this disjunction is disingenuous because it affirms a unity where there is in reality a duality. But the matter does not end here at the equivocal. Instead, at issue is the fact that simple substances like the pure breaths that materialize to accost Roberte are generally disallowed such materialization, such duality, and therefore are incapable of the equivocity that

Roberte glibly passes off as univocity. In thus approximating the equivocal by materializing (the simulacrum of the phantasm), by representing the equivocal, as it were, the pure breaths initiate a movement of reversal that serves to display the hidden bifurcation of Roberte's seemingly unified actions. By mimetically reproducing a simulacrum of the equivocal, they expose the way that Roberte has all along—even before she met her husband, Octave, as we see in the "Roman Impressions" section of *The Revocation*—been miming or simulating the univocal (illustrating Milbank's assertion that "if one says that the equivocal univocally is, then a dialectic after all ensues"). The pure breaths, though they are mute, speak analogously of this simulation and thereby upend any straightforward dialectic that this series of reversals would seem to entail. In a similar fashion, the excessive play of identities between Vittorio and Binsnicht that is dramatized in *The Revocation of the Edict of Nantes* (or between K. and Théodore in *Le Souffleur*, the third book of the *Laws of Hospitality* trilogy) is not so much about locating either a dual or a singular identity as it as about the dizzying oscillation itself. In this regard, Klossowskian analogy privileges movement, even when it is movement immobilized in the *tableau vivant*, or in the photograph in *Roberte Ce Soir* in which Vittorio manages to capture the burning Roberte. Despite their differing assessments of the analogical, Klossowski and Deleuze are joined in their similar attitudes toward movement, something that will be challenged, as we shall see in part 3, in the fiction of Blanchot.

Although Bataille and Deleuze certainly share with Klossowski the same constellation of philosophical and aesthetic concerns, the mobile model of analogy outlined above is one that Klossowski arguably shares with two unlikely bedfellows, Sartre and Badiou. Though Sartre might be seen as an unfailing apologist for existentialist humanism and Badiou as a relentless proponent of what he terms the fidelity to a process of truth, and each in his fashion as expounding a model for political action—and none of these things bearing a resemblance to anything recognizably Klossowskian—it is my contention that the three thinkers nonetheless overlap in their insistence on a mode of dualism that both employs and challenges a model of dialectics aimed at synthesis.

As we have seen, Sartre envisions a two-tiered realm composed of a phantasm-like inert term (the in-itself in *Being and Nothingness*, the practico-inert in the *Critique of Dialectical Reason*) and the privileged active term that reflects the mutual embeddedness (even a sort of synthesis) of both terms (the for-itself, praxis). Insofar as the active term serves as an animating catalyst for the inert term — the way a group of people united only because they are waiting for the same bus (the practico-inert, Sartre's classic model of seriality in the *Critique*) might be transformed into something like a bus riders' union — it might seem that the two blend into one and the same thing, like the simulacrum collapsed into the phantasm. This is one of many ways in which Sartre's dualistic system would seem to aspire to a reconciliation or synthesis of its opposing terms, a utopian univocity not dissimilar to Deleuze or Spinoza. Yet, as in Klossowski's *La Monnaie vivante*, this synthesis is evoked but not properly achieved. For Sartre is ever at pains to keep his terms separate, not so much in the spirit of a multiplicity or equivocity, but rather in the inimitable fashion of carefully opposed terms that nonetheless undergo strange reversals, so that the lesser and more static term becomes suddenly animated (the stone that, seemingly out of the blue, is equated with a god).[23] Though the content of Sartre's and Klossowski's fiction and philosophy could not be more dissimilar, there exists a proximity of method — a sort of antidialectical yet mobile form of analogy — that has never to my knowledge been remarked upon. If Bataille, Klossowski, and Deleuze might all be characterized, and not unfaithfully, as reacting against Sartre, it seems somehow fitting that Klossowski's mode of reaction takes the form of a solecism: an overt nonengagement akin to rejection coupled with a shy if not perverse nod in the form of a shared method.

In a similar vein, Badiou has no obvious affinities with Klossowski and never engages with him explicitly. Indeed his recuperation of questions of truth and universalism are at a far remove from Klossowski's Nietzscheanism (though both share a heterodox fascination for Christianity, Badiou in his celebration of the Apostle Paul, a Judeo-Christian Baphomet if ever there was one). Yet if the force of Klossowski's disjunctions — his superior pornology — resides in the juxtaposition of the corporeal and the theological, or of bodies and languages, Badiou's unavowed and therefore perhaps even more perverse disjunction is within the world of number and numbers.[24] Given his explicit interest in mathematics and set theory, it is fitting that numbers take on the status of conceptual personae in Badiou's work, being not unlike the pure breaths or simple substances of Klossowski's fiction. Put in Klossowskian terms, Badiou's oeuvre might be considered an elaborate choreography between the phantasmatic purity of the One and the dialectical materialism of the Two. Badiou writes in *The Century* that "the century is a figure of non-dialectical juxtaposition of the Two and the One. Is it a desire for division, for war, or is it instead a desire for fusion, for unity, for peace?"[25] His study of the concept of a century, itself a phantasmatic unit, hinges on readings of a series of authors that are marked by a vacillation between a dualism and a univocity (Balzac, Freud, Saint-John Perse, Celan, and Mao are just a few of the figures treated according to this rubric).

Badiou draws directly on Deleuze's notion of disjunctive synthesis yet, like Klossowski, is somewhat at odds with Deleuze's impetus toward the purely univocal. This comes out most forcefully in Badiou's pointed critique of Deleuzian univocity in his *Deleuze: The Clamor of Being*. Badiou states his differences with Deleuze around what he perceives as a noncoincidence of the multiple and the One in Deleuze's thought. Whereas Badiou affirms the category of the multiple, he is suspicious that the purported univocity of the One is actually a two in disguise. As Badiou queries in a fashion entirely parallel to Milbank's defense of analogy outlined above, "Is the nomination of the univocal itself univocal?," and he goes on to gloss why the very assertion of univocity makes visible the fact that univocity also tries to encompass something apart from its nomination.[26] Thus there is a differential between the thing and its nomination (the phantasm and its simulacrum, or as Deleuze puts it in *The Logic of Sense*, the name of the thing and what the name of the thing is called.[27] Badiou maintains that

> what emerges over the course of these experiments is that a single name is never sufficient, but that two are required. Why? The reason is that Being needs to be said in a single sense both from the viewpoint of the unity of its power and from the viewpoint of the multiplicity of the divergent simulacra that this power actualizes in itself. Ontologically, a real distinction is no more involved here than, in Spinoza, between *natura naturans* and *natura naturata*. Yet, a binary distribution of names is necessary; it is as though the univocity of being is thereby accentuated for thought through its being said, at one moment, in its immediate "matter," and, in the next, in its forms or actualizations. In short: in order to say that there is a single sense, two names are necessary.[28]

Although Deleuze compellingly argues, especially in his work on Spinoza, that univocity is expressed as equivocity — with the caveat that the apparent equivocity is really just a function of the multiplicity of expression but does not contradict the notion of a single underlying substance, of being ultimately having just one sense — Badiou sees this "*double movement*" as falling outside a pure and simple univocity.[29]

The attempt to name this errant movement, to pinpoint that thing that escapes from the One, but without which the One wouldn't be one, is remarkably close to the Klossowskian suspension between univocity and equivocity that is at issue here. If Badiou's unabashed espousal of truth grants him a form of orthodoxy, then his animation of numbers into characters that circulate like the pure breaths combines with this orthodoxy to confer on him a reactionary radicalism that is, at least in this respect, worthy of Klossowski's Octave.[30]

CHAPTER FOUR

Cinema and the *Tableau Vivant*

THE ENCOUNTER BETWEEN Deleuze and Klossowski is nowhere better staged than on the terrain of immobility, which is taken up as a central motif in part 3. Immobility serves as a concept for extending Deleuze's work on cinema to a domain that has been evoked but not explicitly mapped out (not unlike what Deleuze himself does with William S. Burroughs's and Foucault's notion of the society of control). If cinema is the stringing together of blocks of movements/duration, if an innovative resistance occurs when a severing takes place between what one sees and what one hears, then what cinematic idea is at stake when we find alongside sound a posed immobility (*tableau vivant*) where we would expect to see movement?

The very concept of the *tableau vivant* is fraught with contradiction and exaggeration, opening up a dialectic of animation and immobility, gesture and pose, and traversing all of Klossowski's oeuvre. The lines preceding Foucault's famous remark about the Deleuzian century from "Theatrum Philosophicum" are rarely cited in full: "I believe that these works [*Difference and Repetition* and *The Logic of Sense*] will continue to revolve about us in enigmatic resonance with those of Klossowski, another major and excessive sign, and perhaps one day, this century will be known as Deleuzian."[1] One of the most excessive aspects of Klossowski's fiction, painting, and philosophy is the way immobility highlights an unbroachable disjunction between bodies and their gestures. What we examined in the second chapter as the disjuncture between body and mind is brought into a gestural space in Klossowski's fiction and painting. And we saw in chapter 3 that in *The Revocation of the Edict of Nantes*, Klossowski poses the opposition between gesture and bodies by way of the Scholastic philosophy professor Octave's discussion of the solecism. Octave, who dabbles as an art critic, occupies a good third of *The Revocation* with lengthy and pedantic descriptions of his art collection, especially his works by the imaginary painter Tonnerre. He begins his ruminations as follows:

> "Some think there is solecism in gesture too, whenever by a nod of the head or a movement of the hand one utters the opposite of what the voice is saying." This passage from Quintilian, quoted at the head of the descriptive catalogue to my collection of paintings—to what does it allude? . . . But if solecism there be, if it is something *opposite* which the figures *utter* through this or that gesture, they must say something in order that this opposition be palpable; but painted, they are silent; or whether, from painting the kind of scenes he chose, he was, to the contrary, trying to demonstrate the positiveness of the solecism which could be expressed only through means of an image.[2]

As noted in chapter 3, solecism is a gesture—often of the hands—that provides a point of contradiction within the image: the hands, for example, seem to beckon even when the body's overall pose is one of defiance or nonchalance. Such solecisms of the hand abound in the curious set of photographs and drawings that accompany Klossowski's quasi-economic treatise *La Monnaie vivante* (Living currency). Taken by Pierre Zucca, these photographs depict Klossowski's wife, Denise Morin-Sinclaire, in a series of sometimes-compromising postures that are loosely based on other fictional works by Klossowski, such as *The Baphomet* and *Roberte Ce Soir*. In one photograph a bearded man places what appears to be a crown on her head. With her body, she leans backward to accept the coronation, yet with her hands extended before her torso she defends herself from some unseen onslaught in front of her, while simultaneously, by way of a slight curvature of the right hand, gracing that same offender with a gesture of waving or beckoning.[3]

In discussing Tonnerre and the genre of the *tableau vivant*, Klossowski's Octave first asks if the *tableau vivant* is not "the basic antecedent to every picture" and then holds up Tonnerre as exceptional in that he reverses this ordering:

> Here, in the case of Tonnerre, I am referring to the fascination exerted upon him by this in itself false genre, very much in fashion during the period. It was the reverse process that took place then; one generally

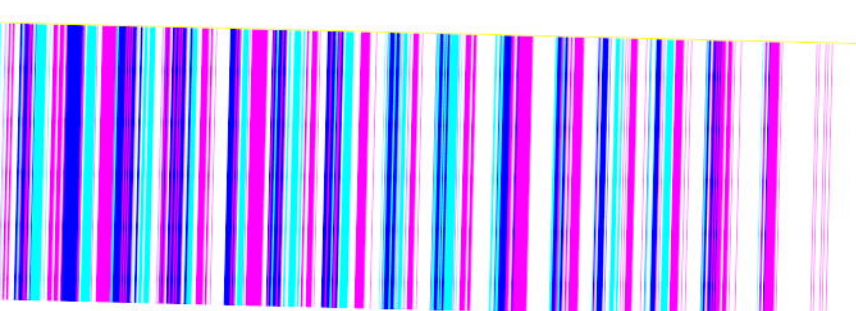

drew one's inspiration from some well-known painting standing clear in everybody's mind, to reconstitute it, usually in a salon, with the help of those persons present, improvised actors, and the game consisted in rendering as faithfully as possible the gestures, the poses, the lighting, the effect one supposed was produced by the masterpiece of such and such a painter. But this was not simply life imitating art—it was a pretext. The emotion sought after in this make-believe was that of life giving itself as a spectacle to life; of life hanging in suspense.[4]

It is precisely this gesture of life hanging in suspense that is at the crux not only of the *tableau vivant* but of Deleuze's reading of movement and immobility in the cinema books. While the *tableau vivant* literally stages an encounter between movement and immobility, Deleuze produces such an encounter in the realms of thought and image (percept, affect, concept). In Deleuze's intricate trajectory from *Cinema 1: The Movement-Image* to *Cinema 2: The Time-Image*, we find at once a complex Bergsonian analysis of movement and immobility and a movement away from movement and toward time.

In discussing "crystals of time" and "sheets of past" in *Cinema 2*, Deleuze redeploys Bergson so as to accentuate the way certain cinematic auteurs produce, through their images, multilayered renderings of time. One example is the way depth of field gives rise to "two poles of a metaphysics of memory. These two extremes of memory are presented by Bergson as follows: the extension of sheets of past and the contraction of the actual present."[5] Deleuze uses Alain Resnais and Alain Robbe-Grillet's *Last Year at Marienbad* as an example of how a film's cast of characters and auteurs may be situated along two different yet mutually inflected axes of time:

> The difference is thus in the nature of the time-image, which is plastic in one case and architectural in the other. For Resnais conceived *Last Year at Marienbad* like his other films, in the form of sheets or regions of past, while Robbe-Grillet sees time in the form of points of present. If *Last Year at Marienbad* could be divided, the man X might be said to be closer to Resnais and the woman A closer to Robbe-Grillet. The man basically tries to envelop the woman with continuous sheets of which the present is the narrowest, like the advance of a wave, whilst the woman, at times wary, at times stiff, at times almost convinced, jumps

from one bloc to another, continually crossing an abyss between two points, two simultaneous presents.[6]

It is interesting that, if anything, it is the feminized present (Robbe-Grillet versus Resnais) that Deleuze seems to favor, and this might be linked favorably to the "eternal present" of the third synthesis of time in *Difference and Repetition*, though such a reading goes against the grain of studies on Deleuze and cinema that emphasize the mobile as opposed to static elements of Deleuze's cinema books.[7] But to the issue at hand, what Deleuze effectively describes in the above passage is a solecism of time, in which past and present inflect one another with a contradictory yet nonetheless sustainable tension. The man's gesture extends to the past, while the woman remains less fixed and in this fluctuation captures the present. What if such an analysis were to be extended backward to the movement/immobility locus of *Cinema 1*, as a quest for the eternal present, perhaps imbued with death, that disrupts the dialectic of movement and immobility?

In the second commentary on Bergson in *Cinema 1*, Deleuze, in a solecism of his own, both invites and dismisses reflection on the posed nature of the *tableau vivant*. He begins by suggesting the virtual potential of both movement and the image: "And how can movement be prevented from already being at least a virtual image and the image from already being at least possible movement? What appeared finally to be a dead end was the confrontation of materialism and idealism."[8] Insofar as movement would be in flux and the image more fixed, their virtual coming together in the movement-image implies neither movement nor stasis as such. This suggests that, at its limit, immobility is also in flux.[9]

By reading Deleuze alongside Klossowski, we see how (like the image that is not just the image but also the disjunction of vision and sound) there is immobility, which is not just immobility but the disjunction of movement and arrested movement. That such a disjunction is imbued with a particular erotics is Jean-François Lyotard's Klossowskian insight in *Libidinal Economy*. Lyotard locates the "acinema" in the noncontradictory space of "extreme immobilization and extreme mobilization," a space epitomized by the Klossowskian *tableau vivant*.[10] In the lengthy passage that follows, Lyotard uses Klossowski to analyze the erotics of immobility:

> Presently there exists in Sweden an institution called the *posering*, a name derived from the *pose* solicited by portrait photographers: young girls rent their services to these special houses, services which consist of assuming, clothed or unclothed, the poses desired by the client. It is against the rules of these houses (which are not houses of prostitution) for the clients to touch the models in any way. We would say that this institution is made to order for the phantasmatic of Klossowski, knowing as we do the importance he accords to the *tableau vivant* as the near perfect simulacrum of fantasy in all its paradoxical intensity. But it must be seen how the paradox is distributed in this case: the immobilization seems to touch only the erotic object while the subject is found overtaken by the liveliest agitation. . . . But things are not as simple as they might seem. . . . We must note, given what concerns us here, that the *tableau vivant* in general, if it holds a certain libidinal potential, does so because it brings the theatrical and economic orders into communication; because it uses "whole persons" as detached erotic regions to which the spectator's impulses are connected.[11]

The intricate erotics to which Lyotard refers revolves around the tension between the corporeal and the incorporeal: (1) while posed in the *tableau*, the characters have no bodily contact either with each other or with the spectator, while at the same time suggesting considerable erotic potential; (2) the characters are immobilized yet clearly full of life, so that, at any point, an abundance of animation and movement might be expected to burst forth; and (3) the posed immobility of the characters highlights and eroticizes certain bodily parts, namely the hands as opposed to the face. In this fashion the tension or solecism in the cinematic *tableau vivant* is not so much concerned with the disjunction between bodies and affective states as it is between bodies and their immobile placement in an otherwise mobile apparatus, here the cinematic apparatus. In *The Cinematic Body*, Steven Shaviro highlights the separation between bodies and affect:

> We cannot read [bodies'] postures, gestures, and countenances as indications of inner emotional states. We are made oppressively aware that corporeal appearance and behavior in fact precede identity, that they are the "quasi-causes" (to use Deleuze's term for the action of the simulacrum) of which identity is a transitory effect, and that such

quasi-causes are themselves incited and relayed by the presence of the movie camera, and by all the codes of cinematic display.[12]

Following from this, we might envision the abstract category of identity not just as a "transitory effect" of corporeal appearance but also as an effect of the interplay between bodies and immobility as it is captured in the solecism, gesture, or pose.

Raúl Ruiz's *Hypothèse du tableau volé* (Hypothesis of the stolen painting) illustrates the way the filmic *tableau vivant* affords, through its reverse logic, a dizzying sensation of motion *within* arrested movement. In this adaptation that condenses several of Klossowski's works of fiction, the comically bombastic art critic–narrator (a version of Octave in *The Revocation of the Edict of Nantes*) presents a continually displaced hypothesis about why one painting in a series of works by the painter Tonnerre is missing.[13] Instead of enacting the narrative, the characters pose in mid-action as the event is being described. We hear the narration of a mesmerizingly incoherent series of events that include games of chess (between two crusaders vying for the affections of a young page), hangings (of the very same page, hanged in a ritual ceremony), metamorphoses (in the *tableau* version of the Diana and Acteon story), and betrayals (the young girl O discovering her beloved marquis conspiring against her), all while the characters at issue remain posed in a single still that stands, in one arrested set of gestures, for the entirety of the narrative. Momentous actions are here rendered in the form of silent and immobile *tableaux*, in which the characters neither speak nor touch. The extremity of the action described is at once betrayed and contained by the living immobility of the characters' poses.

Such a disparity between words and image is in fact characterized by Deleuze as a "cinematographic idea,"[14] one that derives from the cinema of Syberberg, Duras, and Straub and Huillet. He characterizes such a disjunction as an act of resistance, citing the cinema of Straub and Huillet:

> Take the case, for example, of the Straubs when they perform this disjunction between auditory voice and visual image, which goes as follows: the voice rises, it rises and what it speaks about passes under the naked, deserted ground that the visual image was showing us, a visual image which had no direct relation to the auditory image. But what is this speech act that rises in the air while its object passes underground? Resistance. An act of resistance.[15]

It seems for Deleuze this act of resistance is none other than an epiphany of the dialectic: the moving apart of a nondiegetic voice and a diegetic space, two distant worlds that are nonetheless connected by a plane of reference (here, literally the ground). In Ruiz's film the nondiegetic has a minimal presence; in its place, the diegetic space unleashes an intricate array of schisming narratives from the seeming coherence of a fixed field of vision.[16] This schism of coherence and ground, of disjointed voice and image, serve as the dialectical building blocks for a Deleuzian theory of resistance—not a term he usually emphasizes as such and one that is above all a *structure* rather than an *actant* (the question of the structure will be taken up in conjunction with Lévi-Strauss in part 2).

At the beginning of *Hypothesis of the Stolen Painting*, the art critic–narrator describes an illicit "ceremony," in which the painter Tonnerre took part and which was interrupted by the police. At one point the narrator explains that the *tableaux vivants are* the ceremony. He goes on to explain that, with the *tableau vivant*, it is not a matter of illusion but of showing. As he narrates these words from a seated position, the bottom half of two different paintings are barely visible in the background. But just before the punctuated ending of the sentence (after he has pronounced, "Les tableaux mis en scène par le moyen de tableaux vivants ne font pas allusion" [The paintings dramatized by the means of *tableaux vivants* do not allude]), he rises, bringing into full view a painting of a scene that at a later point in the film becomes a *tableau vivant* with bodies posed and hands pointing (one where the young girl O points at the marquis in an accusatory fashion). In this manner, the narrator's body rises as his voice intonates, "Ils montrent" (They show), and the image descends, as it were, to meet the voice and body at a strange impasse. The voice tells us that the *tableaux* are not allusions but the things themselves, while the visible painting depicts scenes that will *become* the *tableaux vivants*. There is disjunction not only between sound and image, live *tableaux* and inanimate painting, and movement and immobility but also between present (the painting) and future (*tableaux vivants*). To evoke Deleuze's analysis of *Last Year at Marienbad* from *Cinema 2*, it is as if the posed woman is once again "continually crossing an abyss between two points, two simultaneous presents," while the narrator's prophetic statement that these paintings are not allusive (for they will soon materialize with an animated immobility) evokes in nothing short of the most philosophical of tenses, the future-anterior (sheets of future?).

"Having an Idea in Cinema" again highlights Deleuze as a thinker of disjunction and dialectic, something that is more fleshed out—literally—in the written and visual oeuvres of Klossowski and Ruiz. Such a juxtaposition with Klossowski and Ruiz also reveals Deleuze as a philosopher of immobility no less than of movement, indeed of the non-oppositional relation of these two terms. This non-oppositional relation will be the explicit topic of the first chapter of part 3, which discusses the literary domain—American literature—that is at once championed by Deleuze and extends his thinking about immobility by making it inseparable from its opposite. Like silence, immobility—and its attendant disjunctions—is at once a withdrawal and a force of resistance. But before taking up the connection between stasis and ontology, I will first address Deleuzian dialectic as it relates to questions of structure.

PART TWO

Structure

This section continues the work of arguing for Deleuze's hidden dialectic, but this time in conjunction with a new grouping of thinkers and a new focus on the question of "structure," another term rarely associated with Deleuze but surprisingly important in his early writings. Following from the brief discussion in the introduction, it begins with an overview of two books on Deleuze, by Žižek and Badiou, that place Deleuze's oeuvre under the sign of the dialectic but also subsume it into each critic's proper system. Whereas Žižek finds a Hegelian if not Lacanian kernel in Deleuze's work, Badiou accuses Deleuze of falsely elevating the notion of the One when in fact a surreptitious two slips into Deleuze's model of univocity. What unites these readings is their attention to structural if not numerical aspects of Deleuzian thought. Rather than a terrain of becoming, nomad thought, lines of flight, and minor literature, they highlight a Deleuze who is first and foremost a thinker of structures, if not exactly a structuralist per se. Even in their disagreements with him or their reappropriation of his work, Žižek and Badiou capture this structural penchant in more precise form than does the majority of critical literature on Deleuze.

Chapter 5 examines this structural penchant in Deleuze's own early engagements with structuralism, above all his essay "How Do We Recognize Structuralism?" and his subtly favorable reading of Lévi-Strauss. Whereas numerous critics of Lévi-Strauss castigate him for being too caught up with structure and form at the expense of the concrete, Deleuze's recognition of Lévi-Straussian analysis being about "the structure itself" is notably more celebratory. Indeed, I signal this as the marker, if there is one to be found, of

Deleuze's so-called poststructuralist turn: it is the enthusiasm for the structure becoming more — and not less — abstract.

Chapter 7 provides a detailed analysis of one of Deleuze's lesser-known essays that is published as one of the appendixes to *The Logic of Sense*. In its reading of Michel Tournier's rewriting of *Robinson Crusoe*, Deleuze's 1967 essay "Michel Tournier and the World Without Others" comes the closest of anything in Deleuze's oeuvre to articulating the position of this book. In reading this essay alongside and against Deleuze's more acclaimed book on Sacher-Masoch, I emphasize Deleuze's structural presentation of the Other as the governing structure of our perceptual field. He then uses Tournier's fiction — and the psychology of perversion and sadism — to imagine something beyond this "structure-Other," namely what he terms the "world without others." In this non-other-dependent domain, consciousness merges with the object of perception, and the human does not disrupt the desert island but consecrates it (*The Logic of Sense*, 311). In short, to return to the terms from Sartrean phenomenology with which I began, this approximates the in-itself that is arrested in time, without past or future. Though Deleuze does not develop the temporal dimension in great detail, this description of the "world without others" serves as a template for the meditation on the phenomenology and ontology of immobility that will be addressed in the concluding section.

CHAPTER FIVE

Betraying Well (Žižek and Badiou)

As with many prominent thinkers, there is a striking imperative that circulates among those who read Deleuze: a drive to fidelity, or more nearly to not betray the master's thought, the trap that so many who write in his wake purportedly fall into. The world of Deleuze criticism is rarely immune from the dialectic of fidelity and betrayal that is arguably so far removed from Deleuze's thought. Of course such a pronouncement is itself a judgment that only repeats this particular logic. It is the merit of Žižek's *Organs without Bodies: Deleuze and Consequences* and Badiou's *Deleuze: The Clamor of Being*, both written from a certain position of infidelity, to dramatize this controversial force of dualism that underlies if not belies Deleuze's oeuvre.[1]

Both Žižek and Badiou are critical of the position of the Deleuzian disciple, each evoking after a fashion the paradox whereby to be truly faithful to the spirit of the master, one must betray the letter of his teaching. As Žižek puts it, "There are, accordingly, two modes of betraying the past. The true betrayal is an ethico-theoretical act of the highest fidelity: one has to betray the letter of Kant to remain faithful to (and repeat) the 'spirit' of his thought. It is precisely when one remains faithful to the letter of Kant that one really betrays the core of his thought, the creative impulse underlying it" (13). In a similar though even more direct vein, Badiou remarks on the problem of betrayal as also a problem that his proper work encounters, implicitly equating his status as a master thinker to that of Deleuze. His target is one shared with Žižek, those Deleuzians who champion radical flux and pure positive libido—in short the body without organs—and those who take the works coauthored with Guattari, namely *Anti-Oedipus* and *A Thousand Plateaus*, as their central inspiration. Badiou characterizes this as a "crucial *misunderstanding*" and comments: "That Deleuze never did anything of an explicit nature to dissipate this [misunderstanding] is linked to that weakness rife among philosophers—in fact, none of us

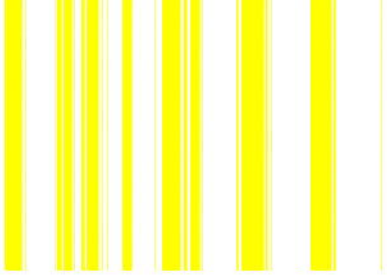

escape it—regarding the equivocal role of *disciples*. As a general rule, disciples have been won over for the wrong reasons, are faithful to a misinterpretation, overdogmatic in their exposition, and too liberal in debate. They almost always end up by betraying us" (96). Here, Badiou, like Žižek, not only denounces the bad betrayals of the disciples, but gives us the hope that his form of betrayal will be a truer and better one.

The correspondence between Žižek's and Badiou's readings of Deleuze, which at a certain level might seem to have very little in common, is an assertion of a latent dualism, even a hidden dialectical energy, in Deleuze's repeated insistence on a Spinozist notion of the One and Deleuze and Guattari's repeated diatribe against the Hegelian dialectic. Though others, most notably Fredric Jameson, have pointed to this underlying dualism,[2] its proclamation—or more nearly implication in the cases at hand—still carries a distinctly heterodox force. This reading against the grain is bound up in the very style of the reading: for Badiou, it is the reduction of all of Deleuze's work to one central and repeated concept, namely the assertion of being as univocal, a problematic from which Badiou hardly strays; for Žižek, in spite of his insistence on engaging with the Deleuze of *The Logic of Sense* over and above the Deleuze and Guattari of *Anti-Oedipus*, what counts as Deleuze is much more all over the map, at times hardly resembling Deleuze at all. Indeed, the second half of Žižek's book (the part called "Consequences," which discusses cognitive science, film—particularly Hitchcock—and cultural politics ranging from fascism to the Zapatistas to Hardt and Negri's *Empire*) does not even mention Deleuze by name with great frequency (not that it need to). This section, if not the whole book, is certainly much more recognizable as peculiarly Žižekian in its broad-ranging series of paradoxical structures whereby the purported bad guy of the situation (the Stalinist, the fascist, the anti-Islamicist, even Bill Gates) is revealed to contain the kernel of the situation's truth, if there could be said to be one. In the middle of Žižek's discussion of fascism, there is a point where he asserts that "two important, interconnected conclusions are to be drawn from such Deleuzian analyses" (190), and it seems a reader's immediate response would be to wonder how exactly these analyses are Deleuzian.

On the one hand, the Deleuzian element in *Organs without Bodies* is somewhat elusive, but on the other, and this is the key, Žižek does something apart from the two main forms of writing on Deleuze: the one exegetical, explicating and elaborating the philosophical implications of Deleuze's work, the other an application, showing how nomadic thought or deterritorialization or what have you is a useful framework for analyzing some entirely different text or problematic. Though Žižek does give extended attention to Deleuze and Guattari's concept of the body without organs (more on this and its relation to Lacan in what follows), he comes at this neither as an exegete nor an applicator but as more of a Judas figure who betrays (and loves) with a kiss. This is altogether fitting given Žižek's remarks on the relevance of Judas in *The Puppet and the Dwarf*, where "betrayal was part of the plan, Christ ordered Judas to betray him in order to fulfill the divine plan; that is, Judas' act of betrayal was the highest sacrifice, the ultimate fidelity."[3] The betrayal lies in Žižek's very form of reading askance, of sometimes making alignments that Deleuze's work invites (such as with Lacan), of bringing out dimensions (such as the Hegelian one) that the work is at pains to negate, and at times not really addressing his work at all. Though Žižek avows that the problematic of *The Logic of Sense* is the central Deleuzian one (and that accords with the general argument of this study, though I also address the importance of other works from the late 1960s), Žižek's text has a way, at least stylistically, of making Deleuze seem very hard to pin down.

By contrast, if Badiou insists that all of Deleuze's work repeats the same thing, he is quite fittingly not out of line from the master, as his compact reading finds different ways to reiterate the same set of links and dissociations between himself and Deleuze. These might be summarized as follows: though both evoke the category of the multiple, Deleuze retains the notion of the One, while Badiou abandons it; moreover, Deleuze elevates the simulacrum that Plato denigrates, while Badiou retains a Platonic notion of truth and abandons the virtual, the virtual being the site of Deleuze's secret Platonism (see Badiou's own summary of the two positions on p. 46). What links Žižek and Badiou is that both delineate, yet usually without naming it in so many words, the latent dualism of Deleuze's thought. Badiou does this by suggesting that Deleuze's professed univocity is really an equivocity in disguise, Žižek by bringing out Deleuze's affinities with Hegel and with Lacan.

Sometimes Žižek translates Deleuze into Hegelian terminology, as when he evokes Deleuze's dialectical materialism, and at other times he analyzes Deleuze through Lacanian models such as the phallus or Lacan's revision of Freudian castration. Whether it is articulated via Hegel or via Lacan, the insight is guided by a similar logic, one that is to my mind the real brilliance of Žižek's reading. It is a reading that bypasses the obvious set of good and bad dualisms in the works coauthored with Guattari (the good molecular versus the bad molar, the good nomad versus the bad state, the good becoming versus the bad being, etc.) in favor of the *structural* dualism that, most simplistically, divides the joint works from Deleuze's single-authored ones. The disjunction at issue is not so much the split between being and becoming as it is the *structural impasse* inherent to becoming itself: in short, there are two becomings; one is a becoming of production and generation, in which the actual is generated from virtual intensities. This becoming is the seemingly more materialist Deleuze of the coauthored works, but in fact the one where Žižek locates a hidden idealism. By contrast, it is the "becoming" of *The Logic of Sense*, in which the corporeal realm instantiates a secondary level of incorporeal effects (effects that retrospectively turn out to be embedded in the very heart of the corporeal), that Žižek favors and regards as the proof of Deleuze's ultimate dialectical materialism. As Žižek puts it,

> Is this opposition of the virtual as the site of productive Becoming and the virtual as the site of the sterile Sense-Event not, at the same time, the opposition of the "body without organs" (BwO) and "organs without body" (OwB)? Is, on one hand, the productive flux of pure Becoming not the BwO, the body not yet structured or determined as functional organs? And, on the other hand, is the OwB not the virtuality of the pure affect extracted from its embeddedness in a body, like the smile in *Alice in Wonderland* that persists alone, even when the Cheshire cat's body is no longer present? (30)[4]

Thus, it is the seemingly immaterial or even transcendental Deleuze of the early works that turns out to be the most materialist, and it is the apolitical single-authored works (interestingly, Žižek refers to the elitism of these works [20], while Badiou refers to Deleuze as an aristocratic thinker [12]) that have the true political potential, though not one that is drawn out by Deleuze himself. As Žižek writes, with the damning formulations that he (and also Badiou, not coincidentally) reserves for vulgar leftism:

The ontology of productive Becoming clearly leads to the Leftist topic of the self-organization of the multitude of molecular groups that resist and undermine the molar, totalizing systems of power—the old notion of the spontaneous, nonhierarchical, living multitude opposing the oppressive, reified System, the exemplary case of Leftist radicalism linked to philosophical idealist subjectivism. The problem is that this is the only model of the politicization of Deleuze's thought available. The other ontology, that of the sterility of the Sense-Event, appears "apolitical." However, what if this other ontology also involves a political logic and practice of its own, of which Deleuze himself was unaware? . . . What if the domain of politics is inherently "sterile," the domain of pseudo causes, a theater of shadows, but nonetheless crucial in transforming reality? (32)

Here, Žižek joins Badiou in an unsparing attack on those who use Deleuze in an overtly political fashion to champion the likes of pure becoming, the multitude, and radical democracy. Žižek does not really explain what a better and alternate Deleuzian politics would look like, but it seems not to be that of Hardt and Negri's *Empire* and later works.[5]

Žižek is at his Lacanian best when he shows how Deleuze's dialectical materialism partakes of the logic of the phallus and castration, asserting that the phallus is exemplary in that it signifies the point of mediation between the two seemingly divergent series (the corporeal and the incorporeal). Žižek shows the castration function to be the link between the corporeal cause and the incorporeal effect, what he terms the Sense-Event:

First, the impassive-sterile Event is cut off, extracted from its virile, corporeal causal base (if "castrations" means anything at all, it means *this*). Then, this flow of Sense-Event is constituted as an autonomous field of its own, the autonomy of the incorporeal symbolic order with regard to its corporeal embodiments. " 'Symbolic castration,'" as the elementary operation of the quasi cause, is thus a profoundly *materialist* concept, since it answers the basic need of any materialist analysis. . . . This is the "phallic" dimension at its most elementary: *the excess of the virtual that sustains actualization*. . . . As it was clear to Deleuze (and not only to Lacan), the notion of castration answers a very specific question: how does the universal symbolic process detach itself from its

> corporeal roots? How does it *emerge* in its relative autonomy? "Castration" designates the violent bodily cut that enables us to enter the domain of the incorporeal. (84–85)

In this fashion, Žižek's explication of the phallic mediating function at once shifts the common emphasis on lack and negativity so frequently evoked alongside the mention of Lacan, and it brings out the twofold structure at the heart of Deleuze's thought, simultaneously showing the two parts to be bound together in a mutually implicated relation.[6]

Insofar as the phallic function represents for Žižek this element of *relation* between the two disjointed series, it serves a transcendental function (a term, in addition to the category of mediation itself, that Deleuze denounces in no uncertain terms): "In this precise sense—shocking as it may sound to vulgar materialists and obscurantists in their unacknowledged solidarity—the phallus, the phallic element as the signifier of 'castration,' is the fundamental category of dialectical materialism. Phallus qua signifier of 'castration' *mediates* the emergence of the pure surface of Sense-Event. As such, it is the '*transcendental* signifier'—nonsense within the filed of sense—that distributes and regulates the series of Sense" (91, my emphasis).[7] Žižek's pronouncement has an interesting if not perverse double twist: precisely by making a strong claim for the mediating and transcendental role of the phallic signifier, it thereby articulates a basic compatibility between Deleuze and Lacan that is often contested or goes unacknowledged by Deleuze scholars. While I have enormous sympathy (probably rare among such scholars) for this compatibility and for the way it elaborates and extends certain unarticulated elements of *The Logic of Sense*, it does seem that this insight is gained by dint of the imposition of a strong form of Hegelian dialectic on Deleuze and Lacan, whereas a weak one, one that made mediation more incidental rather than fundamental, would be to my mind more in order, especially in the case of Deleuze.

Badiou comes closer to the position against mediation outlined in the chapter on Sartre above. He isolates even more precisely how the critical impasse in Deleuze's thought centers on the question of mediation. At one point he notes that "Deleuze's method is thus a method that rejects all recourse to mediations; indeed, this is why it is essentially antidialectical" (32), and yet Badiou points out that the category of relation is never entirely absent, for even the act of evoking nonrelation or univocity gestures to a hidden relational element, an oscillation that is in some sense a mediation. In light of this, Badiou modifies his assessment of Deleuze's dialecticism: "It would seem that it is not very easy to definitively abandon the presuppositions of the dialectic" (85). Badiou thus underscores one of the crucial aspects of Deleuzian difference, that disjunctive series, such as those we have seen and will see to be at issue in *The Logic of Sense*, are not conducive to an easy mediating third term that would show them to be fundamentally autopoetic, though they are also never immune from it. While I concur that the autopoetic mediating quality is not entirely absent in Deleuze's thought, it is always vexed in the way Badiou's modification demonstrates. Mediation is something that appears in spite of Deleuze, and this "in spite of" is crucial, for it is the key to Deleuze's hidden dialectic, which is not quite the easy one Žižek often makes it out to be.

Žižek's *Organs without Bodies* might be characterized by two terms that recur with striking and almost diametrically misplaced frequency. One is a notion of "excess" that Žižek repeatedly situates at the center of Deleuze's oeuvre. He writes, for example, of "the excess of the pure flow of becoming over its corporeal cause" (3), of a "Deleuzian excess of relations . . . [the] excess of the effect over its causes" (112), and even more generally of "Deleuze's affirmation of an irreducible *excess* of the problem over its solution(s), which is the same as the excess of the virtual over its actualizations" (55). While it is Žižek's and Badiou's great insight to locate an excess in Deleuze's formulation of univocity, such that what appears to be one thing (i.e., becoming or the One itself) is actually secretly doubled, I would call this more specifically a question of the difference between the one and the two. To be sure, the two for Deleuze marks a kind of blasphemous excess of the One, but this is not the excess of the multiple, of the outside, of the transgressive à la Bataille. If it is to be called an excess, it is rather an internal excess, an excess of structure that is nearly invisible. It is not simply more than one, as excess would imply, but precisely the upsurge of the two where one thinks there is only one. This is the recurrent theme of Lacan's underrated seminar 6 on desire, though Žižek would align Deleuze with the Lacan of seminar 7 and onward, Lacan of the drive as opposed to desire.[8]

Another term that Žižek, following Manuel DeLanda, uses repeatedly to characterize the Sense-Event over the lesser model of productive becoming is "sterile." Insofar as it describes a realm of incorporeal effects

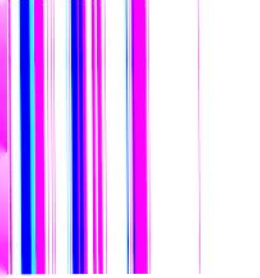

and not the body itself, this term makes some sense. However, following from Deleuze's outline of the incorporeal in *The Logic of Sense* and Émile Bréhier's *La Théorie des incorporels dans l'ancien stoïcisme*, which Deleuze is so indebted to, this realm might be more aptly described as impassive yet limitless.[9] Sterility does not fully capture what Deleuze refers to as "incorporeal splendor,"[10] nor does it convey the alternate temporality of this realm of incorporeal effects, what I have discussed predominantly under the banner of the "unlimited Aion, the becoming which divides itself infinitely in past and future and always eludes the present."[11] While this might seem a minor quibble, the reiteration of sterility (with its various derogatory resonances) seems to work at cross-purposes with what is otherwise a stunning and much-needed recuperation of Deleuze's hidden materialism in what might appear to be one of his most idealistic concepts.

As we have seen, Deleuze repeatedly asserts, in particular in *Difference and Repetition* and in *Bergsonism*, the significance of differences in kind as opposed to differences of degree. If the difference of degree represents an inclusive ecumenical standpoint, then the difference in kind signals the exclusiveness of the cut. This radical separation is something that Žižek does not hesitate to evoke in his examples. He opens *On Belief* with the wonderful example of a *Larry King Live* debate among a priest, a rabbi, and a Southern Baptist minister. Whereas the first two have accepting attitudes toward the belief systems of the others, the minister does not hesitate to assert that the other two are damned. As Žižek glosses it in pointed fashion, "The basic premise of this book is that, cruel as this position may sound, if one is to break the liberal-democratic hegemony and resuscitate an authentic radical position, one has to endorse its materialist version [that of the Southern Baptist]."[12] In *Bodies without Organs*, he is sharply critical of the notion held by many Western academics that political or humanitarian activism can be redemptively integrated with their academic pursuits, for he insists that this is a false mixing of categories that are different in kind, that largesse in one realm cannot be used to justify complicity in another (178–79). (It is interesting to note that Walter Benn Michaels makes much the same point in *The Shape of the Signifier*.)[13]

Badiou's book on Deleuze articulates this strong form of distinction almost to a fault, whereas Žižek's otherwise provocative book might draw out this art of separation, one for which Žižek has an extraordinary gift, even further. Žižek certainly broaches a strong theory of difference when he separates the Deleuze of *The Logic of Sense* from that of *Anti-Oedipus* and when he brings out Deleuze's unacknowledged Hegelianism and Lacanianism. Yet at other points Žižek slips into the other form of difference, the difference of degree and not kind, when he evokes scenarios, especially in the latter part of the book, that are really his own examples and not Deleuze's. Why is this still Deleuze rather than not-Deleuze? Why are these ending meditations not also staged in the form of a betrayal, with the verve of the Protestant minister? There are times that Žižek might betray Deleuze more thoroughly, and in this fashion be even truer, and might employ even more of the disjunctive synthesis, which is after all also outlined by Deleuze and Guattari in *Anti-Oedipus*.

As discussed in the introduction with respect to Hallward's *Out of This World*, these two rather heterodox readings of Deleuze also in their fashion come closest to the argument of this book. They point to a dialectical dimension of Deleuze's thought and above all focus on Deleuze's early work and its relation to structure. Though the precise nature of the structure varies — from perversion and betrayal to series and mediation — of import at this juncture is the interest in the structure itself.

CHAPTER SIX

Lévi-Strauss and the Joy of Abstraction

DELEUZE INSISTS AT DIFFERENT points that the most radical possibility for thought (if not politics) is to become more, not less, abstract. It is this potential for becoming more abstract that I locate as the hinge point between what might be narrated as Claude Lévi-Strauss's structuralism and Deleuze's poststructuralism: in short, Lévi-Strauss never fully crosses into the promised land of abstraction, remaining too insistent on the return to the concrete, whereas Deleuze insists on the need to bring the concrete back to the abstract. This is not to claim that the so-called poststructuralist moment ever really left the fundamental orientations of structuralism (and the mark of this nonabandonment is the continual tension in both domains between the drive to the two- or four-part schema and the concomitant appeal to the univocity of the one single term that encompasses everything). Moreover, traversing both French structuralism and French poststructuralism as it extends from Sartre to Deleuze and on to Badiou, is a preoccupation, often not acknowledged as such, with the inhuman, making this a central term of what I would claim to be a continuous twentieth-century French philosophical project. Insofar as the inhuman numbered structure would seem to reside at the heart of Lévi-Strauss's structuralist anthropology, we might also ask to what degree the "anthropo-" in anthropology is a misnomer. On the one hand, Lévi-Strauss embraces the inhuman structure in all its abstraction, yet on the other he calls for a return to the concrete. By contrast, Deleuze formulates a movement from the abstract to the concrete and back to the abstract, which has an even stronger affinity with Marx's model of capital.

It is first useful to survey a range of critical commentary, some coming from Lévi-Strauss himself, that asserts that his is not a humanist, subject-oriented project. As Christopher Johnson writes in *Claude Lévi-Strauss: The Formative Years*:

> Parallel to the desacralization of the object of anthropology is what one might term the dehumanization of the subject. If anthropology's point of departure is the lived experience of fieldwork, the concrete interaction of the ethnologist with the other culture and his or her testimony of that experience, then in Lévi-Strauss the destination of such experience is the abstraction of structural analysis. . . . The effective suspension of human agency one finds in structuralism is of course already present in the discipline Lévi-Strauss sees as its main inspiration, linguistics.[1]

Johnson's analysis underscores the antihumanist dimension of Lévi-Strauss's oeuvre and, more specifically, the movement from the concrete to the abstract. Whereas the "point of departure" of anthropology centers on questions of "lived experience" and "the concrete interaction of the ethnologist with the other culture," the movement that Lévi-Strauss inaugurates bypasses these dimensions to land at the "destination" of "the abstraction of structural analysis." Even if this antihumanist tendency is already present in linguistics, in the anthropological domain it must follow the trajectory from the concrete to the abstract.

The dominant refrain of critical writing about Lévi-Strauss emphasizes the idea that he comes to rest at the abstract, at the structure itself, and cannot get beyond this. This is often articulated as the shortcoming inherent in Lévi-Strauss's omnipresent structures. In *Elementary Structures Reconsidered*, Francis Korn asserts, "With respect to the concept of 'structure' as used in *Les structures élémentaires de la parenté*, there is no consistent meaning to the term throughout the book. 'Structure' is assimilated by Lévi-Strauss to 'regulating principle,' or to the Gestalt concept of 'whole,' or alternatively to the division of societies into actual institutions such as moieties, sections, and subsections."[2] Not only does everything come to rest at the level of the structure, according to Korn, but structure becomes so general that it encompasses a whole range of categories. Jonathan Culler writes in *Structuralist Poetics*, in reference to Lévi-Strauss's four-part structural mapping of the Oedipus myth, that "it does not really advance our understanding of the logic of myth: the only logic revealed is that of the homologous structure postulated in advance and an elementary logic of class membership."[3] Such an analysis indeed seems aptly applied to Lévi-Strauss's celebrated analysis of the Oedipus myth, where he condenses transhistorical versions of the Oedipus myth into four series: (1) those that overemphasize kinship relations (Oedipus marrying Jocasta); (2) those that deemphasize kinship relations (Oedipus killing his father); (3) those that deemphasize the autochthonous (monsters being killed); and (4) those that emphasize the autochthonous (the relation to the lame or hunched over, the clubfoot, the state of being closer to the earth). In this fashion, 1 and 2 are in a parallel relation of opposition to 4 and 3.[4] Yet at the end of the day, what does this stunning chiasmic mapping tell us about the content of the myth under consideration? Is the content not strangely emptied out by the sheer brilliance of the form? What is striking in the criticisms outlined above is the anxiety—and I locate this anxiety in what follows as intrinsic to the structuralist project—that the sequence not end at the abstract but have some kind of "real life" concreteness or applicability.

It is thus significant that in Deleuze we find a less pejorative analysis of Lévi-Strauss's emphasis on form over content, something entirely in keeping with the drive to be more rather than less abstract. Deleuze writes of Lévi-Strauss in "How Do We Recognize Structuralism?" that "the true subject is the structure itself."[5] He notes that Lévi-Strauss's analysis of the Oedipus myth boils down to a mapping of differential relations and singular points and, moreover, to the identification of more than one series of differential and singular elements, as in the categories of the Oedipus myth. More often than not, it is exactly four series at issue, as in Lévi-Strauss's analysis of "Four Winnebago Myths" or in numerous kinship systems that break down into four interrelated parts.[6] Rather than critiquing the structure for not returning to the concrete, Deleuze's 1972 essay dwells on the complexity opened up by the mapping of differential points into a singular structure—in short, the relation of the four to the one—and the type of thought this enables or forecloses.

Such an approach has affinities to the move that Lévi-Strauss makes in his introduction to the works of Marcel Mauss, where he asserts that what is at issue in Mauss's famous analysis of gift economy as a structure ultimately bound up in reciprocity is not so much the tripartite schema of giving, receiving, and reciprocating that Mauss outlines but rather the singularity of exchange itself. Lévi-Strauss writes, "Why did Mauss halt at the edge of those immense possibilities, like Moses conducting his people all the way to a promised land whose splendor he would never behold?"[7] By understanding that it is exchange itself—the structure itself—and not the already condensed three-part schema (the one rather than the three), Lévi-Strauss sets himself up as the greater visionary to Mauss's Moses.

If Mauss's tripartite dynamic is ultimately about exchange itself, what might it mean in Lévi-Strauss's work for the subject to be the structure, generally the four-part structure, itself? There is ample evidence for claiming that Lévi-Strauss's oeuvre is ultimately about the singularity of the four-part structure, nowhere more so than in the essays that compose the two volumes of Lévi-Strauss's *Structural Anthropology*, which reflect a startlingly original mapping of myths or kinship structures so that what might seem to be endless repetition or inassimilable complexity is in fact a set of four divergent series, often in some form of chiasmic relation to one another. To be sure, Lévi-Strauss can be critiqued for his selective process of reading (only including the parts of the Oedipus myth that support the four-part structure) and for his relegation of the question of the content. And it is in this space of critique or lack of critique, of problematizing or celebrating the landing on "the structure itself," that I would venture to distinguish in broad strokes what might be taken as the structuralist project from the poststructuralist one. Though in many regards difficult to differentiate (some of the canonical works of both structuralism and poststructuralism appeared at exactly the same moment in the mid- to late 1960s, by some of the same authors, such as Barthes, Foucault, and Lacan, who are classified simultaneously in both camps), structuralism and poststructuralism might be distinguished by a difference of tone or, more precisely, by a different relation to the anxiety bound up with excessive attention to form. Though both are preoccupied with structure or form at the expense of human content—there is a strong continuity in the analysis of the inhuman—the structuralist desiring mechanism is one that still privileges a grounding in content, whereas the poststructuralist one is more at ease, if not joyful, in the abandonment of such claims.

Such a logic is illustrated by one of Lévi-Strauss's forays into structuralist poetics, in an essay published in 1960 that analyzes and critiques the then-recent (1958) English-language publication of Vladimir Propp's *Morphology of the Folktale*. In this essay, aptly titled in English translation "Structure and Form: Reflections on a Work by Vladimir Propp," Lévi-Strauss seeks to distinguish Propp's formalist approach to the folktale from his own structuralist approach, the latter developed more in the domain of myth analysis. According to Propp, all the folktales under consideration can be broken down into thirty-one functions, the functions represented by terms such as absence, prohibition, violation, villainy, struggle, victory, and so forth. Notably, these functions are not specific characters or character types but rather single-term attributes that transcend the realm of the personal. Propp analyzes all Russian folktales as combinations of these essential thirty-one functional components, and the types of combinations bring out new nuances of structure — for example, it turns out that the functions implicate one another, that no two functions are mutually exclusive but rather can be grouped in pairs ("prohibition-violation"; "struggle-victory"; "persecution-deliverance," etc.), in sequences ("villainy-dispatch," "decision for counteraction-departure from home," etc.), or according to the sphere of action of the villain ("villainy-struggle-pursuit"; "transference of the hero-liquidation of lack-rescue-solution of a difficult task-transfiguration of the hero," etc.).[8] While such a "formalist" reading of the folktale would seem to have much in common with Lévi-Strauss's "structuralist" analysis of myth, Lévi-Strauss is steadfast in his accusation that formalism privileges the abstract over the concrete — or specifically, in the terms of Propp's analysis, the single-term functional unit over the richness and variation of the detail.

This critique is grounded in the tensions of form and content, or abstract and concrete, but in no way with the fact that the human individuation of characteristics is entirely subsumed by their function in the story. As Lévi-Strauss summarizes: "In order to define the functions, considered as the basic components of the tale, the dramatis personae will first be eliminated, their roles being only to 'support' the functions. A function will be expressed simply by the name of an action: 'interdiction,' 'flight,' and so forth."[9] Lévi-Strauss then proceeds to critique Propp's formalist project for eliminating the content and context of the folktale (or *conte*) at issue, but he never explicitly critiques the elimination of the dramatis personae, the characters, the human actors, as such.

Lévi-Strauss reads in Propp's hierarchy of form over content the essence of the difference between formalism and structuralism: "For [formalism], the two domains must be absolutely separate, since form alone is intelligible, and content is only a residual deprived of any significant value. For structuralism, this opposition does not exist. There is not something abstract on one side and something concrete on the other. Form and content are of the same nature, susceptible to the same analysis."[10] At this juncture Lévi-Strauss would seem to be criticizing the separation between form and content in the formalist project, whereas for structuralism the two are of a piece and not separable. To a certain extent, such a depiction of structuralism as a merging of form and content coincides with the observations, noted above, by those critics who would locate a superior formalism or structure at the heart of Lévi-Strauss's project. Thus structuralism, even in its seemingly equal attention to form and content, might be said itself to be a formalism taken to the next degree. Yet on the other hand, if one takes one of the distinguishing marks of structuralism as the ability to separate terms, to see binary pairs or chiasmic mappings of four-part structures where there might appear to be only one term (for instance, the Oedipus myth), then the very breaking down of oppositions that Lévi-Strauss proposes as a way to distinguish structuralism from formalism seems hardly aligned with the eye to division and separation that is a hallmark of structuralism no less than of formalism.[11]

It is on these very terms of inadequate attention to distinction and division that Lévi-Strauss further distinguishes structuralism from formalism. He writes: "*Formalism destroys its object.* With Propp, it results in the discovery that there exists in reality but one tale. . . . Before formalism, we were certainly unaware of what these tales had in common. Since formalism, we have been deprived of any means of understanding how they differ. One has passed from concrete to abstract, but can no longer come down from the abstract to the concrete."[12] Such a charge of excess abstraction, and beyond that of falling into the very pitfalls he seeks to critique (such as Propp's univocity), is certainly one of the dominant refrains of the critical literature on Lévi-Strauss, from Paul Ricoeur's charge that history provided the "destructive disorder" in Lévi-Strauss's system to Jacques Derrida's famous arguments in *Of Grammatology* and "Structure, Sign, and Play in the Discourse of the Human Sciences" that among other things Lévi-Strauss elevates the very traces of writing (which he is otherwise at pains to attack) into a sort of mystical glue.[13] If Lévi-Strauss would want somehow to return to the concrete, to speak to history, to the importance in anthropology of the oral human tradition, he ends up doing just the opposite, by creating his own inhuman, abstract, often four-part, and all-consuming metastructure.[14]

It is not my claim that Lévi-Strauss somehow succeeded where other critics would say he failed; rather, I wish to dwell on the image of failing to come down from the abstract to the concrete. For such a failure, whether it is attributed to Mauss or Propp or Lévi-Strauss himself, implies a projected trajectory of terms that is itself of great interest. It places the abstract at a sort of summit from which it is difficult to redescend into the realm of the concrete. Thus we have a model on the order of

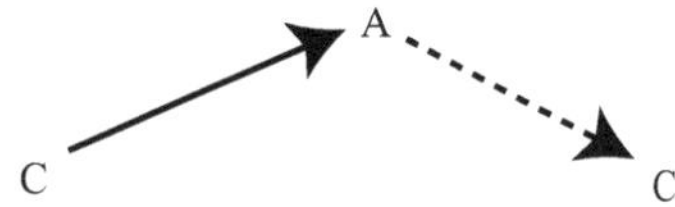

The abstract rests at the summit, much like Moses at the peak of Mount Nebo (Deuteronomy 34), but without being able to descend into the promised land of the concrete. Rather than rest on the drive to the abstract, it is perhaps more meaningful instead to consider the logic that would seek to recuperate the abstract into the concrete, into the real lived experience or use value that would return a balance or proper elevation or reciprocity to the system. This is notable in its affinity with the system that Marx outlines in *Capital* where the commodity is exchanged for money and that money is used to purchase a new commodity that will be of use, effectively producing a C-M-C structure between the commodities and the money (where commodities are concrete and money is abstract). Marx, of course, goes on to formulate the structure proper to capital as that of M-C-M, where money serves as the motor force, one that does not rest with a balanced exchange but builds on the perpetual energy of the surplus it engenders.[15] When one adds to this mixture the important writings on use value and the desire structure it generates, one that is in every way equivalent to the imbalanced economy of exchange (by theorists of "libidinal economy" such as Lyotard, Baudrillard, Klossowski, and Deleuze and Guattari), as well as a Derridean model of gift economy that is based on the unconditional and the nonreciprocal and pitted against Mauss's gift theory that would see an ultimate structure of reciprocity at the heart of all gift exchange, then one finds that if anything could be said to distinguish it definitively from structuralism, the "poststructuralist turn" is centrally bound up with nonreciprocity, pure gift, desire that cannot be returned to simple use or need—in short, an M-C-M structure that draws its energy from a critique of the return to the level of use, the concrete, and the reciprocal.[16]

If there is a difference to be had between structuralism and what follows it, it might consist in the movement from the desire to return to the concrete (C-A-C) to the full embracing of the entropic movement of capital, one that starts with and returns to the abstract (A-C-A).

Indeed, it is with such a movement that I would like to conclude, by drawing on two examples of this A-C-A dynamic, proffered at the moment of structuralism's heyday by Deleuze himself. In this fashion, I hope to underscore, alongside the dialectical and ontological dimension of Deleuze's oeuvre, one that is bound up with the idea of structure, if not structuralism. If it may be argued that Deleuze, like Barthes, Foucault, and Lacan, had a structuralist phase, it would generally be located at the moment of his "How Do We Recognize Structuralism?," which is also the moment of his 1969 *The Logic of Sense*. In the latter book, Deleuze focuses on the series and the serial and defines them in terms that are highly resonant with Lévi-Strauss's structuralism, particularly insofar as they participate in a logic of division that is above all one of duality. The chapters in *The Logic of Sense* are in fact called "series," and the one from which I quote is the wonderfully alliterative "Sixth Series on Serialization": "*[T]he serial form is necessarily realized in the simultaneity of at least two series*. Every unique series, whose homogenous terms are distinguished only according to type or degree, necessarily subsumes under it two heterogeneous series, each one of which is constituted by terms of the same type or degree, although these terms differ in nature from those of the other series."[17] For Deleuze, the series in question are by necessity unequal, though they may in fact share some of the same terms. What is essential, however, is that there is always more than one series, and although these series may have some relation to one another, it is not one of mediation (which takes us back to Deleuze's affinity with Sartre and Badiou, and even more with Klossowski, who all share a drive to a non-mediated dualism).

This binary relation between series is in many respects parallel to the terms and modalities of Saussurean linguistics or Lévi-Strauss's elementary structures of kinship, especially when Deleuze insists on the dualist relation of signifier and signified in the same oppositional terms as Ferdinand de Saussure or Lévi-Strauss: "When we extend the serial method—in order to consider two series of events, two series of things, two series of propositions, or two series of expressions—homogeneity is only apparent: it is always the case that one series has the role of signifier, and the other the role of the signified, even if these roles are interchanged as we change points of view."[18] Such a formulation is entirely of a piece not only with Lévi-Strauss's structural anthropology but also with his claim, contra Russian formalism, that structuralism does not ultimately separate form from content, nor does it collapse them into one term, but leaves them as two terms in chiasmic relation. Yet on the same page of *The Logic of Sense*, we see the gesture to a line of descent that would seem to be the descent that formalism, and Lévi-Strauss in its wake, are unable to fully achieve, like Moses stuck upon the mountain unable to descend.

In the lengthy passage that follows, Deleuze would seem to chart a descent from the abstract theory of the series to the concrete literary instantiation of the serial, yet what ensues is an exemplary excess that more nearly produces an endless chain of signifiers than a coming to rest on a coherent literary signified:

> Jacques Lacan has brought to light the existence of two series in one of Edgar Allan Poe's stories ["The Purloined Letter"]. First series: the king who does not see the compromising letter received by his wife; the queen who is relieved to have hidden it so cleverly by leaving it out in the open; the minister who sees everything and takes possession of the letter. Second series: the police who find nothing at the minister's hotel; the minister who thought of leaving the letter in the open in order better to hide it; Dupin who sees everything and takes back possession of the letter. It is obvious that differences between series may be more or less great—very great with certain authors, or very small with those others who introduce only infinitesimal, and yet equally efficacious, variations. . . . It is easy to cite various authors, who have known how to create serial techniques of an *exemplary formalism*. Joyce, for example, secured the relation between the signifying series "Bloom" and the signified series "Ulysses," thanks to multiple forms which included an archeology of narrative modes, a *system* of correspondence between numbers, a prodigious employment of esoteric words, a method of question and answer and the establishment of currents of thought or multiple trains of thought (Carroll's double thinking?). Raymond Roussel based the communication of series on a phonematic relation ("*les bandes du vieux pillard*," "*les bandes du vieux billard*" = b/p),

and filled up the difference with a marvelous story in which the signifying series *p* links up with the signified series *b*: the enigmatic nature of the story is emphasized in this general procedure, to the extent that the signified series may remain hidden. Robbe-Grillet established his series of descriptions of states of affairs and *rigorous designations* with *small differences*. He did it by having them revolve around themes which, although fixed, are nevertheless suited to almost imperceptible modification and displacement in each series. Pierre Klossowski relies on the *proper name* "Roberte," certainly not in order to designate a character and manifest its identity, but on the contrary, in order to express a "primary intensity," *to distribute difference and to obtain the doubling up of two series*: the first, signifying, which refers to "the husband being unable to imagine his wife otherwise than as surprising herself as she would allow herself to be surprised"; the second, signified, which refers to the wife "rushing into initiatives which ought to convince her of her freedom, when these initiatives confirm only the vision of her spouse." Witold Gombrowicz established a signifying series of hanged animals (what do they signify?), and a signified series of feminine mouths (what is signifying them?); *each series develops a system of signs*, sometimes by excess, sometimes by default, and communicates with another by means of strange interfering objects and by means of the esoteric words pronounced to Léon.[19]

Not only does this long passage mirror in its swift progression the very form of the series that creates, through division, a line of descent, or line of flight (which is also the very form of Deleuzian dialectic), but this also could serve as a model of sorts for a method of literary comparison. Here Deleuze breaks many implicit or explicit rules about the way to do literary analysis. The examples are thrown out, not situated in their context, undeveloped, ranging in seemingly haphazard fashion over myriad national literatures and authors (and the same accusation has been made of Deleuze's mode of filmic analysis in his cinema books). Yet the examples are linked by the singular thematic of the series and its systematic differentials (see my emphases in the passage above) in such a strong fashion that this allows for the breakneck line of comparison that might seem to run roughshod, with a peculiar type of literary dilettantism, over the richness of the texts it evokes. What is gained, however, is not only the precision of the insight but the exhilaration of its staging as a serial line of descent. (How might this serve as a model for the study of comparative literature?)

On this reading Deleuze achieves something that by Lévi-Strauss's evaluation Propp and the Russian formalists fail to do: to descend from the abstract to the concrete. Yet viewed from a different lens, this evocation of the specific literary examples of seriality transitions into its own form of abstraction in the seemingly endless energy of the propagation of the chain of examples at the expense of arrival at a concrete destination. What we witness is the high structuralism of the model devolving into the manic and interminable chain of concrete instantiations that in the very energy of their metonymic deferral take on a still higher level of abstraction. Is such a phenomenon to be signaled as the central gesture of structuralism or the mark of the "post" that would somehow lie beyond? (Given the opening example of Poe's letter, is this what it means to enter the postal dimension?)

In a still earlier work, Deleuze presents a more sober example that conforms more exactly to the A-C-A model of descent into the abstract as opposed to the concrete. In *Proust and Signs* Deleuze provides, as it were, a serial mapping of human affect. At the outset, he discusses the dynamics of jealousy, how jealousy allows for an intensive reading of signs that accesses love's truths far more pointedly than would a less motivated relation of friendship—in effect, jealousy allows for the best possible fine-tuning of the skills of close reading (or in words that are not exactly Deleuze's, for a heightened attunement to the structure itself).[20] Yet Deleuze also focuses on how love's very intensity waxes and wanes in serial fashion. He takes as his example the Proustian narrator's falling in and out of love with Albertine. When the narrator first encounters Albertine, she is indistinguishable from a group of young girls; she is one element in a series. However, as the narrator falls in love with her, she becomes a singular entity, entirely apart from her young peers. So far this seems altogether straightforward and recognizable, but what Deleuze isolates in Proust is the descent from love's singularity back into serial formation. In other words, as the narrator falls out of love with Albertine, she begins to resemble once again the group of young girls from which she emerged. Significantly, Deleuze registers no hierarchy between the two states. If anything, the descent proves more enlightening, because it allows for the perception of the law of the series.[21] Love's singularization is not superior to the receding away from it; indeed Deleuze emphasizes the joy of seriality and its repetitions as illustrated by Proust. That is, Deleuze distinguishes the joy of the form of repetition from the pain of the content. The fact that one's patterns of loving often repeat themselves—hence Deleuze's assertion that "there are so many Albertines," for the relation with Albertine keeps being repeated with other people[22]—introduces a second-order seriality to the first-order seriality of simply falling out of love. Deleuze emphasizes that although the love repetitions are quite painful, there is nonetheless a joy and a pleasure in the often fleeting recognition of the pattern itself and of the love object's being merely a part of a larger serial structure. The hyperbolic curve of the series, the series of amorous repetitions, is the series as it approaches its own law, which is often semi-unconscious.

Deleuze's study of Proust thus stages in more than one fashion the triumph of form and abstraction, presented in what follows as the perception of the law of the series above and beyond the amorous series itself:

> What we repeat is each time a particular suffering; but the repetition itself is always joyous, the phenomenon of repetition forms a general joy. Or rather, the phenomena are always unhappy, and particular; but the idea extracted from them is general, and joyous. For love's repetition is not to be separated from a law of progression by which we accede to a consciousness which transmutes our sufferings into joy. We realize that our sufferings do not depend on their object. . . . There is something tragic about what is repeated, but something comic in the repetition itself, and more profoundly, a joy of repetition understood, or of the comprehension of its law.[23]

This logic of difference and repetition, or of the Nietzschean eternal return, is the promised land that Lévi-Strauss feared to enter. It is the affirmation of joy in landing upon the structure itself, something that Lévi-Strauss's readers all signaled as the hallmark if not the downfall of his work but that Lévi-Strauss approached with extensive reticence if not denial. It is Deleuze who will recognize the desire for the structure and give this desire an affirmative valence, something entirely comparable to Lacan's injunction to not give way on one's desire, or Žižek's imperative to "enjoy your symptom." And it is this joy of abstraction, this desire to remain under its sway rather than reside in the world of the concrete with its ever-repeating content, that may be the true hallmark of the move beyond structuralism, but at a moment and from a vantage point that was confoundingly always within it.

CHAPTER SEVEN

Extreme Formality and the World without Others

THERE ARE NUMEROUS WAYS in which Deleuze's thought might be aligned with a generally recognizable form of ethics: from his beautiful Nietzschean meditations in *Spinoza: Practical Philosophy* on the ethics of good and bad forces as opposed to the morality of Good and Evil, to Foucault's famous designation of Deleuze and Guattari's *Anti-Oedipus* as a "book of ethics, the first book of ethics to be written in France in quite a long time," to what are profoundly ethical late reflections on conceptual personae, philosophical friendship, and even an ethics of "life."[1] This is not to mention the Stoic dictum from *The Logic of Sense* "not to be unworthy of what happens to us."[2] While it is specifically the single-authored work from the late 1960s—if not the year 1967—under consideration in this chapter, at issue is a notion of ethics that might arguably not be recognized as one at all or recognized as in any way resonant with Deleuze. This ethics, perhaps more aptly labeled an "anethics," is a stranger and darker one than the more palatable examples listed above; it is an ethics more in resonance with Lacan as well as a certain structuralist imperative.

Lacan proposes a counterintuitive if not perverse definition of ethics in his 1959–60 seminar *The Ethics of Psychoanalysis*: "And it is because we know better than those who went before how to recognize the nature of desire, which is at the heart of this experience, that a reconsideration of ethics is possible, that a form of ethical judgment is possible, of a kind that gives this question the force of a Last Judgment. Have you acted in conformity with the desire that is in you?. . . Opposed to this pole of desire is traditional ethics."[3] If a Lacanian model of ethics is thus to not "give ground relative to one's desire,"[4] I would propose that Deleuze of the late 1960s—and arguably the Deleuzian oeuvre in its entirety—twists such a dictum to the following formulation without ever stating it as such: *to not give ground relative to that place where desire is stopped in its tracks.* In his extended consideration of *Antigone* in the ethics seminar, Lacan emphasizes the way in which Antigone's "strange beauty" stops desire in its tracks,[5] and similarly it will be emphasized here the way in which the Deleuze who with Guattari would seem to be preoccupied with desire is in fact equally preoccupied with those zones where desire is arrested and, more often than not, arrested at that point where it resonates with a higher notion of structure itself.

The structure in question takes on different forms, which I attempt to delineate in what follows. But all such forms hinge on what Deleuze characterizes as an "extreme formality," and this combination of the formal and the extreme is central to the alternative Deleuzian ethics — or anethics — in question. This combination of formal and extreme is perhaps best articulated in the disjunction Deleuze repeatedly emphasizes between sadism and masochism and, beyond that, the disjunction inherent in the structure of sadism itself, one side of which is precisely that place where desire is stopped in its tracks, a place that is entirely above and beyond the structure of masochism, or even the first order of sadism.

Gilles Deleuze's 1967 essay "Coldness and Cruelty" first appeared in the context of a work devoted to Sacher-Masoch and featuring the latter's *Venus in Furs.* It was translated into English under the title *Masochism*, and in this context the rubric of masochism not surprisingly overshadows that of sadism.[6] What I hope to draw attention to is the curious fact that, in a work that must necessarily speak to the question of masochism, Deleuze brings particularly acute attention to outlining the structure of sadism. Of course it might be argued that such an attention is critical to the understanding of masochism, and to some extent this is the case; but if the two forms do not rely on each other for their definition, why does Deleuze keep returning to the question of sadism in his exposition of masochism? This chapter claims that the structure of sadism, above and beyond that of masochism, is in strong resonance with a series of terms that traverse, in subterranean fashion, Deleuze's work from the late 1960s. Each of these structures points to a modality of ethics that is more nearly something akin to an anethics, insofar as it eschews the categories of the human and even of life but instead focuses on the highest structural order that can be reached within a given system (in this sense, it is not that far removed from Foucault's 1966 *The Order of Things*). Thus, Deleuze's concepts of sadism, the world without others, the third synthesis of time, and the death instinct all mirror one another and reveal not only an extreme formality but an extreme state of stasis and nonbecoming at the heart of Deleuze's early work.

As I discuss in part 3, Deleuze has a somewhat fraught relation to the question of movement. Although he and Guattari are always careful to insist that there need not be actual physical movement for flights or becoming or nomad thought to take place, there is nonetheless a privilege accorded to becoming and the implicit movement it entails, so that a certain dialectic of movement and stasis tends to result, with movement being the favored term. This might be mapped onto Deleuze's privileging of the time of Aion in *The Logic of Sense*, which is that of the past-future conjunction that he opposes to Chronos, the time of the present. In his discussion of the event, we see an implicit premium placed on the movement of becoming:

> The event in turn, in its impassibility and impenetrability, has no present. It rather retreats and advances in two directions at once, being the perpetual object of a double question: What is going to happen? What has just happened? The agonizing aspect of the pure event is that it is always and at the same time something which has just happened and something about to happen; never something which is happening.[7]

In the realm of the Aion, what counts is what has just happened and what is about to happen. There is a movement in two directions at once, but it is not a movement of cancellation. It appears that even in the intemporal form of time that is Aion, there is still a hint of movement—and this is what distinguishes the Aion from Deleuze's third synthesis of time in *Difference and Repetition*.

As I suggest on the chapter on Blanchot in part 3, Maurice Blanchot embraces more fully than Deleuze, at least in the twentieth-century French tradition, a being of pure inertia and immobility, so that, for Blanchot, movement or action ultimately leads to a more radical state of inertia, an *inertia of being* (as opposed to a seemingly more Deleuzian notion of becoming). Blanchot's fictional works present, much like those of Kafka, Beckett, and Melville's "Bartleby," characters who remain stuck in a hemmed-in interior space, a hotel room or apartment or concentrationary universe from which there is no escape, even if in some instances it would seem that the characters are free simply to walk away. This Blanchotian state of arrestation surpasses even the intemporality of Deleuze's *Aion* and invokes an interminable and immobile present over and above a convergence of past and future. Such an endless present marks a radical dwelling in being that in no way resembles the *parousia* of being or presence that is often under assault by Derrida and others. (Indeed Derrida's *Demeure*, as the culmination of a series of writings on Blanchot throughout his career, captures this Blanchotian modality of dwelling, of remaining, or living on — but as *désoeuvrement* rather than *parousia* — as perhaps nobody else has done, though without an open embrace of its ontological ramifications.)[8]

Thus, in comparing Deleuze and Blanchot, it is not difficult to affirm that Blanchot has a more developed notion of stasis, immobility, and inertia, especially compared to the Deleuze of becoming over being, of nomadology, of lines of flight, deterritorialization, and so forth. But I want to suggest that there is a register in Deleuze's early texts that runs entirely against this divide and is often best discerned by registering which terms receive a positive or a negative valence in Deleuze's thought. (Of course that does sometimes change.) So, for example, in "Coldness and Cruelty," when Deleuze writes, "while Sade is spinozistic and employs demonstrative reason, Masoch is platonic and proceeds by dialectical imagination" (CC, 22), any reader remotely familiar with Deleuze's philosophical trajectory would know that Spinoza is always cast on the side of the good and Plato more nearly (though not uniformly) on that of the bad. Similarly, the dialectic (here associated with Masoch) is for Deleuze generally, though not exclusively as I have tried to show, cast on the side of the bad. Of course, it is never this simple: Deleuze has some surprisingly good things to say about Plato (this reader would even claim that Deleuze is perhaps, after Badiou, one of the most Platonic philosophers in the twentieth-century French tradition, although this study is if anything an attempt to recuperate his more Aristotelian side). Still, we have to take note, when seeing Sade so blatantly tethered to Spinoza and Spinozist ethics, that there must be something of enormous appeal for Deleuze in the structure of sadism, which, as he emphasizes at practically every juncture in "Coldness and Cruelty," is fundamentally different in kind from masochism. For Deleuze argues that sadism and masochism are not complementary structures, and to lump them together is conceptually inaccurate.

I will return to "Coldness and Cruelty" in what follows, but for now I ask the reader simply to consider the hypothesis that there may be something that Deleuze finds particularly compelling about sadism in terms of its structural purity — and it must be emphasized that these are impersonal structures above and beyond anything else, more than they are attributes of individuals. This is in no way to claim that Deleuze unilaterally disfavors the structure of masochism, to which he gives greater attention in this early study, for in fact sometimes masochism (as well as the neurotic, to take another somewhat comparable example) is described with epithets to which Deleuze gives negative valence (Platonic, dialectic, etc.) and at other times with epithets that are favored (humor, suspense, suspended gestures). To this end, masochism is the harder structure to pin down because it goes in several directions at once, whereas sadism has a purity that masochism can only aspire to.[9] And, as we shall see, sadism and its attendant ethics, or anethics, has a remarkable affinity with at least three other distinctive structures in Deleuze's early works, works written in the late 1960s and concentrated in the year 1967.

Published that year is the essay noted previously on Michel Tournier's rewriting of the Robinson Crusoe story in his acclaimed novel *Friday*, entitled "Michel Tournier and the World without Others." This essay provides a crucial if indirect elaboration of the structure of sadism, which is also a structure or space of extreme intemporality and stasis (and such a space recurs in Deleuze's single-authored work from the 1960s and even appears to some degree in the joint works with Guattari, above all *Anti-Oedipus*). Here, Deleuze describes the world that the protagonist Robinson comes to inhabit on the desert island, which is the world without others. It is not simply that the Other is missing from the desert island, which it is, but at stake is the opening that this absence provides, an opening onto an impersonal and inhuman perceptual space that is entirely beyond the realm of other people. Deleuze writes:

> In the Other's absence, consciousness and its object are one. . . . Consciousness ceases to be a light cast upon objects in order to become a pure phosphorescence of things in themselves. Robinson is but the consciousness of the island, but the consciousness of the island is the consciousness the island has of itself — it is the island in itself. We

> understand the paradox of the desert isle: the one who is shipwrecked, if he is alone, if he has lost the structure-Other, disturbs nothing of the desert isle; rather he consecrates it.[10]

Evoked here is something akin to a pre-Kantian notion of the thing in itself, a vision precluded by what Quentin Meillassoux terms the "correlationism" that is inaugurated by Kant, in short the idea that everything must be described as *relative* to the perceiving consciousness and not in and of itself.[11] We see something like Sartre's "in-itself," a level of pure being or essence that is not usually equated with Deleuze. And this vision of thing-being, of island-consciousness, is also an opening to an ontology of nonrelation. If ethics might be said to be about relations, and human relations at that, then the particularly Deleuzian ethology of this period is an ethics beyond anthropomorphic being and relation, an ethics beyond ethics, indeed what I am also calling an anethics.

The realm of the world without others is notably intemporal yet also eternally present. It is hard to know where to fit it into the temporalities mapped out in *The Logic of Sense*, whether it would fall into the past-future conjunction of becoming that is Aion or the disfavored chronological time of the present that is Chronos. Ultimately, it is not clear that the world without others fits into either of these temporalities. Deleuze notes that, under the regime of the structure-Other (which is a highly Lacanian, if not Hegelian and Sartrean, model of the other as a structural field, one that is endemic to language and falls under the register of the possible—a term that, on the whole, appears in Deleuze's work as pejorative),[12] spatial and temporal distribution and organization dominate the field, but in the absence of the structure-Other they no longer obtain. As Deleuze writes: "How could there be a past when the Other no longer functions?" (WwO, 311). It would seem that the past, or even the past-future conjunction of Aion, is something like a preliminary stage that is then subsumed by the world without others.

Furthermore, this world without others is curiously described as an "eternal present." Deleuze writes, "[L]acking in its structure, [the Other's absence] allows consciousness to cling to, and to coincide with, the object in an eternal present" (WwO, 311). Such a notion of the present is decidedly not the time of Chronos, which is another kind of present, but rather an eternal present. As outlined in the introduction, Aquinas, one of Deleuze's proclaimed enemies, evokes a divine temporality that has striking affinities with Deleuze's eternal present. In God's time, there is no past or future and no succession. For Aquinas, God cannot be the result of anything, since he is the prime mover, inhabiting an intemporal eternal present that is very much like the world without others.[13] The crucial point of distinction between Aquinas's eternity and Deleuze's notion of the "eternal present" as accessed in the world without others can be accounted for by Deleuze's concept of difference. Because the world without others is itself generated through a process of difference (it is not itself the primary substance, or first mover) and is itself the *product* of genesis, it is formed by an entirely different process than Aquinas's divinity, which by definition cannot be preceded by anything. It is this that distinguishes Deleuze's intemporal eternal present from a purely theological one: for Deleuze the world without others (or third synthesis of time) is not a primary order but a secondary one, which for Deleuze generally makes it better, something that is not the case for Aquinas.

Therefore, unlike Aquinas, Deleuze's eternal present is not primary but secondary or tertiary. While Deleuze is critical of a certain dualism present in modern psychology, and even in Husserl, a dualism for example between the matter "of the perceptual field and the pre-reflective syntheses of the ego" (WwO, 308), he affirms a dualism inherent in the workings of the structure-Other, one that is produced through a genetic process that stems from a difference in kind. Thus he insists:

> The true dualism lies elsewhere, it lies between the effects of the "structure Other" of the perceptual field and the effects of its absence (what perception would be were there no Others). We must understand that the Other is not one structure among others in the field of perception. . . . *It is the structure which conditions the entire field* and its functioning, . . . [it is] the a priori principle of the organization of every perceptual field. . . . Real dualism then appears with the absence of the Other. (WwO, 308–9)

Not only is this a consummate articulation of Deleuze's particular form of dualistic but nonmediated dialectic, but it is also an articulation of the hierarchical structure of the succession of orders, the paradox being that the higher secondary order crucially dispenses with a notion of temporality based on succession. In short, the structure-Other is primary, whereas the world without others, which is the higher order for Deleuze, is secondary. One might think that the world without others would be some sort of primordial, chaotic state from which the proper structural relation to the Other emerges (like an elemental Imaginary from which the Symbolic order issues, or something of the sort, though Lacan is never that straightforward). But that is not at all the case, for it is the reverse principle of order and process of genesis that is critical to the concept, because the world without others is a product, and a higher product, of the structure-Other.[14]

As discussed above, we see this same ordering in *The Logic of Sense* with respect to the incorporeal, which is at a higher level than the corporeal but also issuing from it, and the same holds with the rather elaborate hierarchies of art in the Proust book (all of these notably works from this same period in the 1960s).[15] Almost invariably in Deleuze's work from this period, it is the second order, or the third order if there are three, that is the higher one, the more intemporal, immaterial and pure order, and the one generated from the preceding order or orders. Deleuze writes in *Difference and Repetition* of "the formless as the product of the most extreme formality," and this is the relentless if not cruel logic that connects all the examples at issue here.[16] It is thus the recognition and description of this higher level that takes on its own sort of anethical imperative in early Deleuze.[17]

Such a logic traverses *Difference and Repetition*, more systematically than in *The Logic of Sense*, where it appears at its most acute in the appendixes. If the time of the Aion in *The Logic of Sense* might still fall under the category of a generalized movement or becoming, the third synthesis of time in *Difference and Repetition* falls squarely outside of it and resonates in profound fashion with the description of "the world without others" that concludes *The Logic of Sense*. Moreover, if *The Logic of Sense* anticipates some of the major thematics of *Anti-Oedipus*, above all in the early formulation of the body without organs, then *Difference and Repetition* reads as a quasi-paean to Freud in a fashion that is no longer operative in *Anti-Oedipus*.

To begin with the third synthesis, it is delineated in opposition to the first synthesis, which is that of habit and the more Chronos-like present, and even to the second synthesis, that of memory and the past (which to a certain degree resembles the time of Aion in *The Logic of Sense*). By contrast, Deleuze characterizes the third synthesis, invoking Hamlet, as "time out of joint":

> [T]ime out of joint means demented time or time outside the curve which gave it a god, liberated from its overly simple circular figure, freed from the events which made up its content, its relation to movement overturned; in short, time presenting itself as an empty and pure form. . . . [Time] ceases to be cardinal and becomes ordinal, a pure *order* of time. . . . We can then distinguish a more or less extensive past and a future in inverse proportion, but the future and the past here are not empirical and dynamic determinations of time: they are formal and fixed characteristics which follow *a priori* from the order of time, as though they comprised a static synthesis of time. The synthesis is necessarily static, since time is no longer subordinated to movement; time is the most radical form of change, but the form of change does not change.[18]

Of import here, in addition to the articulation of the concepts, is the order of their presentation. Just as the cinema books might be said to be ordered according to the overcoming of movement by time, so too the height of Deleuzian genesis entails first a surpassing of movement and secondly a surpassing of time. The ultimate attainment is an empty and pure form, which is also a pure order, and with that, static. Time at its most radical is divorced from movement and is static. As we proceed, then, through the Deleuzian syntheses of time, we ascend to the higher, intemporal, static third order.[19] Indeed, if much of what is considered to be Deleuzian ethics revolves around a type of becoming that avoids the stasis of morality, then at stake here is a rarefied kind of stasis that approximates being above and beyond becoming yet also in its formless (*informe*) quality escapes the realm of morality and its attendant judgments. It is the triumph of Kant's second critique, which Deleuze himself alludes to in select moments in his writings on Kant, and this is taken up in what follows.

It is in this context that I wish to come full circle (though Deleuze's notion of the circle in *Difference and Repetition* is ambivalent at best) and return to "Coldness and Cruelty," because it is through Freud, of all unlikely Deleuzian models, that we can see formulated most clearly the connection between the third synthesis, the world without others, the structure of sadism, and the question of ethics. This connection is made via Freud's notion of the death instinct, as outlined in *Beyond the Pleasure Principle*, which "masterpiece," according to Deleuze, "is perhaps the one where [Freud] engaged most directly—and how penetratingly—in specifically philosophical reflection" (CC, 111). In *Difference and Repetition*, Deleuze clearly links the third synthesis of time to the Freudian death instinct, where he writes in the abovementioned discussion of the three syntheses of time: "Time empty and out of joint, with its rigorous formal and static order, its crushing unity and its irreversible series, is precisely the death instinct. The death instinct does not enter into a cycle with Eros, but testifies to a completely different synthesis. . . . [It is] a death instinct desexualised and without love."[20] And these are precisely the terms used to characterize Robinson on the desert island. In the third synthesis, we see all at once the alignment of (1) time out of joint; (2) a rigorous, formal and static order; and (3) the death instinct. Rather than dwelling on *Difference and Repetition* and the complexities of its syntheses of time, which have been capably treated elsewhere,[21] I wish to use this alignment of concepts to argue that, despite the neutrality of tone and evenhandedness with which sadism and masochism are taken up in "Coldness and Cruelty," it is above all the structure of sadism that resonates most fully with this extreme space of stasis and intemporality in the work from the late 1960s.

Although Deleuze links both sadism and masochism simultaneously to the pleasure principle and to the death instinct, he takes care to distinguish between, on the one hand, death or destructive instincts, which are in a dialectical relation to Eros and governed by the unconscious, and, on the other hand, the Death Instinct (which he puts in capital letters), which is a pure, silent, and absolute negation that is not connected to the unconscious, since, as Freud puts it, there is no big No (or pure negation) in the unconscious (CC, 30).[22] Deleuze links such an absolute negation to the second-order negation in Sade. The first order is a personal form of Sadean negativity that is imperative and descriptive (good sense?), and the second and related but higher order is one that is impersonal and absolute, even delusional (CC, 19). Deleuze writes that "the second and higher factor represents the *impersonal* element in sadism and identifies the impersonal violence with an Idea of pure reason, with a terrifying demonstration capable of subordinating the first element. In Sade we discover a surprising affinity with Spinoza—a naturalistic and mechanistic approach imbued with the mathematical spirit" (CC, 19–20). As indicated above, for Deleuze one cannot surpass "the Christ of philosophers" and author of the *Ethics*, and it seems that this passage must be read, above all, as an extraordinary paean to the second level of sadism and its surprising Spinozisms.

In a similar vein, we also see the gesture toward an absolute if not divinely violent form of pure reason that in its extremity might explode and overcome reason's law, and here it is not insignificant that Deleuze cites Lacan's 1963 essay "Kant with Sade" (CC, 137n26). Deleuze develops this connection to Kant in the section of "Coldness and Cruelty" titled "Humor, Irony, and the Law," when he notes that Kant's second critique is more revolutionary than the first, for if the first weds us to the subject, the second establishes the law at such a level of pure form that it opens the path—a formal one—to its overturning. I quote this passage in its entirety:

> The Copernican revolution in Kant's *Critique of Pure Reason* consisted in viewing the objects of knowledge as revolving around the subject; but the *Critique of Practical Reason*, where the Good is conceived as revolving around the Law, is perhaps even more revolutionary. It probably reflected major changes in the world. It may have been the expression of the ultimate consequences of a return beyond Christianity to Judaic thought, or it may even have foreshadowed a return to the pre-Socratic (Oedipal) conception of the law, beyond to the world of Plato. However that may be, Kant, by establishing that THE LAW is an ultimate ground or principle, added an essential dimension to modern thought: the object of the law is by definition unknowable and elusive. (CC, 83)[23]

This passage sets up the paradox of the form or structure that, when pushed to its extreme, is static and formless, essentially Deleuze's claim in his essay "How Do We Recognize Structuralism?" that Lévi-Strauss's "empty square" is at once the arrival point and motor force (the "secret glue") of his structuralist project. Are there not so many occasions when one does something out of principle, out of a strange and possibly even self-destructive loyalty to the form something should take, above and beyond the content or value? If push comes to shove, can it be explained *why* the principle is held to with such tenacity, even if the outcome matters little? It is this imperative to hold to form, and the attendant stasis or dissolution that may be produced—quite literally stuck on the formality—that Deleuze explains on an ontological level. But following Lacan, can such an imperative be divorced from desire, and when it is divorced from any desire for content, does it not become an insistent ethics of form, one which then leaves desire itself somewhat stranded and by the wayside? Clearly such an insistence on laws of form can be taken to very bad ends, but it is hoped that the unflinching pursuit of an understanding of the *structure* may pave the way for different — and more positive — alternatives.

Deleuze continues his discussion of Kant and law with an analysis of the way in which masochism and sadism, each in its way, subvert the law. In masochism this is done through humor, through the downward movement of exploding the law from within by observing its very letter to the point that its absurdity is brought into full relief. But with sadism it is an issue of principle, and the overturning is transcendental. Through Sadean institutional anarchy, evil subverts Platonism and transcends the law from on high. Whereas the masochist is "the logician of consequences," the ironic sadist is "the logician of principles" (CC, 89). While the relation between heights and depths is indeed a fraught one, above all in *The Logic of Sense*, I would claim that, without ever stating this as such (indeed Deleuze writes that the masochist "overthrows law as radically as the sadist, though in a different way" [CC, 89]), it is hard to come away from a thorough reading of Deleuze's work from this period without remarking on the Deleuzian proclivity for heights over depths, for the superego over the ego, for the raging molecules over the agrarian, for thought over imagination, and for the thinker over the visionary. The former terms are all used to describe sadism, the latter terms masochism. Admittedly, there may be some ambivalence in the terms, and certainly they are not simple opposites of one another, to return to the oft-reiterated central thesis of "Coldness and Cruelty." It may be contentious to claim that the thinker or philosopher takes precedence over the visionary or artist, but is anything ever higher than thought for Deleuze?[24] Even in the book on Proust, where art would take on the loftiest space in all of Deleuze's works, it is art's formality and purity, things accessed by the philosopher, that give it its high status. Creativity, after all, may proceed dialectically, but pure form, and pure thought, do not. Pure thought is the product, and the higher project, of an initial and more primary structure.[25]

It is also notable that in his brief discussion of Kant, Deleuze introduces a rare form of speculation as to what produced this shift between the first and second critiques, making the second more revolutionary. Leaving aside the Judeo-Christian hypotheses, which might be mapped more decisively into thinkers such as Derrida, Agamben, and even Badiou, it is notable simply that Deleuze makes a fleeting reference to "forces in the world," for the world is decidedly not the realm that serves as the backdrop for his analysis (and on this point I concur with the focal point of Hallward's *Out of This World*, if not its precise conclusions). Indeed, like the libertine sequestered in his "*tour abolie*," Deleuze does not present a program for "applying" the structures of sadism and masochism to the "real world," not that they cannot be so applied in his wake. Rather, he focuses on the question of structure as such, at least in the work from this period, and on this count alone, sadism, in its purer and more absolute structural logic, must necessarily be the higher form.

On the concluding page of "Michel Tournier and the World without Others," Deleuze notes that in Sade's work, victims are not at all grasped as others (WwO, 320) and he goes on to note that "the world of the pervert" (i.e., Robinson on his desert island, with his "desert sexuality," as Deleuze calls it) "is a world without Others, and thus a world without the possible." (Again, Bogue's argument notwithstanding, the possible is almost always inflected negatively for Deleuze, so this seems to be a solid tribute to that world without others.) He continues, "This is a strange Spinozism from which 'oxygen' is lacking, to the benefit of a more elementary energy and a more rarefied air" (WwO, 320). This is an extreme state of negation, lack of oxygen, death, purity, sadism, intemporality, incorporeality, and an eschewal of the other and of communication and relation that traverses the work from the late 1960s and forms the hidden kernel of Deleuze's philosophical project, which is on some level quite a dark one. It is Deleuze's own dark precursor,[26] which is not so clearly visible from the vantage point of the later work or the joint work with Guattari, and which does not present a palatable ethics in the form of *Spinoza: Practical Philosophy* or some of the late writings. In fact it presents something quite contrary to these easier ethics, but something that is nonetheless an ethics of relation, if not to others then to the forces of the impersonal, the law, and structure itself.

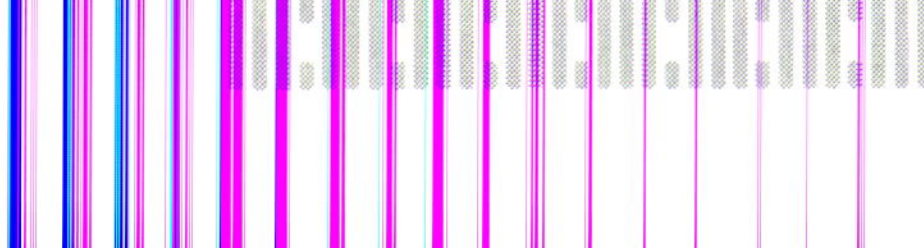

PART THREE

Being

Part 3 focuses on a range of primarily literary texts that develop the connections between mobility and immobility and between becoming and being. Deleuze was an avid and laudatory reader and critic of American literature, and he seems particularly drawn to American novels that depict extreme mobility and movement (such as Kerouac's *On the Road*, discussed in chapter 8 alongside Nabokov's *Lolita* and several novels by Paul Auster). In this regard, Deleuze is part of a lineage of French writers from Tocqueville to Baudrillard who express a marked fascination with the American landscape. Deleuze, however, goes the farthest in questioning some of the easy associations made between infinite movement and lack of thought. In linking thought to movement, he opens a new line of questioning that is developed in more extreme fashion in the progression of this section's five chapters: if thought can happen alongside movement, and if one can stand still and still move according to Deleuze, is there a type of thought that might also (and not simply in negative fashion) accompany extreme immobility or stuckness?

With this guiding question, the five readings move from a discussion of American road-trip novels in chapter 8 to Melville's "Bartleby, the Scrivener" in chapter 9 to the fiction and philosophy of Blanchot in chapter 11 and finally to the architecture of domestic space in chapter 12. Chapter 10 is an interlude that reflects on small-town and underclass American landscape and perception. If "Bartleby" captures the attention of an array of European critics (at issue here are essays on "Bartleby" by Rancière and Agamben that respond directly to Deleuze's much-cited essay on the story), there is a concomitant tendency, inaugurated by Deleuze, to read Bartleby's

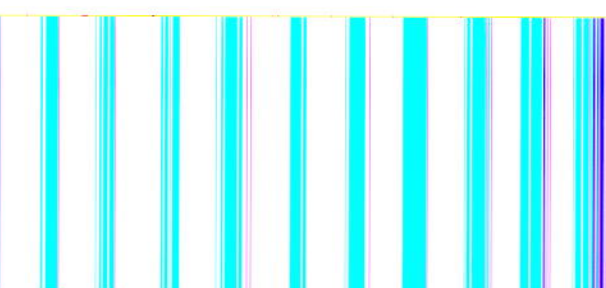

language (his repeated "I would prefer not to") above and beyond his physical presence. By shifting attention to Bartleby's stuckness in front of the wall, I suggest that this extreme immobility is the domain that Deleuze constantly gestures to but refuses to fully embrace. By contrast, Blanchot's fiction, like Melville's, depicts a maddening state of inertia and inaction that may be dissociated from a strict logic of becoming. Such a modality of becoming is for Deleuze located at the conjunction of the past and the future (the temporality of Aion), but my reading proposes an ontology of the immobilized present more in line with the analysis of the third synthesis of time in chapter 7.

The concluding chapter translates these questions to an architectural and phenomenological realm, to the skewed perception offered by the spaces of the house (above all from the upside-down view of a child who turns the house's ceiling into its floor). It tries to reintegrate Deleuze's concept of the virtual into the terms of this study by asking if its implicit static ontology might allow a new and formidable way of viewing those states and spaces that often go unrecognized or, worse, become pathologized (as is Bartleby's condition by the story's narrator) as less than livable.

French Thought and the Space of American Literature

IT IS SOMETHING OF A truism that America is integrally connected to the concept of vast unbounded space and, more precisely, to unbounded movement through that space. In other words, freedom of movement across virtually uncharted territory is taken as a cornerstone of a specifically American form of being. This connection of America with movement through limitless space is especially common among French intellectuals, who, from Alexis de Tocqueville to Jean Baudrillard and Deleuze himself, have made something of a small cottage industry of charting out the philosophical ramifications of American space. While briefly outlining some of these Franco-American lineages and several works of American literature that illustrate them, I aim to reverse and reorient the omnipresent emphasis on movement and vast space as definitional of an American essence. I wish to examine the way in which American space is also—and sometimes simultaneously—bound up with enclosed spaces and immobility. As we will see in the other chapters in part 3, Deleuze's work both opens this perception and, like Moses at the edge of the promised land, does not take it far enough.

In surveying the genre of French intellectual writing that unabashedly conflates America with unrestrained—and unthinking—movement, there is no better place to begin than with Tocqueville's two-volume classic, *Democracy in America*. Suffice it here to note only the points of departure for each volume, for they establish the framework for a long trajectory of French theorization of American space. The first chapter of volume 1 is entitled "Exterior Form of North America," and it provides a detailed climatic and geographical description of the North American territories. Tocqueville begins the chapter as follows:

> North America presents in its external form certain general features which it is easy to discriminate at the first glance. A sort of methodical order seems to have regulated the separation of land and water, mountains and valleys. A simple but grand arrangement is discoverable amidst the confusion of objects, and the prodigious variety of scenes.[1]

This reading of "general features" in "external form" and "methodical order" in a "simple but grand arrangement" provides the very formula and methodology for an entire lineage of French thinkers who take on a spatio-philosophical analysis of America. For it is precisely the "external form" and the "grand arrangement" of American space and American landscape that give rise to what are now commonplace notions about an American way of being or, more precisely, of being in movement.

Of crucial importance to this Americanness—as defined by movement through vast space—is its accompanying absence of speculative thought. Once again, this is nowhere better defined than by Tocqueville, this time in the first chapter of volume 2 of *Democracy in America*. Entitled "Philosophical Method among the Americans," this chapter begins with the following sentence: "I think that in no country in the civilized world is less attention paid to philosophy than in the United States."[2] From this provocative opening, Tocqueville goes on to explain how Americans nonetheless do have a logic all their own, but one that does not pronounce itself as philosophical. As one might suspect, this method is bound up with individualism, pragmatism, a quest for plain truth, and the lack of a sense of history,[3] and it leads Tocqueville to two striking conclusions:

> In the midst of the continual movement which agitates a democratic community, the tie which unites one generation to another is relaxed or broken; every man readily loses the trace of the ideas of his forefathers or takes no care about them.[4]

> This disposition of mind soon leads [the Americans] to condemn forms, which they regard as useless and inconvenient veils placed between them and the truth.[5]

These statements are significant not so much in themselves but in the way they are implicitly linked together. Indeed, the implicit or explicit linkage of "continual movement" with "this disposition of mind . . . [that] condemns forms" is at the crux of many French—and American—readings of the way Americans inhabit their spaces. There are at least three propositions here that are worth putting into question: (1) that America is somehow synonymous with continual movement, (2) that America is not synonymous with thought, and (3) that movement and thought do not go together.

These same propositions are omnipresent in twentieth-century French writings on America. An amusing example can be found in the "American civilization" installment of the popular "Que Sais-Je?" textbooklet series. In a section entitled "The Movement Factor," author Jean-Pierre Fichou writes that "designated by the term 'M Factor' is this element of American culture that gives it an appearance of perpetual agitation, or incessant activity. . . . In contrast with what takes place in certain cultures that have erected contemplation into a system, the notions of progress and movement are omnipresent."[6] This analysis would imply that, since it possesses the notorious "M Factor," America is not one of those cultures driven toward contemplation and, moreover, that movement and contemplation are mutually exclusive. One might be led to ask, especially in light of Baudrillard's celebrated analysis of America, whether it is possible for an exercise-obsessed American to think while jogging—or working out at the gym.

"Most certainly not" would seem to be the resounding conclusion of Baudrillard's *America*, in which joggers exemplify a state of pure movement in which the only possible thought is a purely corporeal "ecstasy of fatigue."[7] From the outset of *America*, Baudrillard underscores how the hypermobile/hyposentient construct of America that he is looking for (avowedly inspired by Tocqueville) is precisely the America that he finds: "I went in search of *astral* America, not social and cultural America, but the America of the empty, absolute freedom of the freeways, not the deep America of mores and mentalities, but the America of desert speed, motels and mineral surfaces."[8] In short, all that is interesting about America is to be found on the surface, in the perpetual movement from place to place, and never in a rootedness or immobility, which in any case would not be comparable to what one finds in Europe.

What Baudrillard captures—and in an even purer form than Tocqueville—is a vision of America in which exteriority determines everything and interiority nothing. From his analysis of the "psychology of the automobile," Baudrillard concludes that all this creates a new experience of space, and, at the same time, a new experience of the whole social system. All you need to know about American society can be gleaned from an anthropology of its driving behavior. That behavior tells you much more than you could ever learn from its political ideas. Drive ten thousand miles across America and you will know more about this country than all the institutes of sociology and political science put together.[9]

In short, Baudrillard reiterates, in the most blatant possible fashion, the three assumptions culled from Tocqueville, namely that America equals movement (and fast movement at that) through vast space, that it is anti-intellectual, and that movement and intellect could never go together.[10]

Although Deleuze repeats many of the same truisms about American space and intellect, he does so in a more complicated fashion. While still equating America with movement and geography, he brings thought back into the picture, both with respect to America and with respect to movement. Moreover, he reverses the system of philosophical values expressed thus far, making the Anglo-American fashion of being-in-movement — as opposed to the French predilection for stasis and history — the more philosophically nuanced modality. Such a being-in-movement is more properly characterized by the term "becoming," so central to Deleuze and Guattari's philosophical lexicon. Deleuze elucidates the multilayered relationship between becoming, American literature, American geography, and France at the beginning of his dialogue (with Claire Parnet) "On the Superiority of Anglo-American Literature":

> Anglo-American literature constantly shows these ruptures, these characters who create their line of flight, who create through a line of flight. Thomas Hardy, Melville, Stevenson, Virginia Woolf, Thomas Wolfe, Lawrence, Fitzgerald, Miller, Kerouac. In them everything is departure, becoming, passage, leap, daemon, relationship with the outside. They create a new Earth; but perhaps the movement of the earth is deterritorialization itself. American literature operates according to geographical lines: the flight towards the West, the discovery that the true East is in the West, the sense of the frontiers as something to cross, to push back, to go beyond. *The becoming is geographical.* There is no equivalent in France. The French are too human, too historical, too concerned with the future and the past. They spend their time in in-

> depth analysis. They do not know how to become, they think in terms of historical past and future.[11]

Given Deleuze's emphasis in *The Logic of Sense* on Aion, the temporality that unites past and future, it is striking that in the context of American space such a temporality is denoted as being characteristically French (much in the fashion of Deleuze's derogatory quip about Bataille, cited in chapter 3). While the properly American temporality is presumably more present-oriented yet still characterized by movement, geography, and surface, Deleuze gives these qualities a positive valence rather than using them to devalue America with respect to France.[12]

Moreover, Deleuze goes on to attack the French model and to redefine what constitutes movement, suggesting that thought and movement might actually go hand in hand. He continues:

> To flee is not exactly to travel, or even to move. First because there are travels in the style of the French—too historical, cultural and organized—where they are content to transport their own "egos." Secondly, *because flights can happen on the spot, in motionless travel.* Toynbee shows that nomads in the strict, geographical sense are neither migrants nor travelers, but, on the contrary, *those who do not move, those who cling on to the steppe, who are immobile with big strides*, following a line of flight on the spot, the greatest inventors of new weapons. But history has never begun to understand nomads, who have neither past nor future. Maps are maps of intensities, geography is no less mental and corporeal than physical in movement.[13]

Here we see not only the dismissal of the past-future conjunction that was so diligently outlined in *The Logic of Sense* but also Deleuze's most extreme paean to immobility. This paean is developed in the form of oxymoronic characterizations: "because flights can happen on the spot, in motionless travel," or the discussion of nomads who "cling on to the steppe, who are immobile with big strides." Chapter 11 of the present volume, on Blanchot, asks what is left when you remove the second term, "travel," from "motionless," or the "big strides" from "immobile" (and it proposes that it is something akin to "being" itself). Yet in the context of a discussion of American space, Deleuze provides an alternative conception of what movement might entail. Instead of pertaining simply to travel, speed, and the body, movement for Deleuze is to be thought also in terms of immobility, intensity, and mind. Following such a logic allows for a reversal of all of the three suppositions outlined above. Thus, (1) America might be linked not only to movement over vast space but also to interior movement and even to immobility, (2) America might have a substantial relation to mind and intellect, and (3) movement and mind might actually go together.[14]

In what follows, this set of relations between movement, mind, and American space is drawn out in three variously canonical twentieth-century American writers. The first and most straightforward is one hailed by Deleuze, Jack Kerouac. It is hard to talk about unbounded movement and American landscape without signaling Kerouac's 1957 best seller, *On the Road*. And it is also easy to use *On the Road* to support a Baudrillardian reading of America. Indeed, *On the Road* perfectly illustrates the first of our truisms, that America is synonymous with continuous movement. Charting as it does a series of spontaneous and aimless road trips, this novel bolsters Baudrillard's notion that the essence of America is in an astral movement from place to place, in pure speed, and that actual locations are, for all intents and purposes, radically indistinguishable. We see this, for example, in the narrator's description of riding a bus into downtown Los Angeles: "We got off the bus at Main Street, which was no different from where you get off a bus in Kansas City or Chicago or Boston—red brick, dirty, characters drifting by, trolleys grating in the hopeless dawn, the whorey smell of a big city."[15] What would seem to be of import here is not the specific big cities but the very act of moving in and out of them, a monotonous movement that defies further elaboration.

Yet through the eyes of Dean Moriarty, one of the novel's central characters, this very modality of unreflecting movement takes on its own form of mysticism. In the following passage, Dean provides a similar description of movement in America, while the narrator, Sal, gives it a spiritual gloss:

> "You see what I mean? God exists without qualms. As we roll along this way I am positive beyond doubt that everything will be taken care of for us. . . . Furthermore we know America, we're at home; I can go anywhere in America and get what I want because it's the same in every corner, I know the people, I know what they do. We give and take and

> go in the incredibly complicated sweetness zigzagging every side." There was nothing clear about the things he said, but what he meant to say was somehow made pure and clear. He used the word "pure" a great deal. I had never dreamed Dean would become a mystic.[16]

This passage interrogates our third proposition, the one that states that movement is not synonymous with thought, for here movement is part and parcel of a new form of "mystical" thought. For Dean and Sal, movement both reflects and induces a new form of perception.

This perception is legible in the landscape itself. So, for example, in an interesting twist that both echoes and rewrites Baudrillard, we find that Sal prefers "reading" the American landscape as opposed to a newly acquired French book: "At dawn my bus was zooming across the Arizona desert. . . . Then we swung north to the Arizona mountains, Flagstaff, clifftowns. I had a book with me I stole from a Hollywood stall, *Le Grand Meaulnes* by Alain-Fournier, but I preferred reading the American landscape as we went along. Every bump, rise, and stretch in it mystified my longing."[17] Not only is landscape readable in the fashion of a book, but it is also not-readable: it is illegible in a way that both evokes the mystical and mystifies desire. That is, contrary to appearances, movement across American landscape is by no means clearly opposite to thought. In fact, in a car trip that follows on the heels of the bus trip mentioned above, Sal embraces the road as a soulful inducement to thought: "I drove through South Carolina and beyond Macon, Georgia, as Dean, Marylou, and Ed slept. All alone in the night I had my own thoughts and held the car to the white line in the holy road."[18] That driving and thinking might go hand in hand is of course no great insight in its own right, but in the context of the most American of stories in which movement, to borrow the words of Auden, "makes nothing happen," it becomes significant to emphasize that thought nevertheless happens (that thought indeed always happens), significant in unmasking one of the most pernicious ideologies about America, namely, that its interior landscape and daily life are impermeable to philosophical nuance.

What *On the Road* alludes to—and what another road trip narrative (of sorts), Vladimir Nabokov's *Lolita*, makes more explicit—is that movement is not always about movement; indeed, it is often about its opposite. If movement through America is on the one hand a quest for a sort of

Baudrillardian pure speed, on the other it may be about the opposite impetus, immobility. Nabokov's controversial classic from 1955, which portrays a middle-aged man's obsession for Lolita, his preteen ward, is arguably about all manner of literary things — passion, allusion, language, and transgression, to name a few — and negligibly about travel in America, except that a good portion of the book details the narrator Humbert Humbert's yearlong aimless road trip across America with the young Lolita as his emotional and sexual captive. What, then, if not pure movement, is the function of such an unbounded crossing and recrossing of the American landscape? Arguably, it is precisely a method of stalling, of maintaining a fragile status quo in which Humbert and Lolita are absolutely alone and absolutely undetectable. It is a way of arresting a moment in time by means of a continuous catapulting through space, and here, not insignificantly, American space.

Humbert Humbert avowedly employs movement across the United States as a means of remaining immobile, and Lolita uses landscape as a means of seeing nothing. In Humbert's words,

> By putting the geography of the United States into motion, I did my best for hours on end to give her the impression of "going places," of rolling on to some definite destination, to some unusual delight. I have never seen such smooth amiable roads as those that now radiated before us, across the crazy quilt of forty-eight states. Voraciously we consumed those long highways, in rapt silence we glided over their glossy black dance floors. Not only had Lo no eye for scenery but she furiously resented my calling her attention to this or that enchanting detail of landscape; which I myself learned to discern only after being exposed for quite a time to the delicate beauty ever present in the margin of our undeserving journey.[19]

A central question to be asked of this passage is why exactly is the journey undeserving? Perhaps the answer, that Humbert Humbert was up to no good ends and moreover that he and Lolita failed really to see America, seems obvious. Such an answer is virtually given by Humbert two chapters later, as he narrates the journey's end:

> We had been everywhere. We had really seen nothing. And I catch myself thinking today that our long journey had only defiled with a sin-

> uous trail of slime the lovely, trustful, dreamy, enormous country that by then, in retrospect, was no more to us than a collection of dog-eared maps, ruined tour books, old tires, and her sobs in the night—every night, every night—the moment I feigned sleep.[20]

Whereas this passage merely alludes to Humbert's regret for having betrayed Lolita, it strongly asserts Humbert's regret at having betrayed the American landscape. The really shocking thing about *Lolita* is not so much the transgenerational desire it portrays but the fact that this desire is maintained at the cost of perpetual movement across the pristine American landscape. *Lolita* undermines not so much a set of sexual mores as a set of ideological truisms about how movement through American space should or should not be perceived. In rendering geography inconsequential, in making travel the same as never leaving the hotel room, *Lolita* immobilizes movement through America and suggests that, insofar as America is bound up with movement, it is equally and more provocatively tied to immobility.

One of the most intricate and expansive dynamics between movement and immobility is found in the fiction of Paul Auster. Nearly all of his novels deal in some way with a protagonist who vacillates between plummeting errant movement across the American landscape or across a particular city and totalizing immobility or confinement, usually within the space of an apartment or room. It is interesting to speculate why and how this might account for the fantastic success of Auster's fiction in France as opposed to its relative obscurity in the United States.[21] In terms of our initial propositions, reversing the order of the second and third, Auster's work (1) makes *both* movement *and* immobility synonymous with America, (3) brings thought into conjunction with both, and (2) by implication, brings thought into an integral relation with America.

Auster's *The Music of Chance* begins with a sentence that is dramatically reminiscent of *Lolita*: "For one whole year he did nothing but drive, traveling back and forth across America as he waited for the money to run out."[22] Yet Jim Nashe, the protagonist in question, moves not so much to remain immobile, in the fashion of Humbert Humbert, but in order to perceive and think. When he accidentally takes the wrong highway ramp one day (after having just inherited an unexpected sum of money), Nashe decides to keep on going in the wrong direction. He does this as a way of contemplating the intricate relation between choice, freedom, and solitude: "It was a dizzying prospect—to imagine all that freedom, to understand how little it mattered what choice he made. He could go anywhere he wanted, he could do anything he felt like doing, and not a single person in the world would care."[23] For Nashe, such a form of movement becomes a refuge for thought and an escape from the body:

> After three or four months, he had only to enter the car to feel that he was coming loose from his body, that once he put his foot down on the gas and started driving, the music would carry him along into a realm of weightlessness. . . . Empty roads were always preferable to crowded roads. They demanded fewer slackenings and decelerations, and because he did not have to pay attention to other cars, he could drive with the assurance that his thoughts would not be interrupted.[24]

Such is Nashe's experience of the road trip, one where smooth movement is employed to provoke thought rather than to efface it. It might follow that if here movement is connected to thought, then immobility might somehow disrupt it. This is put to the test when Nashe falls in with a young gambler, Jack Pozzi, and loses all his money and his car in a diabolical gambling match. In this fashion, he finds himself stuck in a bizarre scenario in which he and Pozzi are confined to a trailer at the far end of their creditors' estate, where they are forced to erect a huge stone wall in order to pay back their debt. Surprisingly, instead of uniformly resenting his confinement, Nashe is allured by its contemplative possibilities:

> His money was gone, his car was gone, his life was in a shambles. If nothing else, perhaps those fifty days would give him a chance to take stock, to sit still for the first time in over a year and ponder his next move. It was almost a relief to have the decision taken out of his hands, to know that he had finally stopped running. The wall would not be a punishment so much as a cure, a one-way journey back to earth.[25]

In his newfound immobility, Nashe soon reestablishes a routine as well as many of the same thought patterns that he had while on the road: "Nashe was not nearly as restless as he had thought he would be. Once he accepted the fact that the car was gone, he felt little or no desire to be back on the road, and the ease with which he adjusted to his new circumstances left him somewhat bewildered. It made no sense that he should be able to abandon it all so quickly."[26] The sense to be made from this is perhaps that the very ability to think movement and immobility as one and the same thing is itself a form of abandoning it all. Or, in other words, insofar as the thought of movement tends toward immobility and the thought of immobility toward movement, the experience of both as belonging to the same perceptual structure signals a radically different mode of existing in the world.

It is such a different mode of existence that Deleuze and Guattari gesture toward when they write in *A Thousand Plateaus* that "movement has an essential relation to the imperceptible; it is by nature imperceptible. Perception can grasp movement only as the displacement of a moving body or the development of a form. Movements, becomings, in other words, pure relations of speed and slowness, pure affects, are below and above the threshold of perception."[27] Following from this, it is at those points where movements and slownesses intersect the threshold of perception that new thoughts are produced. Moreover, to turn these terms back on themselves, it is at the specific point where movement and immobility are shown to be *perceptually the same* that a new *form* of thought is produced. Sometimes indiscernible from madness, this form of thought is a hallmark of Auster's writing and, I would suggest, of a certain strain of American literature that runs from the poetry of Emily Dickinson through Charlotte Perkins Gilman's *The Yellow Wallpaper* and Melville's "Bartleby" (the subject of the next chapter), eventually to land with Auster in the twentieth century.

A final and brief example of this dynamic—where first movement equals thought, then immobility equals thought (or vice versa), and finally the perception of the imperceptibility of the difference between the two equals a new form of thought—is to be found throughout Auster's acclaimed *New York Trilogy*. Each of the three novels in this volume recounts the story of a man who, in detective fashion, gets into the skin of another man, generally a double of sorts, by retracing his life, charting his every movement, and stalking him mercilessly. Such a pursuit entails a combination of seemingly random movement (as when Quinn meticulously maps Stillman's daily peregrinations around New York City in *City of Glass* or when the narrator of *The Locked Room* suddenly goes to Paris to retrace the details of Fanshawe's life there) and abiding, painstaking immobility (as in *Ghosts* when Blue is paid to follow Black, who does virtually nothing but sit in the apartment across the street and write in a notebook, or when Quinn in *The Locked Room* decides to camp out for months in the alley across the street from the entrance to the Stillmans' apartment). Unlike Nashe in *The Music of Chance*, the characters in each of the three novels in *The New York Trilogy* are not forced into immobility, for they could easily walk away from the odd predicaments in which they find themselves. Instead, they willingly and even willfully embrace the immobility into which they are cast, for it provides access (and better access than mobility) to a world of uncharted thought. This is how Blue in *Ghosts* explains what immobility does to his ability to think:

> Now, suddenly, with the world as it were removed from him, with nothing much to see but a vague shadow by the name of Black, he finds himself thinking about things that have never occurred to him before, and this, too, has begun to trouble him. If thinking is perhaps too strong a word at this point, a slightly more modest term — speculation, for example — would not be far from the mark. To speculate, from the Latin speculatus, meaning to spy out, to observe, and linked to the word speculum, meaning mirror or looking glass. For in spying out Black across the street, it is as though Blue were looking into a mirror, and instead of merely watching another, he finds that he is also watching himself.[28]

The same effect can be read not only in the play of doubles and mirrors throughout Auster's work but also in the play of mobility and immobility, which alternate and double each other as a means of access to new speculation and insight. Here, the dynamics of immobility are such that whenever the body stays in one place, thought is sure to move to a place it has never before traveled. In this sense, where there is immobility, there is also movement, yet not unthinking movement through unbounded space in the fashion of Tocqueville and Baudrillard, but rather a movement of becoming (that may not be linked to actual physical movement) in alternation with an immobility of being. That such an interplay of thought, movement, and immobility is an abiding refrain in the work of Auster is undeniable, and that such an interplay also governs a whole strain of American literature — and a strain of contemporary French philosophy — is the ultimate stake of this argument. This will be taken up in the next chapter with the example of Melville's "Bartleby" and that story's abiding fascination for Deleuze and French philosophy.

CHAPTER NINE

Bartleby, the Immobile

These questions of immobility and of transatlantic fascination are supremely condensed in the figure of Melville's Bartleby. As discussed in the preceding chapter, there is a powerful disjunction between a rampant tendency to generalize about America and a refusal to view the American literature of interiority—of which Bartleby is a preeminent example—as in any way a precursor to twentieth-century French literary and philosophical texts that are also preoccupied with interiority. Moreover, "Bartleby" points to the disjunction at the heart of Deleuze's thought that is perhaps best illustrated in his writings on American literature, namely, the loud paean to nomadic mobility and the quiet openness to the stasis of being.

There is, as discussed in the preceding chapter, a significant disjunction between a thought of infinite mobility and one of closed interiority. In the texts I will be examining here, this disjunction is manifested as the tension between a European preoccupation with, on the one hand, the vastness of American space and all that it implies and, on the other hand, a veritable obsession with Bartleby, the antihero of Melville's 1853 short story. Bartleby, a Wall Street law copyist, slowly refuses some of his copying tasks (to the chagrin and amazement of his lawyer boss), then refuses to do any work whatsoever, and eventually refuses to leave his boss' office. Each refusal is punctuated with the quiet yet firm statement "I would prefer not to."[1] This is by all accounts one of the most extreme cases of immobility in American literature. It is avowedly the polar opposite—extreme movement—that most fascinates French intellectuals when they write about America. As we saw in the preceding chapter, from Tocqueville to Baudrillard, three related truisms repeatedly surface: that America is synonymous with infinite movement over vast landscapes; that Americans are an unreflective, pragmatic people who do not like to think; and that movement and thought in no way go together.

Given this equation of America with movement, it would seem to be the height of paradox that few works of American literature have been more discussed by contemporary French and European philosophers than Melville's "Bartleby."[2] Why, then, this fascination with the enclosed and immobile Bartleby (who, as the lawyer boss slowly discovers, never leaves the boss's office)? Why this fascination alongside an equally strong fascination, albeit not as focused on one particular text, with what would seem to be Bartleby's opposite, infinite movement and open space? While the question of immobility and its relation to ontology is developed more fully in chapter 11 (on Blanchot), we might pose the problem initially in terms of this bifurcated fascination and how one might truly differentiate between these two poles of movement and immobility.

Following the claim in the previous chapter that extreme mobility and extreme immobility are distinct in their differences but proximate in their extremity, it is not surprising that "Bartleby" also resonates with a twentieth-century European literary and philosophical tradition that returns over and again to depictions of enclosure and interiority. Alongside Kafka, there are the similarly excessive examples of Beckett and Blanchot. All of these writers portray characters that enter a diabolical house or apartment space and never leave. Similarly, in contemporary French and Italian philosophy, there has been sustained attention to the concept of unworking (*désoeuvrement*), which suggests both the cessation of work (as in labor) and the undoing of the work (as in the *oeuvre*, or work of art). The fact that the first thing Bartleby stops doing is writing (albeit the writing is copying) unites the two aspects of *désoeuvrement*, for Bartleby stops working on the *oeuvre* that is the copied (legal) text. This critical gravitation toward "Bartleby" is therefore entirely in keeping with a philosophical lineage that questions the valorization of a work ethic, as it concerns both work as labor and the work of art.[3] It is thus quite understandable that such thinkers would gravitate toward "Bartleby." What is curious is that neither the first category, the quest to find the essential Americanness, nor the second category, the attention to unworking (which Bartleby perfectly exemplifies), is in fact the issue in much of the continental "Bartleby" criticism. We find responses from Deleuze, Rancière, and Agamben that are grounded in linguistic concerns rather than those of American space or of *désoeuvrement*. The essays in question focus on the character of Bartleby (and with scant attention to other characters, such as the somewhat unreliable lawyer-narrator, who is so often a significant focal point), above and beyond the action of the story. It is more nearly in Rancière's diagnosis of Deleuze's *proper désoeuvrement* (rather than Bartleby's) that this problematic surfaces at all.

Deleuze's essay, entitled "Bartleby; or, The Formula," highlights, as the title implies, Bartleby's repeated formula "I would prefer not to"—the response he gives first when asked if he would like to proofread legal copy, again when asked if he would do any work at all, and finally when asked if he would vacate the premises. Deleuze is generally disinclined to direct great attention to questions of language, especially if the language is English. Yet here he insists repeatedly on what he terms the agrammaticality of the utterance "I would prefer not to," comparing it to E. E. Cummings's line "he danced his did" (which this reader regards as entirely more of a defamiliarization of English than "I would prefer not to"). For Deleuze, this formula produces what he refers to at several junctures as a "zone of indetermination": "The formula I PREFER NOT TO excludes all alternatives. . . . [I]t hollows out a zone of indetermination that renders words indistinguishable, that creates a vacuum within language."[4] While such an argument for linguistic indeterminacy might be more (but not altogether) typical of a French philosopher such as Derrida, it is not at all typically Deleuzian. And indeed, when Deleuze uses the term "zone of indetermination" to characterize Bartleby's immobility (as opposed to the lawyer-narrator's flight), it is once again in the realm of language that these terms are explored. Deleuze describes Bartleby as

> someone who is born to and stays in a particular place, while the attorney necessarily fills the function of the traitor condemned to flight. . . . It is the attorney who broke the arrangement he himself had organized, and from the debris Bartleby pulls a trait of an expression, I PREFER NOT TO, which will proliferate around him and contaminate the others, sending the attorney fleeing. But it will also send language itself into flight, it will open up a zone of indetermination or indiscernibility in which neither words nor characters can be distinguished—the fleeing attorney and the immobile, petrified Bartleby.[5]

Rather than reading these poles of mobility/immobility and the resulting zone of indetermination as somehow characteristic of the concept of America itself (which would seem to be the more characteristic French philosophical move), Deleuze instead holds up the *language* of the formula as that which opens up the indeterminacy function. America by contrast is in no way associated with this glorious indeterminacy. Here, as elsewhere, Deleuze makes only the most determinate characterizations of America: for example, the idea that Bartleby, like America more generally, "is the one who is freed from the English paternal function" to instead constitute a nation of states, or as Deleuze terms it "a society of brothers."[6] Thus, for Deleuze, America is very resolutely the land of the brother and Europe that of the father—and this while the nexus of mobility/immobility is unconnected to America and remains happily indeterminate.

Rancière's reading of Deleuze's "Bartleby" essay, "Deleuze, Bartleby, and the Literary Formula," brings these contradictions to the fore, suggesting that Deleuze rewrites the tension that D. H. Lawrence locates between the Christian idealism of Melville and the democratic fraternalism of Whitman. Rancière writes: "Deleuze seems to resolve the tension by reversing Lawrence's logic. He gives Melville the reasons of Whitman. He transforms Bartleby, the voluntary recluse, into a hero of the American open road."[7] It seems that this formulation by Rancière captures something that Deleuze would want to do but does not do explicitly in this essay: to claim one of American literature's most stuck and immobile characters as the hallmark of an American openness that is not about mobility per se but nonetheless shares some of the spirit or mystique of the open road that we saw in the readings of Kerouac, Nabokov, and Auster in the previous chapter. Yet like Moses (and Mauss and Lévi-Strauss, as we saw) stranded on Mount Nebo, this is the space over into which Deleuze does not exactly cross. Without endorsing Rancière's overall reading of "Bartleby," one that would anchor the text in debates around mimesis that seem far removed from its greatest source of strength, or Rancière's subtle critique of the way Deleuze fails to achieve a workable notion of politics or equality (which might be read as a merit rather than a shortcoming), I would claim that Rancière touches on a profound dilemma in Deleuzian thought, which thought he reads as being sent into the wall.[8]

Rancière makes a strong distinction between the Aristotelian counterpoles of character and action, and in so doing, he opposes Deleuze to Flaubert, the latter preferring action but sacrificing becoming, the former (that is, Deleuze) choosing character and maintaining the modality of becoming. Rancière writes:

> It seems, then, that the molecular revolution of literature returns, in other terms, to the old Aristotelian alternative, the choice between privileging action or character. Flaubert chooses *haecceities* over characters and the law of the *cogito*. But by doing this, he sacrifices the *becomings* to the story. Deleuze, however, makes the opposite choice. By privileging the anti-narrative power of becomings, he concentrates power in the exemplary character, who becomes the operator of becomings and the emblem of becoming.[9]

In other words, Deleuze, who, along with Guattari in *A Thousand Plateaus*, will favor the *haecceity* (the thisness, or the eventness) of things, is here forced to build his topology from an opposing theory of strong characters. Thus, if Rancière opposes Flaubertian to Deleuzian character, yet Deleuze, following Scotus, champions *haecceity* repeatedly in other contexts, then this discrepancy helps us see a split in Deleuze's work, one, put simply, between becoming and being. Furthermore, and in support of Rancière's contention about Deleuze and character, Deleuze indeed singles out Melville's fiction as depicting the two types of profoundly original character, the greatly strong or evil character (Ahab, Claggart), and the greatly good or weak one (Billy Budd, Bartleby), *Billy Budd* having the particular merit of having two of them together in one setting, "the demonic and the petrified."[10] Notably, and parallel to this, Deleuze remarks in *Cinema 1* that Herzog's films portray either the very large character (Fitzcarraldo, Aguirre) or the very small (Woyzeck, Kaspar Hauser), all of them characters, like Billy Budd and Bartleby, of such dominating originality that the distinction between the name of the work and the name of the character runs together.[11]

As Rancière notes with respect to Deleuze's essay on Bartleby, all attention falls to Bartleby and very little to the equally fascinating narrator, who is not one of these great original characters according to Deleuze. Rancière does not say this in so many words, but he seems to critique an implicit hierarchy of character—and hence of thought—in Deleuze, which goes along with his veiled critiques of Deleuze's *Proust and Signs*, a study replete with hierarchies, the highest term being the realm of art. Deleuze is fundamentally *not* starting from an axiom of equality or democracy (something that in my analysis is not necessarily a bad thing, simply one that is rarely commented upon),[12] and it may in fact take another thinker (Rancière) who is working absolutely from an axiom of equality to perceive this difference.

How does Bartleby figure as a limit for Deleuze's theory of becoming? Rancière focuses on a line from Deleuze's essay that evokes "a wall of loose, uncemented stones, where every element has a value in itself but also in relation to others."[13] Rancière views this image as opposed to "the innocence of vegetable proliferation that is contrasted with the architectural order" (perhaps the rhizome of *A Thousand Plateaus*?).[14] Moreover, he poses the problem of "separating 'nomadic' thinking from that universal mobilism [*mobilisme*] to which it is so easily linked."[15] Again, Rancière does not say this in so many words, but it seems he helps isolate a Deleuze of the mobile, indeterminate, rhizomatic vegetable (the Deleuze of Deleuze and Guattari's *A Thousand Plateaus*) from the earlier, hierarchical, structural, mineral Deleuze of *The Logic of Sense* and even the Proust and Bergson books (the former being devoted to the question of aesthetic hierarchy and in fact somewhat undermining Rancière's reading of Deleuze on Proust).[16]

To return to the question of mobility and immobility, Rancière sees in late Deleuze (1989) something that serves as a limit for, indeed runs counter to, a Deleuzo-Guattarian theory of becoming (and as I hope to have shown in the preceding chapters, there is ample evidence of a greater devotion to being than to becoming in early Deleuze as well). Rancière notes that Deleuze "sings of the great highway of souls set free" but ends by describing "the wall of stones." But then Rancière rightly asks: "[W]hy does the image of the whole in motion that must guide the explorers on the great road have to be the image of a wall?"[17] He goes on to suggest, alongside an excellent critique of the easy way in which Deleuze and Guattari's notion of nomadism is so facilely linked to mobility, that in order to make a political difference in this kind of Deleuzian world, one needs a strong ontology or a Platonism, two things Deleuze would seem to be most staunchly opposed to. However, it has been my claim throughout this book that such a strong ontology, albeit rather more Aristotelian than Badiou's Platonic one, is in fact the luminous underside of Deleuze's thought, which comes to the foreground in Deleuze's early works and actually brings him closer to a thinker like Badiou than most would concede or imagine. In short, the question of how to read Bartleby behind his green screen and up against his wall marks the impasse of these two strains of Deleuzian thought (being and becoming), an impasse I would claim is not a zone of indetermination or a structure of "both/and" but instead represents the true dialectical power of the "or."

In Giorgio Agamben's essay "Bartleby, or On Contingency," it is not so much a characterization or lack of characterization of America that is at issue but rather the way that Agamben's essay, with respect to Deleuze's earlier essay, takes on a symptomatic repetition of what might be termed a Bartleby effect. In Melville's story, Bartleby's language becomes thoroughly infectious. Even when Bartleby's coworkers and boss are most disgruntled with his refusal to work, they nonetheless start unconsciously employing the language of preference. Both the lawyer and the fellow copyists nicknamed Turkey and Nippers start using "prefer" all the time. The lawyer points this out to Turkey, and Turkey replies:

> "Oh, *prefer*? oh yes — queer word. I never use it myself. But, sir, as I was saying, if he would but prefer — "
>
> "Turkey," interrupted I, "you will please withdraw."
>
> "Oh certainly, sir, if you prefer that I should."
>
> As he opened the folding-door to retire, Nippers at his desk caught a glimpse of me, and asked whether I would prefer to have a certain paper copied on blue paper or white. He did not in the least roguishly accent the word prefer. It was plain that it involuntarily rolled from his tongue. I thought to myself, surely I must get rid of a demented man, who already has in some degree turned the tongues, if not the heads, of myself and clerks. But I thought it prudent not to break the dismission at once.[18]

In a similar fashion, Deleuze's formulations about Bartleby seem to be taken up unconsciously, as it were, by Agamben. This comes out most notably in the title and subheadings of Agamben's piece. Deleuze's essay is entitled "Bartleby; or, The Formula" (perhaps itself an echo of Melville's earlier work *Pierre; or, The Ambiguities*). Using the same formula of a proper name followed by an "or," Agamben titles his essay "Bartleby, or On Contingency" and its three parts "The Scribe, or On Creation," "The Formula, or On Potentiality," and "The Experiment, or On Decreation." The two-part title separated by "or," like the language of preference, is here taken to excess. In the section entitled "The Formula, or On Potentiality," Agamben cites Deleuze and extends Deleuze's notion of the "zone of indetermination" (here, translated as the "zone of indistinction"): "As Deleuze suggests, the formula thus opens a zone of indistinction between yes and no, the preferable and the nonpreferable. But also . . . between the potential to be (or do) and the potential not to be (or do)."[19] This oscillation between the potential to be or to not be is the crux of Agamben's argument.[20] Once again, the very form of the argument (potential to be or to not be) is structured around the pivotal "or," which is here the contagious marker of oscillation or indeterminacy.[21] The "or," then, becomes something like the "both/and," something that breaks down readability and the dialectic of opposites.

Yet it is precisely this "or" as zone of indetermination that drops out of the picture whenever America comes into the picture. All of the intricacies of mobility are clearly and readably synonymous with America and its landscape, while Melville's "Bartleby" is eminently applicable to a range of discussions in French philosophy (or ancient Greek philosophy as Rancière would have it). However, these two poles refuse to come together. On the one hand, there is the America of movement, on the other, the excitingly European and indeterminate immobility of Bartleby. This either/or opposition is not unlike that between the two clerks Turkey and Nippers, whose contrary humors are outlined in great detail at the beginning of Melville's short story. The elderly Turkey works best in the morning but becomes decidedly too energetic and reckless in the afternoon. Nippers, by contrast, is nervous and suffers from indigestion in the morning but is quite docile in the afternoon. Bartleby is introduced into the system and proceeds with all his preferring to wreak havoc on the nicely refined dialectical polarities of Turkey and Nippers. By the same token, it seems that "Bartleby" the story carries the as-yet-untapped potential to introduce into French philosophy a vision of America that is indistinguishable from the eminently European characteristics of immobility and unworking. French critics, while avowedly fascinated by America, have invested immense energy in casting it as mobile, readable, and outside of any zone of indetermination. By linking Bartleby more resolutely to his native America, we might begin to challenge a series of truisms and suggest that a nineteenth-century American literature of immobility is in fact paradigmatic and not accidental to the establishment of a twentieth-century French literary and philosophical canon that is preoccupied with precisely the same issues. Yet that very project must acknowledge the generative dimension of the impasse between a certain model of European thought and another model of American mobility and not simply leave it as a zone of indetermination. The next three chapters situate this Bartleby-esque encounter with the wall as also and simultaneously an encounter with being.

CHAPTER TEN

In the Middle of Things

A BREATHTAKING, TERRIFYING VERTICALITY emanates from the skyscrapers in New York City. This verticality reflects a certain vision of space, one that is monumental, urban, large scale. Here I wish to speak of another kind of space, one that is not urban — or not necessarily so — one that is small scale to the point of not even being recognized as existing, yet equally monumental in its intensity. This space has its own verticality, which is the verticality of vast flatness, occasionally set of by a small yet pivotal elevation. This space is marked by what I'd like to call a plane of slight elevation, which could range anywhere from the space of about a story high to the space of not being yet six feet under — or to the space of thought itself.

In *The Fold: Leibniz and the Baroque*, Deleuze describes the space of the baroque house as punctuated by two levels, the lower level forming a façade, a sort of infinite space for perception, the upper level being a pure, closed interiority.[1] These two floors are separated by a fold, which both sets them apart and reflects the tension of their inextricable belonging to each other. Deleuze writes (and this will be analyzed in more detail in chapter 12), "We are dealing with two cities, a celestial Jerusalem and an earthly one, but with the rooftops and foundations of a same city, and the two floors of a same house."[2] My pursuit here is this fold, or this plane of elevation, as it is figured in nonurban space.

Living on the coasts of this country, one often encounters the mind-set that not only is the middle of the country devoid of urban space and all the culture and cosmopolitanism that it implies, but this middle, for all intents and purposes, is devoid of existence period, other than constituting that liminal space which one flies over to get from New York to California. In *America*, Jean Baudrillard is greatly taken by the pure verticality of New York City and the pure expanse of the desert. He highlights the superiority of the two American coasts when he writes: "We in Europe possess the art of thinking, of analyzing things and reflecting on them. No one disputes our historical subtlety and conceptual imagination. Even the great minds across the Atlantic envy us in this regard. But the resounding truths, the realities of genuinely great monument today are to be found along the Pacific seaboard or in Manhattan. It has to be said that New York and Los Angeles are at the centre of the world."[3]

There may be some sense in which this is true, but it is precisely not the center I wish to regard but the middle, which exists in a thoroughly different space. Baudrillard writes a great deal about speed—he says that "speed creates pure objects"—and a great deal about driving, which, he says, "produces a kind of invisibility, transparency or transversality in things, simply by emptying them out."[4] We saw such examples in Kerouac, Nabokov, and Auster in chapter 8. Here, I wish to look not at the driving, which produces a kind of invisibility, transparency, or transversality in things, but rather at the things that produce a visibility, plenitude, and plane of elevation in the driving.

If you drive on the Kansas Turnpike from Emporia to Topeka, you see on your right the Flint Hills of eastern Kansas. These hills have little foliage. They are small, discontinuous grassy mounds that bring into stunning relief the flat grandeur of the landscape. Driving on the turnpike, one comes to a rest area every thirty to forty miles, and at the rest area in the Flint Hills region, in addition to the Hardee's that serves pretzels and banana milkshakes, stands a large plaque erected in memory of the famous football player and coach Knute Rockne, who died when his plane crashed in these hills during a lightning storm.

One summer evening a no-longer-young couple, with a child waiting to be born, drove alone in their car through the Flint Hills at the height of a torrential midwestern thunderstorm. They wondered just how secure their car was when it came to lightning because, when they thought about it, set apart as they were even from the hills, they were the tallest thing on the landscape. What was their speed compared with the speed of death, from that terrifying plane of elevation, that plane which was their yellow '54 Chevrolet? No matter how fast they drove, they remained immobilized by the forces above, their speed being that of the terror from within.

On the Will Rogers Turnpike, between Tulsa and Oklahoma City, there is a small town called Stroud, which also features one of the scarce turnpike rest stations. The station, here a Howard Johnson's, is on one side of the highway but is fortuitously connected to the other side by a small pedestrian overpass. From this narrow overpass one can look out on the highway's receding, its diminishing toward either Tulsa or Oklahoma City. The Tulsa side features a lengthy vista of highway as it first stretches over a long straightaway and then gradually winds up into a slightly raised hill. However, on the side that leads to Oklahoma City, one encounters right away a sharp bend in the road, so that only a very small stretch of highway is visible from the overpass.

On the overpass stands a little child, maybe eight or nine. This child will barely speak to people, but she likes to greet the cars as they pass there underneath at Stroud. With the cars that she loves, she plays a vicious game of interpellation. As the cars approach her at their speeds, she stands there, waving furiously. And as she stands there, the immobile greeter, she makes small statistical calculations. She finds the trucks most favorably inclined to return her greeting: almost one of two waves back and even smiles. And she never quite knows if it's because they're just friendlier in trucks or because they're closer to her plane of elevation. (After all, Laura Ingalls on the TV show *Little House on the Prairie* decided to climb a whole mountain just so God could better hear her prayers.) And in the regular cars, the child notices a strange discrepancy. On the side facing Oklahoma City, where the cars abruptly round the bend, she finds the response to her wave to be nearly as good as the trucks — say, one in three. But, on the Tulsa side, where the cars have about a mile's driving time in which to spot her hand, they largely neglect her — maybe one in five, one in six, waves back. It seems that those cars had the space and time to gracefully feign ignorance of the small child above. But the Oklahoma City cars, caught as they were in the stillness of their speed, in the encounter with the immobility of the plane of elevation, didn't have a full-blown chance not to respond.

About ten miles down the highway in the Oklahoma City direction is another small town, even smaller than Stoud. That town has a Tastee Freez and a diner called Fendy's with a funeral parlor right next door. It has a small motel and several churches — Protestant — with one Catholic church. On the outskirts of town is a beautiful and spacious cemetery called Oaklawn with seemingly more inhabitants than the town proper. As in most cemeteries, you can walk around Oaklawn and see many gravestones of people who belong to the same family. But they're not all together. It's not a family-tree kind of logic but one of an unpredictably expansive subterranean root structure, for the roots arrive in their own disordered order, some of them never even coming. And if you are bent on decoding the tombstones, you find that the name on the front is often quite misleading, because in many instances there's one last name on the front side of the stone but another, a maiden name, on the back, and thus you find, for example, that it's another one of those dead Deans. And you wonder what all those dead Deans are doing down there, in that red Oklahoma soil, rooted in the madness of their scattered proximity. Do you think they have the concept of family reunion from six feet under? When you stand still, underneath a large tree, in that space of elevation above them, it's nice to think in reverse perspective, like turning your head upside down and pretending the ceiling of a house is the floor (this example is taken up again in the concluding chapter). If you think of them, then, as a city of souls and bodies looking at we who stand above, you have to wonder what form their vision takes and what form of movement is spawned by the electric immobility of the dead.

If you take the Will Rogers Turnpike back east through Tulsa, where it becomes the Turner Turnpike, and continue well past Vinita—the other, more majestic rest stop–diner that connects both sides of the highway and also allows for the waving game—you find the road once again changes names when you cross the Missouri state line. Now it's Interstate 44, which in the old highway system was the famous Route 66. Past Joplin and Springfield, before Phillipsburg and Lebanon, there's a town in the middle called Conway—another little town with a cemetery. If you get off at Conway and take the exit ramp to its full height, you see there alone on the landscape a middle-sized structure named McShane's but more properly called The Home of the Little Round Pie, because in this highway diner live little round pies. The little round pies are half the size of regular pies but overflow with the fullness of their pie stuff. There are apple pies, raisin pies, peach pies, pineapple pies—any kind of pie you can name. It's not unlike the passage from Marvell: "Let us roll all our strength, and all / Our sweetness, up into one ball, / And tear our pleasures with rough strife / Through the iron gates of life."[5] Compressed into this small portion of round pie space is a nearly infinite density. It's the density of stuff standing still, awaiting its imminent incorporation, yet by reverse always incorporating the incorporator.

I return to Baudrillard, who writes: "When I see Americans, particularly American intellectuals, casting a nostalgic eye towards Europe, its history, its metaphysics, its cuisine, and its past, I tell myself that this is just a case of unhappy transference. History and Marxism are like fine wines and haute cuisine: they do not really cross the ocean, in spite of the many impressive attempts that have been made to adapt them to new surroundings."[6]

To the north of Conway, in the middle spaces of Missouri, is another small town called Hallsville. Just outside this town is a girl named Sue, who grows up on a farm. She has a little friend from the neighboring town, a bigger town, and this friend isn't entirely used to being on a farm. But Sue and her friend are up in the hayloft of Sue's barn, engaging in some trifling indiscretions as they talk. Sue asks her friend: "When we grow up, will you take me around the world with you?"

Here I should add that there are all sorts of towns in Missouri that share their names with bigger places like Mexico, California, Cuba, Lebanon, New London, Nevada, and Versailles (pronounced Versales), and Sue and her friend, who have hardly ever crossed the state line, like to talk about how they're going to travel to the real London, the real Mexico, the real Cuba—to all those big places, countries, cities. And the friend tells Sue, "Yeah, I'll take you around the world with me. We'll travel, we'll go to France, we'll speak real fine French, we'll go to the real Versales, you name it."

Sue and her friend never travel around the world together; they grow up and fall out of touch, but, after a period of many years, they talk again. The first thing that Sue says (and I should add that at the friend's house there was one of these early electronic games—TV table tennis—which the two girls liked to play together, and in this game, when the little pellet on the screen successfully hit the racket apparatus, there was this very peculiar beep that sounded), ending those many years of silence, is "I thought of you just today—I heard this beep that was just like the one on your TV thing."

It seems that that beep has been resonating for years, that beep as their space of travel. Because they *have* traveled together, if not exactly around the world, then around. For they traveled as they sat there, as they sit there, in the middle of that thing called America, like being in the eye of the storm, the lull of that most stupendous of violences. They never went to France together, but the speed that they traveled was faster than any Concord jet, the beeping in their heads more deafening than any airplane roar. It was the dizzying implosiveness of what they had, and still have, lying there, immobile, in that hayloft in Hallsville, looking down at the cows and the electric fence from their plane of slight elevation. The force of that immobility is as great as the vertical bombardment of all the skyscrapers in New York put together.

Certainly these girls missed the range of experiences they could have had had they lived somewhere else, had they lived in a big city. In fact, they probably could have stayed put in any metropolitan space and traveled just as far and just as fast. But the point is that they were where they were, in the middle, out in the middle of nowhere. And perhaps it will have taken them a lifetime, or more, to know — really know — the intensity that was had, that is always had, just sitting still.

CHAPTER ELEVEN

Midnight, or the Inertia of Being

THERE IS HARDLY A MORE consistent thinker than Maurice Blanchot. His work is disarming in its weave of fiction and philosophy, in its timeless anonymity, its undoing of the dialectic, and the affirmation of worklessness and the community of those who have nothing in common. Though in a sense elusive, this work is also infinitely substitutable. Almost any paragraph of Blanchot's is quintessentially Blanchotian. It is daunting, then, if not impossible, to suggest and delineate a fissure that runs through Blanchot's oeuvre, a fissure between the liminal, atemporal, fleeting instant and the more weighty inertia of presentness, the inertia of being. It is this fissure that also marks a profound yet barely palpable divide between the thought of Blanchot and Deleuze, especially with regard to the realms of temporality and ontology. While Blanchot's notion of Midnight resonates most strongly with a Deleuzian insistence on temporal becoming (as opposed to present being), it also gestures to a state that is beyond becoming in that it is too unworkable, too inert. It is my claim that this inertia, rather than marking a lesser or pathological state, may point to a new path for ontology.

Midnight would seem to be always to come, or always just past. It is never purely present, but another time composed of the interplay of past and future, the time of infinite becoming. As we have seen, Deleuze terms this time of becoming Aion, as opposed to the static being of present time, or Chronos. Indeed, Deleuze evokes Blanchot's separation between "personal and present death" (the death the self chooses to die) and "impersonal and infinitive death" (the Other death that chooses you, where there is no longer a self to choose) in the process of elaborating how the atemporal time of Aion is, like the Other death, at odds with an immobile presentness.[1] In this regard, Midnight's "out-of-timeliness" marks a strong convergence between Deleuzian and Blanchotian formulations of an atemporal temporality, a state of becoming as opposed to being that conjoins past and future but is outside of present, static, chronological time. It would seem, too, that Deleuze and Blanchot coincide in their mutual eschewal of the dialectic insofar as it stands in for a present and positive ontology (or at least in so far as Deleuze would seem to disavow the present and Blanchot the positive). If there is a difference at stake between Blanchot and Deleuze, it is a difference that centers on ontology's movements, or lack thereof. If Deleuze redeems being by perceiving its hidden potential for movement, Blanchot affirms being by perceiving its disarming potential for inertia.

It is hard to be, really, in the presence of inertia. Inertia is deceptive in that it might appear to be going somewhere (I am working to clean up the house and move out of here), while at the same time quietly asserting itself in its active inaction. As discussed above, Deleuze writes of American literature that "the becoming is geographical. There is no equivalent in France. The French are too human, too historical, too concerned with the future and the past. . . . To flee is not exactly to travel, or even to move. . . . Flights can happen on the spot, in motionless travel."[2] It is interesting to note that, among their mobile contemporaries, Deleuze and Blanchot stand out as two great twentieth-century French thinkers who did not travel, did not move. Yet, if there is a difference to be distilled between these two thinkers, and even within Blanchot's corpus, it is to be found around the issue of movement. As we have seen, always at issue for Deleuze is a movement of thought, which is a movement of becoming, even if one does not travel, even if one stands still. In this regard, although both Blanchot and Deleuze look askance at the dialectic, there is nevertheless a hidden dialectic punctuated by the uneasy relation between movement and stillness: even if there would seem to be a stoppage of physical movement, there is still the potential for a movement of thought.

On the one hand, Blanchot is quite close to Deleuze, though in what follows I seek to locate a distinct space of difference. In the vein of Deleuze, it would seem that all of Blanchot's work hinges on the enunciation of a type of textual movement. This is a movement of circularity and repetition that characterizes both Blanchot's critical work and his fiction and that is articulated with particular clarity in *The Space of Literature*. The movement of Blanchot's thought is one of excessive repetition; yet this repetition is always slightly displaced—it is not repetition in the strictest sense but rather a movement that doubles back upon itself in a circular fashion. A series of sentences from a three-page span of *The Space of Literature* illustrates this circular movement:

> To write *is* to surrender to the fascination of time's absence. The time of time's absence has no present, no presence. . . . The time of time's absence *is* not dialectical. . . . The reversal which, in time's absence, points us constantly back to the presence of absence. . . . The dead present *is* the impossibility of making any presence real. . . . Here fascination reigns . . . and fascination *is* passion for the image. . . . Fascination *is* solitude's gaze. . . . To write *is* to enter into the affirmation of the solitude in which fascination threatens.[3]

Blanchot explicates, in a definitional way, a series of terms that are related yet metonymically displaced. Here, this chain of displacements circles around the word "fascination," though almost all of Blanchot's sentences could be mapped in a similar fashion onto other sentences which they repeat and enhance through the same circular movement of displaced repetition. This formal movement indeed mirrors the content of Blanchot's statements, for, like "the time of time's absence," it would appear not to be dialectical, to have no presence as such, no temporality as such, just a reign of fascination. Blanchot's writing, his phrasing, is at one with the theme of movement that does not move, that reverberates as a central tenet of Blanchot's thought, and that also resonates so clearly with Deleuze.

Certainly Blanchot's insistence, at the level of the verb, on the ontological in the form of the "is," is of a piece with the slightly displaced repetition of his writing style. His incessant repetition of the verb "to be," usually in the form of the word "is" (emphasized in the quote above), is simultaneously a stylistic and a theoretical motif in his writing, one of the many points where the form and the content of his work merge. Blanchot frequently relates a certain idea of being, one encapsulated by the words "it is," to his notion of literature or the work of art. He writes that "the work—the work of art, the literary work—is neither finished nor unfinished; it is."[4] Also, "the poem—literature—seems to be linked to a spoken word which cannot be interrupted because it does not speak; it is."[5] This "isness," this ontology of the work of art, is also its impossibility, for its supreme moment of becoming is also its dissolution:

> But this exigency, which makes the work declare being in the unique moment of rupture—"those very words: *it is*," the point which the work brilliantly illuminates even while receiving its consuming burst of light—we must also comprehend and feel that this point renders the work impossible, because it never permits arrival at the work. It is a region anterior to the beginning where nothing is made of being, and in which nothing is accomplished. It is the depth of being's inertia [*désoeuvrement*].[6]

On the one hand, this "is" marks the juncture of being and becoming, that point where being becomes nothingness. Such a juncture is also the space of Blanchot's text. Marked by the recurrent "is" of being, Blanchot's writing propels this "is" along in a circular and repetitive movement that is the mark of becoming. This is a type of movement that never really attains a goal or even a concrete expression of thought. If anything, the movement works to obscure thought, but in this act it illustrates thought of another order, an even more exterior form of thought (what Foucault would term "thought from the outside"). Yet, on the other hand, is "the depth of being's inertia," being's seeming unworking, not also beckoning to an ontology of its own, even while resisting such a fixedness of being? Is this, moreover, the slight difference between the "it is" and the "there is" (*es gibt, il y a*)? While both express an ontological encounter, the *il y a*, with all its Heideggerian and Levinasian inflections, would evoke a being toward something, an ontological state where some form of movement is at issue, whereas the "it is" is what stops movement, is much more emphatically inert, all that there is (like the *en-soi* or in-itself).

This interpretative bifurcation is nowhere better emblematized than in the Blanchotian figure of Midnight. For all its fleetingness, Midnight's ever-receding presence nevertheless suggests an ontology of the present that is to some extent at odds with the tenor of Blanchot's oeuvre. Midnight, which Blanchot discusses in *The Space of Literature* in his chapter on Mallarmé's *Igitur*, serves as a figure for the circular movement of Blanchot's thought. Midnight marks both the repetitiveness and the perpetual displacement of time. Midnight indeed recurs every day, comes back around in a circular motion—actually the motion of a double circle—but it is never the same midnight as the day before. Some midnights are more officially commemorated than others, such as the midnight that is

New Year's Eve, and these midnights signal the passing of a greater expanse of time, recalling as they do the previous year's midnight instead of the previous day's. But in all its forms, midnight is a unique entity that punctuates the repetitiveness, the doubling back, and the circularity of time. In this regard, it serves as a mis en abyme for the movement of Blanchot's thought, which is characterized by the same patterns. Blanchot himself comments on the import of the circular nature of thought: "Whenever thought is caught in a circle, this is because it has touched upon something original, its point of departure beyond which it cannot move except to return."[7]

Midnight thus bears witness to the convergence of being and becoming that is registered in Blanchot's use of "is." Midnight is, in a sense, always in the process of becoming. It is something that, except for the briefest instant, is either about to happen or already just past. As Blanchot writes, "Midnight is precisely the hour which has never yet come, which never comes, the pure, ungraspable future, the hour eternally past."[8] This evocation of Midnight is remarkably similar to Deleuze's depiction of Aion, the time of the event, discussed previously:

> The event in turn, in its impassibility and impenetrability, has no present. It rather retreats and advances in two directions at once, being the perpetual object of a double question: What is going to happen? What has just happened? The agonizing aspect of the pure event is that it is always and at the same time something which has just happened and something about to happen; never something which is happening.[9]

The instant of Midnight's being is the momentary present of pure nothingness. Midnight is not the marker of anything tangible—there is nothing out there but darkness and night—yet, because of this daily moment of nothingness, time is made to repeat its continual circle of becoming. Midnight itself never really "is"; it is an absent presence, one that is only registered as presence because of the movement of its becoming. In this, it would seem to be the pure parallel of Blanchot's writing.

Yet alongside this incessant becoming lurks an almost uncanny persistence of being ("the agonizing aspect of the pure event"?), for the nothingness of Midnight inaugurates and mediates the movement of time and in this respect enables time's presence to be measured. This presence that comes from absence leads to an affirmation that is not counterbalanced by negation. Blanchot explicates this in his reading of Mallarmé and once again gestures to a hidden ontology:

> One can say that Mallarmé saw this nothing in action; he experienced the activity of absence. In absence he grasped a presence, a strength still persisting, as if in nothingness there were a strange power of affirmation. . . . It is in unreality itself that the poet encounters the resistance of a muffled presence. It is unreality from which he cannot free himself; it is in unreality that, disengaged from beings, he meets with the mystery of "those very words: it is." And this is not because in the unreal something subsists . . . but because when there is nothing, it is this nothing itself which can no longer be negated. It affirms, keeps on affirming, and it states nothingness as being, the inertia of being [*le désoeuvrement de l'être*].[10]

In this passage, Blanchot is at his most Deleuzian in that he repeatedly emphasizes the power of affirmation over negation, the affirmation of nothingness. Yet here, in muffled resonance with Sartre, this affirmed nothingness is also being in its most pure and elusive state.[11] This being is signaled by the "mystery" of "it is." However, this being is also something beyond movement, beyond an ever-fleeting march and retraction of time. It is precisely, once again, "the inertia of being." And yet, how is this inertia also an affirmation of nothingness? For isn't inertia in some sense a surplus of presence, a plenitude of "stuckness," and in this sense not entirely nothing?

The inertia of being is dramatized throughout Blanchot's fiction, which, if such a narrative-defying oeuvre can be categorized according to any one narrative rubric, is constantly restaging a scenario in which people are stuck in living spaces—houses, apartments, infernal institutions, hotel rooms. Often they just walk in and stay put, as in *Aminadab* and *When the Time Comes*. Sometimes we don't entirely know how they got there, as in the strange concentrationary institution of "The Idyll" or the elongated hotel room of *L'Attente, l'oubli* (*Awaiting Oblivion*). But in almost every case, the most striking thing is that they don't or don't want to or cannot leave, even when it seems like that wouldn't be the hardest thing to do (reminiscent of Buñuel's *The Exterminating Angel*). It is never clear why the narrator of *When the Time Comes* appears unannounced one day at the apartment of his friend Judith and her friend Claudia, whom he has not met before, and just stays there, barely acknowledging that there is a world outside (not unlike Robinson's "otherless" world with Friday in Tournier's fiction). In one of the rare moments where there is any mention of a space outside the apartment, the narrator rather incongruously maintains that he could just walk out the door and join this outside world:

> If it hadn't been so great, the deception would have been final. I would have left. I, too, would have gone into the front hall, and from there rejoined the tranquil flow of the rue de la Victoire and gone down towards the Opéra, which I liked at that hour, and I would have been happy.[12]

Yet, like the dinner-party guests in *The Exterminating Angel* who remain unable simply to cross the threshold and leave the space of the imprisoning house, Blanchot's narrator remains stuck behind the immaterial boundary of the space of the apartment, too immobile to leave despite his perception that he might happily do so.

It seems that what makes the characters and situations in Blanchot's *récits* so disarming is that they don't leave when they might, that they are driven by a relentless yet almost lighthearted inertia. As noted above, this is one reason Blanchot's fiction is sometimes evoked alongside the likes of Beckett or Melville's "Bartleby," for who can surpass these writers in portraying such incredible stuckness so calmly? What is disarming in these writers is that the customary weight of such profound immobility also has such a lightness, even though, as in Bartleby's case, it may be deadly. One might even say there is a mobility or affirmation or becoming to this stuckness. But does that mean it can then be located in the atemporal time of Deleuze's Aion, of the past-future disjunction? While to some degree it does partake of the temporality of Aion, this stuckness conjures more nearly an arrested, endless present over and above a convergence of past and future. Such an endless present marks a dwelling in being, a sticking with being, far beyond the ordinary. In other words, great stuckness seems to be, if anything, an excess of being—pure, immobile, profound being. For usually being is not this stuck and not this pure. Usually being is grounded in a narrative, in a task at hand, in something that makes it unstuck and undead. If Midnight is always arriving and always past, yet never exactly there, Blanchot's characters are on the contrary minimally arriving and never leaving, always entirely there, so much so that they might paradoxically seem not to be, because their "thereness" is hard to fathom. Like Bartleby, who moves in to his boss's office and refuses to vacate the premises, this intensity of not leaving is its own form of aggressive passivity.

It is easy to comprehend movement. Globalization and cosmopolitanism and travel and exile may be subjected to and incorporated into a range of critical positions, but on a fundamental level, they are not challenging to understand. One might debate the stakes and goals and nexus of power behind such movements on the global scale, but the fact that movement happens, and that movement is basically a good thing even if it is the product of bad forces, would seem to be the unstated assumption behind the logic of globalization. But what about people who fall outside this framework? (There is, to be sure, a whole ecological world—trees, rocks, etc.—that falls outside this framework, but since it doesn't bother most people that a tree or a rock, as opposed to a human being, would be stuck and not moving, I will leave aside this line of speculation).[13] People who don't move, whether willfully or not, form the least examined aspect of cosmopolitan discourse. Though much attention may be given to the question of the local, it is generally not at the level of the phenomenology of what it means to inhabit the local, for anyone trying to analyze or write about that realm is almost necessarily, and by definition, not in it.

We are trained not to look for immobility or, if we find it, not to stare at it in the face. If someone never leaves his house or crosses his state line, it seems like a lesser way of being, at least from the world of the mobile intelligentsia. But could it be that what such a form presents is not so much a state to be pitied but a state that is too challenging to look at because it represents a fullness of being that we are not accustomed to encountering, at least we in the classes of the largely mobile community of scholars? Deleuze writes of Herzog's films that they comprise two forms, the Small and the Large (just as he argues that Melville's fiction portrays the greatly good and the greatly evil).[14] He notes:

> In both cases—the sublimation of the large form and the enfeeblement of the small form—Herzog is a metaphysician. He is the most metaphysical of cinema directors . . . . When Bruno asks the question: "Where do objects go when they no longer have any use?" we might reply that they normally go in the dustbin, but that reply would be inade-

quate, since the question is metaphysical. Bergson asked the same question and replied metaphysically: that which has ceased to be useful simply begins to be. And when Herzog remarks that "he who walks is defenseless," we might say that the walker lacks any strength in comparison with cars and aeroplanes. But, there again, the remark was metaphysical. "Absolutely defenseless" is the definition which Bruno gave of himself. The walker is defenseless because he is he who is beginning to be, and never finishes being small.[15]

What I wish to suggest is that there is yet another bifurcation apart from that between the big and the small, or between the past and the future. It is that very weightiness of an endless present, that state that Deleuze describes as "beginning to be," that is the unthought and underside of the big/small and past/future disjunctions. It is not so much the oscillation between the small and the large that is crucial but the fact that at either extreme, one is more proximate to a realm of pure being. In this regard, the crucial split is not between the opposing terms of becoming (becoming smaller, becoming larger) but between the movement of becoming they both invoke and the realm of being that is their (utopian or dystopian) limit.

This bifurcation between becoming and being resides at the spatial margins of Thomas Carl Wall's beautiful chapter on Blanchot in *Radical Passivity: Levinas, Blanchot, and Agamben.* In his reading, which is focused in particular on Blanchot's *L'Arrêt de mort* (*Death Sentence*), Wall emphasizes at several junctures that there is no present but only a disjunction of past and future in the time-space of Blanchot's récits. He writes:

Not a plural text, *L'Arrêt de mort* is a text emptied of all presence and, what is more, it violently empties time of all presence. Put more simply and more abruptly, *L'Arrêt de mort* destroys time. The past—the things that happened to the narrator in 1938—are not offered to the reader, to the present, but instead offered to a futurity whose coming our reading already echoes. The récit is absolutely indifferent to "my time," "my death." It skips over the present moment.[16]

These sentences reach to the heart of Blanchot's thought, for surely, if anything, it is a thought that upends any chronological or ordinary notions of time and space. If for Wall the death of J. in *L'Arrêt de mort* defies chronological time,[17] then the narrator's strange noninhabitation of his apartments is equally defiant of spatial "presentness."

Wall analyzes the extraordinary example of the narrator's drive to simultaneously rent or sublet several apartments at once as a way of deflecting his presentness in his space, of being proximate to himself rather than present to himself. Wall writes the following in his gloss of Blanchot:

> For example, one day I may return home with a strange desire to move to another apartment and, after a few weeks, I may do just that. But then I may wish to move to yet another apartment, and then yet another, and another, and so on and so on—until I am no longer able to "return" "home." I may even, like the narrator in *L'Arrêt de mort*, maintain three or four flats at the same time. What can compel someone to maintain several apartments at once, since he or she cannot inhabit them all simultaneously? I may give in to this mad impulse because in any one of my apartments I could enjoy my absence from it as well, and at the same time. . . . By virtue of taking pleasure in the possibility of his flight from room to room, the narrator encloses himself in himself and he enjoys the separation of subjectivity. The enjoyment is precisely that each "here" is also an "elsewhere." It is not the presence of this room in its actual particularity that contents him, but his savoring of its proximity to each other room he rents out. That which he enjoys is not present, is not consumed or used up, not even partially.[18]

Here, Wall succinctly touches on the core of Blanchot's otherworldly sense of spatiality, especially the spaces of apartments and houses. The inhabiting of several apartments simultaneously so as to better appreciate the proximity of habitation and nonhabitation, to perceive oneself in the nonhabitation of one's space, and thus outside oneself, beyond oneself, to achieve through disjunction a continuity of perception—this Blanchotian motif is, once again, not only echoed throughout Blanchot's oeuvre but is also in strong resonance with the work of Deleuze. Yet do these emptyings of the present of space and time also foreclose an equally Blanchotian motif, one that addresses, albeit in a fashion so similar that it might not seem really to be distinct, the opposite temporal and spatial dimension, that of staying inexorably put in one space and time?

Wall touches on this dimension when he writes about the question of a pure possibility of history. Here, he comments on the fact that in *L'Arrêt de mort*, the narrator notes that the larger political events of the late 1930s dominated every aspect of life, yet strangely in the aftermath of the war, it was those seemingly trifling and mundane aspects of daily life that lingered with him more than the large-scale historical events that he participated in in his work as a journalist:

> While the events of the war years are dead, these inconsequential happenings have managed to live on and remain undead and unrecorded by virtue of their insignificance. . . . They are what the journalist did not write about at the time because they were inessential events, of secondary importance, mere everyday life. They were already supplementary to the time of the coming war. . . . But in a certain sense, these everyday events are purely historic. They are history purged of historic events, or, the everyday as the pure possibility of history.[19]

It seems that Wall's formulation of "history purged of historic events," or "the everyday as the pure possibility of history," is subtly at odds with his nonlocalizable and nonpresent notion of Blanchotian time and space. Indeed, what makes for pure history is the fact of a strange stability of locale and present daily life in the midst of such worldly upheaval. How is such a being in the mundane present to be represented against the omnipresent sense looming in the late 1930s of an ominous futurity and the retrospective vantage point that would necessarily situate this time within what would be its dominant (wartime) context? To remember above all the aspects of daily life would seem to be a blasphemous form of narrating history. While the two might blend together—the dailiness of the present and the more grandiose future anterior of the event—they must also and even more emphatically be at odds.

I now turn briefly to another work of fiction, written in the early 1950s just before Moroccan independence, that is focused so intently on the daily lives of the inhabitants of a small rural village that it was accused of being negligent of the larger and more dominant world events and therefore improperly historical. This work is Mouloud Mammeri's *La Colline oubliée* (The forgotten hill), which details the intricate social dynamics of an Arabo-Berber village in the Atlas Mountains of Morocco during World War II. What is most striking is that this narrative refuses to engage with the war — a war that takes the men away from the small village and brings back only some of them — except in the most perfunctory of ways. Instead the villagers are preoccupied primarily with a local case of potential wife repudiation.

In one of the novel's early passages, when news of the imminent outbreak of World War II has just reached the small village of Tasga where the story is set, the narrator describes a sense of listlessness in the village, an anxious waiting for something to happen, whatever the results of the awaited event — where even the outbreak of war seems to be more desirable than nothing at all. The narrator characterizes this state of waiting as an unnamable malady:

> Indeed for a long time our city suffered from a strange, imperceptible malady. It was everywhere and nowhere; it seemed to disappear for several months, then it would rise up abruptly, terribly, as if to seize the short respite it had left us. We tried all remedies; nothing worked, and even worse no one knew exactly what caused the ailment.[20]

According to Mammeri's critics, the imperceptible and unnamable malady described in this passage should be designated in a more absolute fashion and given the name of colonialism.[21] However, the most challenging part of the narrative is that it is precisely this sense of the absolute that is being put into question. Whether it be named colonialism or World War II, it seems that Mammeri is at least putting forth the possibility of there not being a recognizable change in the community at Tasga, whether or not World War II breaks out, whether or not Morocco gains its independence. It is this possibility of there not being a noticeable difference, or there not being an absolute standard for decidability, that is the real point of crisis. As Blanchot writes in *The Writing of the Disaster*, "I will not say that the disaster is absolute; on the contrary, it disorients the absolute."[22] It is this sense of disorientation, one brought on by an excessive, even obscene focus on the everyday, that Mammeri captures most forcefully in this first novel.[23]

This might be reformulated in the words of Ann Smock, who glosses Blanchot's notion of disaster in the following fashion in her introduction: "That there should be no difference (no difference as difference is ordinarily understood) between disaster and none at all: this is the disaster."[24] It seems that the community in question retains a state of quiet explosiveness whether or not many of its central members are present, and whatever the outcome of the larger political events. The fact that the community of Tasga itself contains its own possibility for dissolution is, more than anything, the unpronounceable disaster.

To return, then, to Wall's reading of the pure history of the everyday that emerges alongside the overdetermined events of World War II, at issue once again is the repressed question of being, and being static. Wall writes eloquently of "the time of radical divergence of past from future" and how "this discontinuity or radical uncertainty insinuates itself into continuous time"; indeed "this void-time is the very hollowing out of time that makes continuity possible in the first place."[25] I would concur, following Deleuze and the German mathematician Dedekind, who put it in stronger form, that this radical disjunction is indeed what makes the thought of continuity possible.[26] And one need not go any further than this. Yet when all is said and done, I would claim that to think the pure history of the everyday in the face of larger events — to think staying in one apartment all the time rather than inhabiting several simultaneously — to really think these things is to venture to a different and perhaps more vexed domain that is not squarely the atemporal domain of the past-future disjunctive synthesis. For this vexed domain is not on the order of becoming; rather, it is unbecoming, and unbecoming so deeply stuck that it ventures on being itself.[27]

As noted above, this is not far removed from Sartre's in-itself in *Being and Nothingness* and his practico-inert in *Critique of Dialectical Reason*, terms that Sartre subjugates to the more properly political and dynamic notions of the for-itself and praxis respectively.[28] These debased terms are challenging because they fall short of the proper, just as it is improper to live in a small rented apartment for forty-five years and not leave it or fix it or buy property or work at a job or go anywhere or straighten up the avalanche of accumulated papers. This would seem to be the irredeemable marker of a life gone awry. Yet I would propose that this is the outpost or limit of the Blanchotian universe, which is first and foremost that disarming atemporal and aspatial terrain that Wall and others so forcefully describe. And that Blanchotian terrain, marked as it is by a disjunction of past and future, the ability for the narrator to distance himself from himself by renting multiple apartments, is both striving toward and conditioned by that other singularity where there is only one apartment that is never left, only one time that is endlessly present, only one death and one night and one midnight that shimmer behind the doubleness of Blanchot's two nights, Blanchot's two deaths.

If the desire to be proximate to oneself by inhabiting multiple spaces is one of *becoming*, then how different is it really from the *being* still of the Bartlebys who inhabit with exclusivity their home or their office? Perhaps they are just two sides of the same operation in that the ones who remain in one place are also proximate to the space across the street, just by staying put where they are. Surely in this way becoming and being access the same thing. But to strive for proximity is nonetheless different from being proximate, even if the difference seems indiscernible. Blanchot must be credited, in addition to his Orpheus-like striving and losing, for also being, in his silent retreat, beyond that striving, maybe not superior to it, but nonetheless dwelling in a realm of being that is beyond, not because it is immune from becoming, but because it has wholly incorporated, wholly become, becoming. To perceive this distinction, not sustainable and even against the very fiber of Blanchot's thought, is nonetheless to perceive that the one trapped in becoming aspires to the utopia of being, while the one in that latter ethereal realm can only speak of it unsentimentally as a prison to be someday escaped. But the perception is to see that maybe becoming will never reach its utopia of being, and being will never leave the dystopia at which it long ago arrived. Is the perception of this enough to sustain serenely the force of it, which would seem also to be shattering?

By way of conclusion, I consider this question of the difference or indifference between becoming and being as it is simultaneously evoked and foreclosed by two critics attuned, very much in the fashion of Wall's *Radical Passivity*, to the phenomenology of passivity and inertia. In *What Is There to Say?* Ann Smock describes with characteristic finesse the suspension of the fissure I have been at pains to outline between becoming and being. She poses it in terms of a choice at stake in Melville's *Billy Budd*, the choice to speak or to kill, which is also one that, for Smock, links Melville and Blanchot and, later, Louis-René des Forêts:

> Blanchot has scarcely stated the bleak choice — either speak or kill — when he adds that speech founds this very alternative. To choose speech (when the sole choice is between speech and murder) turns out not to consist in choosing so much as in maintaining the wavering, un-

> decided movement of the either-or. . . . What concerns me, in other words, is an opposition abruptly neutralized. When human beings draw near to one another, the difference is sometimes suddenly suspended between the impatience and the inertia in them.[29]

This notion of choice that is also an infinite suspension of choice or difference is the recurrent Blanchotian motif of Smock's study. Yet it also raises the question of whether it then might be possible to choose to not suspend, to let the suspension go, so that it is no longer a matter of suspension between impatience and inertia but just inertia itself. Is this possible, and does it look any different?

Smock herself gives an example of what this might look like, one taken from des Forêts's story "Un Malade en forêt." Here, a stranded South African pilot who will betray himself if he speaks, because his English will betray him to the Germans, becomes so ill that it is not clear whether he will remember the prohibition against speaking. Playing dead so that he won't have to speak, he turns out, to the surprise of his comrades, actually to be dead. As Smock glosses the occurrence,

> Indeed, there is something striking in the still body of the dead RAF pilot—in the indisputable presence, lying flat on a stretcher in the sun by the side of the road, of the verdict that rules any such verdict out. The South African's motionless form can just fleetingly be felt to embody the insignificance of the gravest sentence—the one that decides, once and for all, but not anything. One feels in this motionless person the gravity that is proper to the perfectly inconsequential alone.[30]

There are so many words in these lines that indicate weightiness, stillness, gravity, inertia: "something striking in the still body," "in the indisputable presence," of the "motionless form," "lying flat," "the gravest sentence," "the gravity that is proper," and "in this motionless person." Unmoored slightly from their context—one that emphasizes suspension and hanging—these words point to something beside suspension, to an inertia that is here the inertia of deadness caught by surprise. Such a surprised deadness is paradoxically all the more alive for the very fact of the startle it produces, for the fact that it catches the comrades and the reader off guard, but off guard in a way that, as Smock indicates, precludes any verdict being reached. If we linger not so much on the absent verdict but on the present inertia, then it would appear that obliquely, quietly, alongside the choice that is not a choice, there is also a parousia of inertia so full it must announce its own singular ontology in the very process of seeming to undermine it. My claim, then, is that standing beside, indeed enabling, the suspension of difference that Smock reads in Blanchot and Melville and des Forêts is an unsuspended ontology of inertia.

This very phrase is echoed in another critical essay that focuses on a certain languid strain of American literature, specifically on a "Hawthornesque lassitude" that is transmitted even while being questioned and rejected by Melville and James. In "Postponing Politics in Hawthorne's *Scarlet Letter*," Christopher Diffee situates *The Scarlet Letter* as a nodal point in a trajectory of lethargic writing. If this lethargy comes to infect the likes of Melville and James (and one can certainly see the resonances, as Diffee points out, not only in "Bartleby" but also in James's "The Altar of the Dead" and "The Beast in the Jungle"), they nevertheless distance themselves from it to locate it all the more squarely with Hawthorne alone. As Diffee writes, citing Melville, "Melville charges Hawthorne with being neither harmless nor profound but in having 'too largely developed' his undevelopment, hence not veiling what he did not do and so appearing to be 'a sequestered, harmless man, from whom any deep and weighty thing would be [*sic*] hardly be anticipated.'"[31] If Hawthorne eschews weightiness or, according to Diffee's gloss of James on Hawthorne, "Hawthorne's essence is itself inessential," there is a paradoxical momentousness to the very lack of weightiness, to the inessential itself.[32] As with Smock, this paradox permeates Diffee's very text. In discussing James on Hawthorne, he writes:

> James's final word about Hawthorne's imagination is to pronounce it essentially sterile and arid, a passivity so withdrawn as to become a ghostly absence. . . . Reluctant to "produce himself," even hesitation fails to end but lingers on — in observation, expectation, contemplation — reproducing in parenthetical aside what falters as sense. The oddity of Hawthorne emerges not through a positive assertion — as if there could be an ontology of inaction — but when one is put in the awkward situation of realizing a fondness for absence "on almost any occasion."[33]

Once again, there is a torrent of terms indicating a plenitude of stillness and absence: "essentially sterile," "a passivity so withdrawn," and "even hesitation fails to end but *lingers on*" (my emphasis). Given this, it seems incongruous that Diffee characterizes Hawthorne's oddity as not emerging through positive assertion. To be sure, this lack of positive assertion accurately captures a certain essence of Hawthorne's (and Melville's and James's and Blanchot's) oeuvre, but it also belies the full-blown absoluteness of a passivity that lingers to the point of becoming an essence in its own right. It is odd, then, that Diffee would place "an ontology of inaction" in a twisted conditional—"as if" there could be one (but surely there is not)—for it seems that such an ontology of inaction is precisely what Diffee's reading, along with Smock's and Wall's, captures but does not claim as such, preferring not to maintain any sort of pure being when it can be credited to something else. But isn't the emphatic preferring not, as in the case of Bartleby, so antithetical to the presumed passivity that the passivity is itself ontologized into action?

All the more striking in Diffee's analysis is the network of texts that he reads, the attenuated inertia at the heart of the classics of the American canon. Blanchot (and all the more so des Forêts) might seem like an esoteric and obscure writer, even within the French tradition, and the questions of radical passivity, of being and becoming, to which his oeuvre gives rise, might seem peculiarly French and not universalizable questions. However, if one perceives that this inertia of being is also at the heart of the national literature that would seem to be the most movement-focused (portraying endless road trips and mobility, as discussed above), then it might lead one to conclude that perhaps such movement, such infinite becoming, is equally the mask for the inertia that is so entrenched as to become invisible. The ones who have no choice but to inhabit this inertia fully are the unwitting and disrespected guideposts to an ontology that is so present as to seem pathological, or not to seem at all.

CHAPTER TWELVE

Living Virtually in a Cluttered House

IN *THE POETICS OF SPACE*, Gaston Bachelard proposes a new field of investigation or perception, one that would be attuned, like psychoanalysis, to inner psychological states, yet also attuned to the way architecture and space affect those states. He terms such a field "topoanalysis" and defines it as "the systematic study of the sites of our intimate lives."[1] Central to a topoanalytic approach is an attentiveness to the nuances and registers of the space of the house. Bachelard focuses on the intimate and solitary relation of the home dweller to the space of the house:

> And so, faced with these periods of solitude, the topoanalyst starts to ask these questions: Was the room a large one? Was the garret cluttered up? Was the nook warm? How was it lighted? How, too, in these fragments of space, did the human being achieve silence? How did he relish the very special silence of the various retreats of solitary daydreaming? . . . And all the spaces of our past moments of solitude, the spaces in which we have suffered from solitude, enjoyed, desired and compromised solitude, remain indelible within us, and precisely because the human being wants them to remain so. He knows instinctively that this space identified with his solitude is creative; that even when it is forever expunged from the present, when, henceforth, it is alien to all the promises of the future, even when we no longer have a garret, when the attic room is lost and gone, there remains the fact that we once loved a garret, once lived in an attic. . . . In the past, the attic may have seemed too small, it may have seemed cold in winter and hot in summer. Now, however, in memory recaptured through daydreams, it is hard to say through what syncretism the attic is at once small and large, warm and cool, always comforting.[2]

In Bachelard's phenomenology, the space of the house leaves a lingering trace that, when revisited through memory or dreams, recreates very palpably the precise nooks and crannies of the former lived space but does so through a different perceptual lens. This new and different lens might be described as virtual both in that it regards the house space from a spatio-temporal vantage point of some distance and in that the atmospheric conditions it conjures up are in some sense mutually exclusive — a space both big and small, a temperature both warm and cool — that yet can be perceived as existing simultaneously. For Bachelard, such a perception is linked to the state of distance, to the fact that one no longer actually lives in the space in question. In this fashion, the space of the house has perceptual import insofar as it is linked to a distant past, generally that of childhood: "Through this permanent childhood, we maintain the poetry of the past. To inhabit oneirically the house we were born in means more than to inhabit it in memory; it means living in this house that is gone, the way we used to dream in it."[3] Repeated here are terms of distance: "childhood," "poetry of the past," "inhabit in memory," "house that is gone," "used to dream in it." The unique and beautiful form of perception that Bachelard captures is critically dependent on a state of distance, both in space and in time. What would happen if we were to retain this form of perception but rethink its seemingly exclusive link to a state that is past?

As we saw in the introduction, Deleuze opens *The Logic of Sense* with an example similar to Bachelard's but locates it at the conjunction of past and future rather than strictly in the past:

> *Alice* and *Through the Looking-Glass* involve a category of very special things: events, pure events. When I say "Alice becomes larger," I mean that she becomes larger than she was. By the same token, however, she becomes smaller than she is now. Certainly, she is not bigger and smaller at the same time. She is larger now; she was smaller before. But it is at the same moment that one becomes larger than one was and smaller than one becomes. This is the simultaneity of a becoming whose characteristic is to elude the present. Insofar as it eludes the present, becoming does not tolerate the separation or the distinction of before and after, or of past and future. It pertains to the essence of becoming to move and to pull in both directions at once: Alice does not grow without shrinking and vice versa.[4]

This example does not oppose past and future but instead collapses them and opposes both together to the present. As we have seen, the present (Chronos) is clearly in a subordinate relation to the conjunction of past and future (Aion). Nonetheless, and in the fashion of the preceding discussion of Blanchot, I would like to linger on the question of the present—especially as it intersects with the notion of the everyday—and pose the following question: is it possible to reach "the essence of becoming" (is this in fact being?), to perceive virtually in a space that is lived-in in the present, to make of everyday house-space something that is also virtual?

In this light, I will examine the space of the lived-in house and the way in which the architecture of everyday life might be said simultaneously to give rise to new virtual worlds. To start with an example of how the virtual inheres in real-life time and space, one might picture what would happen if the space of the house were literally turned upside down. Perhaps it is the child's game mentioned earlier in which you turn your head upside down so that the house's ceiling becomes its floor, and you perceive the huge moldings that would have to be straddled to pass from one empty room into another. This is an exhilarating and spacious game, for there is no stuff cluttering the ceilings, just empty rooms bordered by foot-high fences; it is a minimalist and ethereal space uncluttered by the objects below. The upside-down ceiling world of the house is entirely composed of actually existing space, yet it is a space viewed from such a skewed angle as to seem altogether otherworldly. Furthermore, the ceiling world exists on a level that is in between. Assuming one is on the first floor, the ceiling world forms a sort of mezzanine between the first floor and the invisible second floor, which from this topsy-turvy vantage point becomes the ceiling world's basement.[5]

I wish to apply such a vantage point to a reading of several disparate texts—spanning the domains of philosophy, architecture, literature, and cultural geography—that each highlight a point of convergence between virtual architecture and everyday space. The central text is Deleuze's *The Fold: Leibniz and the Baroque*, which argues for a unique relation between the baroque house and virtual perception. Deleuze begins this unorthodox study of Leibniz with a detailed analysis of the space of the baroque house, which is defined by the fact that it has only two levels, with a folded space that separates them. Deleuze distinguishes baroque space as follows: "The universe as a stairwell marks the Neoplatonic tradition. But the Baroque contribution par excellence is a world with only two floors, separated by a fold that echoes itself, arching from the two sides according to a different order."[6] At issue here are, on the one hand, the demarcation of two distinct floors or levels and, on the other, the liminal or boundary space — the fold or point of inflection — where the two levels come together.

The two levels of the baroque house would appear to be diametric opposites: the lower level is large, open, public, and spacious, while the upper level is small, windowless, private, and closed. Furthermore, the lower level corresponds with the body, while the upper level corresponds with the soul. Deleuze distinguishes the two levels with a series of characteristics that are repeated with slight variation throughout *The Fold*:

> The lower level is assigned to the façade, which is elongated by being punctured and bent back according to the folds determined by a heavy matter, forming an infinite room for reception or receptivity. The upper level is closed, as a pure inside without an outside, a weightless, closed interiority, its walls hung with spontaneous folds that are now only those of a soul or a mind.[7]

This passage illustrates the way in which, in Deleuze's reading of the baroque house, the two levels are at once entirely distinct yet everywhere imbued with the same stuff, here the stuff being the folds themselves: "the lower level . . . punctured and bent back according to the folds determined by a heavy matter" and "the upper level . . . , its walls hung with spontaneous folds." The fold then, exists both between and within each level of the baroque house. The fold both sets the two floors apart and reflects the tension of their inextricable belonging to each other. Deleuze writes, "We are dealing with two cities, a celestial Jerusalem and an earthly one, but with the rooftops and foundations of a same city, and the floors of a same house. . . . For Leibniz, the two floors are and will remain inseparable; they are really distinct and yet inseparable by dint of a presence of the upper in the lower. The upper floor is folded over the lower floor. One is not acting upon the other, but one belongs to the other, in a sense of a double belonging."[8]

The example of the baroque house highlights the complex dynamic of two interconnected spatial entities. On the one hand, the spaces are clearly distinct: a given room exists on one floor and not the other (unless the house collapses). On the other hand, both floors are composed of the same materials, at least in their points of contact, and are part of the same larger entity. Moreover, the second floor would not exist without the first floor, or else there would just be the first floor. Then again, and this will be taken up in what follows, the question remains as to whether a single floor is really single or whether it also presupposes a virtual second floor. It seems that the latter is the case at least in France where the numbering of floors begins with what in American terminology is already the second floor. Such conundrums might be puzzled out further, but what matters is that they have real bearing on the way we perceive the space around us and thus real bearing on the way lives are lived, particularly in nonextreme moments, which is most of the time.

This question of the "double belonging" or adjacency of two distinct yet inseparable entities comes to the foreground in the relation between mind and body, to which we briefly return. Using the framework of the baroque house as a point of departure, Deleuze connects this framework on numerous occasions to the mind-body question. Deleuze's model of baroque space in fact also serves as a conceptual model for a similar relation between body and soul. In elaborating this connection, Deleuze begins with a reference to religious art:

> We move from funerary figures of the Basilica of Saint Laurence to the figures on the ceiling of Saint Ignatius. It might be claimed that physical gravity and religious elevation are quite different and do not pertain to the same world. However, these are two vectors that are allotted as such in the distinction of the two levels or floors of a single and same world, or of the single and same house. It is because the body and the soul have no point in being inseparable, for they are not in the least really distinct. . . . From this point on any localization of the soul in an area of the body, no matter how tiny it may be, amounts rather to a *projection* from the top to the bottom, a projection of the soul focalizing on a "point" of the body, in conformity with [Desargues's] geometry, that develops from a Baroque perspective.[9]

By this account, the body and the soul coexist in an adjacent and mutually dependent relation (as discussed in chapter 2) that parallels that between the two floors of a same house. Just as he poses the two floors as distinct yet inextricably connected, so too does Deleuze, in a double move, both affirm a mind-body duality and affirm that mind and body are not really separable.[10]

It is this coexistence of seemingly competing realities that Deleuze, drawing on Leibniz, characterizes as incompossibility.[11] Incompossibilities, Deleuze implies, may be negotiated by means of differential perspective and projection ("From this point on any localization of the soul in an area of the body, no matter how tiny it may be, amounts rather to a *projection* from the top to the bottom, a projection of the soul focalizing on a 'point' of the body"). In other words, just as a room looks quite different depending on whether it is viewed with the head upright or upside down, though it is all the while composed of the same space and objects, so too could the body and soul be said to belong to the same space yet appear entirely different when projected onto that space from different vantage points. This concept of using an unusual angle of projection to conjoin two incompatible worlds is essentially what Lacan designates by the term *anamorphosis* in *The Four Fundamental Concepts of Psychoanalysis*. He writes,

> In my seminar, I have made great use of the function of anamorphosis, in so far as it is an exemplary structure. What does a simple, non-cylindrical anamorphosis consist of? Suppose there is a portrait on this flat piece of paper that I am holding. By chance, you see the black-board, in an oblique position in relation to the piece of paper. Suppose that, by means of a series of ideal threads of lines, I reproduce on the oblique surface each point of the image drawn on my sheet of paper. You can easily imagine what the result would be—you would obtain a figure enlarged and distorted according to the lines of what may be called a perspective.[12]

Lacan goes on to discuss Holbein's painting *The Ambassadors*, in which a skull in the foreground is so distorted by anamorphosis that it is virtually unrecognizable. Anamorphosis illustrates, as it were, the blind spot or incompossibility between the gaze that regards the object in its "normal" appearance and the other gaze that is destabilized by the distortion. Through this differential, it effectively reveals the distortion inherent in all perception.

Whereas the anamorphic relation represents a differential between two extremely dissimilar perspectives, the line of inflection also differentiates but does so between nonextreme points. Deleuze characterizes inflection as follows: "[T]he infinite fold separates or passes between matter and soul, the façade and the closed room, the exterior and the interior. The line of inflection is a virtuality that never ceases to differentiate: it is actualized in the soul but realized in matter, each on its own side."[13] While Deleuze refers to the question of inflection in a number of instances, this concept is more fully developed in Bernard Cache's *Earth Moves*, a work that takes up the Deleuzian notions of inflection and the fold and elaborates them within a more architectural framework.[14] According to Cache, points of inflection are distinct from those points that can be mapped as the minima or maxima of a curve.[15] Whereas the minima and maxima can be easily pinpointed and defined because they are at either extreme, points of inflection are precisely those points in the middle that generally go unnoticed because they reside between extremes. In other terms, Cache writes: "Let it be given that the world is the set of the best possible images, and also of the best images possible. On the surface, inflection is the mark of images that can't be the best and that are thus outside the world and its inclines, though they are a part of it."[16] The space of inflection, then, is that space that would almost pass unnoticed in favor of its more noticeable and striking proximate spaces.[17] It is the little world that, when caught at the right angle and from the right perspective, shows itself to be a rich and varied inner world residing at the heart of what appears to be something else.

Inflection, then, is not entirely different from the more radical and dialectical notions of incompossibility and anamorphosis, but it enacts them on a more minor scale. And it is precisely in its ability to designate a minorness of scale that I am highlighting inflection as the term most appropriate to a reimagination of everyday space and objects. Inflection concerns ordinary details of actual space that do not require an elaborate conceptual system in order to be decoded, yet at the same time these details are often so ordinary as to appear banal and unworthy of extended reflection. In this regard, inflection is not unlike a strategy of defamiliarization, except that it is not so much a sustained strategy or method as it is a momentary bracketing of conditioned modes of perception.[18] It is by definition something that can only be sustained briefly. As Cache writes,

> When, in the images that surround us, we are able to concentrate only on inflections, we accede to another regime of images that we call primary ones. This perception is necessarily fleeting and variable, since we can't become "used" to it. We can't settle into it through the determination of a best reaction; it is a mobile image in which an unlocatable position eludes our comfort.[19]

Concentrating on inflections thus produces what by most standards is a skewed perception: it is akin to pretending the floor of the room is its ceiling, or focusing on an object or space that by all objective standards has very little interest or merit but, when viewed from the right angle, casts an entirely different light on everything. The point of inflection, since it is in the middle and does not partake of the extremes, not only goes largely unnoticed but, when it is noticed, appears as a sort of continuous minimalist space.

As in the example from chapter 10, one generally hears (if one lives on one of the United States coasts) midwestern landscape evoked as being just about the most dull and monotonous landscape to be found. Beyond that, Kansas is frequently singled out as epitomizing this endless and dreary landscape. When confronted by such truisms, I can't help but wonder what the people speaking them were seeing when and if they drove through the Flint Hills of eastern Kansas. These rolling mounds, rising only a few stories above the plane of the horizon, are to my mind as breathtaking as any scenery in the United States, breathtaking because they mark such a slight, yet for this reason monumental, departure from the line of the vast landscape. From this perspective, each mound is an austere mountain recasting the line of the plain below. Here, the line of inflection inheres in two perspectives at once. On the one hand, it is flatness in all its nonminimal and nonmaximal monotony ("nonscenic" from many vantage points). On the other hand, it is the minute variation, the slight departure that the low mound makes from the plane of consistency. In both cases, the point of inflection inheres in a minimalist continuum yet refocuses that continuum in such a fashion as to highlight its singularity.

In *Earth Moves*, Cache revisits the link between minimalist continuity and modernism. He views the emphasis on continuity as a modern impulse that has been too summarily dismissed in the wake of postmodernism. He writes that "modernism has been ostracized today in the name of a postmodernity whose eclecticism barely conceals its sterility."[20] Furthermore, the modern continuum, like the baroque house, integrates discrete levels or domains while allowing those domains to retain their distinctions. By contrast, the postmodern is often portrayed as smoothing out all values and points of fixity (though in any given instance, it most likely comes closer to the above description of the modern). Cache glosses the relation between the modern continuum and its unnamed opponent as follows:

> [M]odern optics speaks of this chiasmus where great causes have small effects and vice versa. But nonetheless, this plane has its own topography. On a continuum without values, everything can dissolve into inconsistency; however, if we negotiate its inflections, we can ensure continuities between the most disparate registers, between the most distant eras. . . . Each postulate of the modernist movement, once rid of the principle of unity, can be understood as the expression of a desire for continuity between the social, the technical, and the formal. . . . Instead of simply quoting inconsistent and gratuitous images, our epoch takes up the modern challenge of continuity. If collage appeared to be the paradigm of modernism, it is because it allowed our eye to seek out that invisible line that traces a continuity between images, fields of knowledge, and the most diverse practices. . . . It seems that inflection is precisely the new sign of the modern continuum.[21]

Beyond the overt apology for modernism, Cache is more nearly interested in contemporary appropriations of specifically modernist traits and techniques. Cache finds such traits and techniques—like the flat roof in architecture or the collage in painting—noteworthy in the way they fold disparate aesthetic and political registers into a useful continuum. This is not unlike the virtual ceiling world of the two-story house, which might bring an otherwise unremarkable or even impoverished house space into a noncontradictory continuum with what might appear to be nothing but rarefied high aestheticism (the minimalist ceiling world). Simply put, at issue is the possibility of a perception that would inject into the most ordinary of spaces an aestheticized or defamiliarized otherness. It might be argued that such a mode of perception devalues the very real social or economic conditions that permeate and overdetermine the dwelling conditions of the given abode in favor of a depoliticized aestheticism. But such an argument takes as a fundamental assumption that the aesthetic is somehow incompatible or negligible when the living conditions become harsh enough and fails to consider that aesthetic perception has no natural and exclusive affinity with the privileged and educated classes.[22]

It is precisely such an assumption that inheres in an otherwise compelling study of the link between modernism and the idea of the noble household. The study is Vincent Pecora's *Households of the Soul*, a meditation on the literary, philosophical, and economic dimensions of modernism.

Pecora's aim is "to understand how an imaginary household emerged within modernism at large"[23] and how such a household also functions in the domains of language and literary theory. Pecora links this imaginary household to a nostalgia for a "noble household" that is aristocratic and not everyday. Drawing on close readings of Conrad, Joyce, Yeats, and Lawrence among others, Pecora argues that "the modern invention of the archaic and courtly household—a largely masculine, heroic, and 'noble' affair . . . —is thus for me a rather basic reaction to the economic rationalization of civil society and the feminization of the bourgeois domestic sphere, but a response with manifold implications."[24] These implications, which Pecora spells out in extended close readings of multiple high modernist texts, point to a retrograde and conservative, if not imperialist, longing for an era of precapitalist sovereignty in which the noble estate served as a place of refuge for the aristocratic.

Although Pecora masterfully supports this thesis with examples that range over both canonical and more obscure modernist texts, he does not consider the potential non-elitist implications of the noble household, nor does he consider in any detail descriptions of the actual physical space of the households in question. For example, in his reading of *Time Regained*, the last volume of Proust's *In Search of Lost Time*, Pecora locates the stately Guermantes mansion as inspiring Marcel's series of past recollections not because of the objects it contains or its associations with childhood but because it abstractly represents the "charm" of the aristocratic for a young bourgeois boy. The one object Pecora focuses on is the "beautiful first editions" in the Guermantes library, which for him underscore the link between noble household, aesthetic recollection, and writing.[25] Although these connections are certainly valid, they undermine any specificity of space or objecthood within a particular house. As Pecora writes, "[F]or the adult Marcel, it is the ancestral, princely household represented by that name and neither simply a specific house (which, after all, was often one of many for the nobility) nor the actual family that matters."[26] While the Proustian and other modernist households Pecora analyzes unquestionably have an elitist function, it seems improbable that this is their only function. Indeed, an attentiveness to the actual space and objects within the house alongside an attentiveness to their class and social functions might produce other angles of analysis. With regard to the first editions, though they are markers of privilege, they also mark how objects and impressions are modulated by time. As Marcel himself explains, "[T]he first edition of a work would have been more precious in my eyes than any other, but by this term I should have understood the edition in which I read it for the first time."[27] Marcel, like Bachelard, uses objects and spaces as a conduit for reexamining and remapping life-defining events.[28] That such a form of perception is only available in aristocratic spaces seems itself to be an elitist presumption.

Such an attentiveness to everyday physical space and household objects is central to Denis Wood and Robert J. Beck's *Home Rules*, a study that takes a supremely localized point of departure. Whereas Pecora focuses on the abstract idea of the household as a recurrent motif in a vast array of literature and literary theory, Wood and Beck focus minutely on specific objects and spatial relations and produce a reading so detail oriented (a sort of *S/Z* of the suburban home) that it too attains a high level of abstraction, albeit from a completely different vantage point—which underscores that it is the context that makes abstraction value laden and not abstraction per se. In contrast to Pecora, Wood and Beck suggest that the virtual spaces of the house are not necessarily spaces of privilege but rather spaces that open up new perspectives on those things that seem most common. In *Home Rules*, which brings the domains of architecture, geography, anthropology, and structuralism into unique convergence, Wood and Beck analyze the elaborate codes that inform the Wood family's mode of dwelling in their North Carolina home. In considering the complex interpersonal and spatial rules that govern such household minutiae as "the screen door," "the radiator by the stair," "the plant on the floor in front of the easel," and "the piece of wire on the mantleshelf," Wood and Beck defamiliarize basic household objects to such an extent that they are ultimately transformed into new and virtual entities.

This virtual perception of the everyday, this making strange of the everyday, is foregrounded repeatedly by Wood and Beck. They frequently point out, as in the following description of the radiator, how common household objects are generally disregarded except when their form or function makes them stand out: "It is easy to overlook the radiator, easy to let it be swamped by the many things clamoring for attention. It is easy to lose it in the space below the window, to let the wall absorb it. Unless it's winter and the snow is falling . . . then the radiator becomes the very *raison d'être* for being in the room, for turning the rocker round to face the window: to watch the weather across the toasting toes."[29] Under special circumstances, a little-noticed object—the radiator—undergoes a transformation such that it becomes the focal point of its surroundings. What is striking here is that the radiator becomes the visual focal point of the room precisely because of its nonvisual attribute: its ability to produce heat. Although the form of defamiliarized perception at issue has been outlined predominantly through visual examples, this perception is in no way the exclusive domain of the visual. Indeed, the most memorable examples of phenomenological association (Proust's madeleine, Bachelard's house that is both hot and cold, Merleau-Ponty's example of two hands touching)[30] rely on the less hegemonic senses of taste and touch. Nonetheless, the very description of these other sensory modes of perception is never at far remove from the visual: hence the formulation "to *watch* the weather" in its stunning juxtaposition with "across the toasting toes."[31]

Watching the weather outside from the vantage point of the radiator-warmed inside also underscores a strong dualism operative not only in Wood and Beck's analysis but also in Deleuze's description of the two-story house. In addition to objects such as the radiator, Wood and Beck also scrutinize the house's walls, floors, and ceilings. The analysis of the ceiling is particularly striking in its resonance with Deleuze's model of a tiered or twofold entity. Here, instead of first and second floors, the two levels—modeled after each other yet in fundamental opposition—are the ceiling and the sky. In a singularly lyrical passage, Wood and Beck describe the ceiling:

> It is nothing of the exosphere, the ionosphere, the stratosphere, the troposphere. It is nothing of the atmosphere. It is not of air. It is not of nature at all. . . . It will constitute itself as anti-sky. Where the sky is hyalescent, the ceiling will be both matte and opaque. Where the sky is blue, the ceiling will be white. Where the sky is proteiform, the ceiling will be changeless (or only a little more grimy year after year). Where the sky is immaterial, the ceiling will be indurate. Where the sky is deep, the ceiling will be flat. Where the sky may rain, the ceiling will always be dry. The ceiling will be a matte, opaque, unchanging, indurate, dry, flat whiteness. It will be paper. It will be harder than paper. It will be chalk. It will be marble.[32]

At every point, the ceiling is comparable to the sky, although they exist at opposite ends of the sensory spectrum. Wood and Beck go on to argue that the ceiling perfectly doubles or mirrors the sky so as to better renounce it (along with the natural world and those who live directly underneath the sky).[33] In a similar fashion, the ceiling/floor division partakes of the same relation of oppositional doubling: "the ceiling is nonetheless forced to constitute itself as anti-floor (the room cannot afford to obliterate the paradigm . . .)."[34]

Wood and Beck imply that the ceiling's function is loftier and more cultured than that of either the floor or the sky. This accounts for the fact that the rules of the house — designed primarily for the two children who live there — are much more stringent about keeping dirt off the ceiling than off the floor. From the children's vantage point, then, the ceiling has a pristine and untouchable quality that would perhaps account for the desire to reverse the household order by a turning of the head which makes the ceiling into the floor. Such a game would also subvert the strict opposition between the codes surrounding ceiling and floor, at least in the household featured in *Home Rules*. This household functions by a logic of doubles similar to those of Deleuze's baroque house (the first and second floors in Deleuze, the ceiling and floor in Wood and Beck). Both the ceiling and the second floor carry with them an unacknowledged privilege, yet neither could exist without its inextricable belonging to the lower term: on the one hand, the ceiling as it is perched over the floor, on the other, the second floor as it is supported by the first floor. Whether one chooses to focus on the fundamental dualism or the interpenetrability of the two terms is itself a matter (and not an innocent one) of perception.

In conclusion, I return to another and more devious version of the upside-down ceiling game as well as to the question of what takes place if the house under consideration has only one floor. In the fashion of Wood and Beck, we might play a sort of hologram game with a certain first floor, a floor packed to bursting with stuff, a floor belonging to a house so full there is only one place to sit and one path by which to navigate, a house so decrepit that it would be unthinkable to fix the stove, the termite-ridden floorboards, the cracks in the walls, the heating — a house so solitary that only one guest is ever asked in. Yet that guest finds in this cluttered, decrepit house a sublimity that the host, who never leaves the house, cannot fathom and would not want to. The guest sits at a portion of the kitchen table that has been cleared off, the space on which to write a letter or a book as the host sleeps. Somehow amid the broken television, the hot plate, the bowl of sugar packets, the stack of meticulously arranged secret notes, the loaves of white bread, the little lamp, the vitamin bottles, the candle, the seven-year-old plant cutting, the hand-carved plaque that reads "Something Good Is Going to Happen" — somehow amid all those objects that encroach upon the guest with years' worth of weight, somehow that guest perceives only spaciousness and hears only silence. The uncluttered section of the table seems as if it were stretching to infinity, the objects that stare back too familiar to be real, too transparent to take up weight and space. The point is that, resting as they do in the guest's ever more skewed plane of perception, these objects, this real-life clutter, is as virtual as the undifferentiated space of the celestial ceiling world.

Maurice Blanchot provides a somewhat different model of the virtual house in his inexpressibly strange novel *Aminadab*. In this story, Thomas, the central character, enters a house one day, drawn by the beckoning wave of a woman standing by the window on one of the upper floors. Upon entering, he finds himself not in a regular building as he had thought but, instead, in the machine of an infernal house where he is ushered from room to room by guardians and housekeepers and servants, never returning to the room he had previously entered, and never gaining access to the elusive second floor. This hermetic house-world is divided between tenants (which he is) and servants, both of whom keep changing and rarely if ever reappear in their former guise. At one point, Thomas is chained to an unknown companion; at another he sees a tenant with a face painted over his real one; at still another he tries to stop a rebellion in which the inhabitants decide to walk up to the second floor, something that is forbidden and that proves disastrous. At every point, Thomas tries to pin down the elusive laws that govern the house's monotonously indecipherable series of encounters, tortures, and comings and goings. The house is a minefield of virtual maps, each pretending to hold the code to the ever-unfathomable floor plan. At a singularly eventful moment, Thomas learns that he is the house's executioner.[35]

By way of commentary on the virtual house of *Aminadab*, I return to the cluttered house mentioned above. At one point in time, a certain dweller of this cluttered house (one who is no longer there) devised a plan for making the cluttered house more spacious, a plan in fact suggested by a stranger off the street to whom had been offhandedly confided the problem of the clutter in the house. The plan was to add a whole second floor that would extend upward from the broom closet of the little one-story house. The child in the house was told of the plan and constructed a virtual second-floor world to play in. There the child would have a room of its own from which to supervise imaginary brothers and sisters and recalcitrant stuffed animals. There in the world of the second floor the child might reinvent the strange laws by which its actual house was governed, reinvent them and make them stranger.

Unfortunately, since the house was a rented one, such an addition on the part of the tenants was by definition impossible, just as in Blanchot's novel it is similarly impossible for the tenants to go up to the second floor. But the child had not understood this impossible law of capital properly, and so the virtual world of the second floor grew and grew each day, constantly adding new laws and dispensing with old ones, and eventually bumping up against the houses of Deleuze and Blanchot with all their similar second-floor virtuality, giving the child, as it were, a home away from home, a home that resembled the little cluttered house and at some moments and spaces was indeed the very same house. But this story, too, has its own horrible point of recognition, the recognition that, indeed, this lovely and mythical little child has all along been, and in fact still is, that cluttered house's executioner.

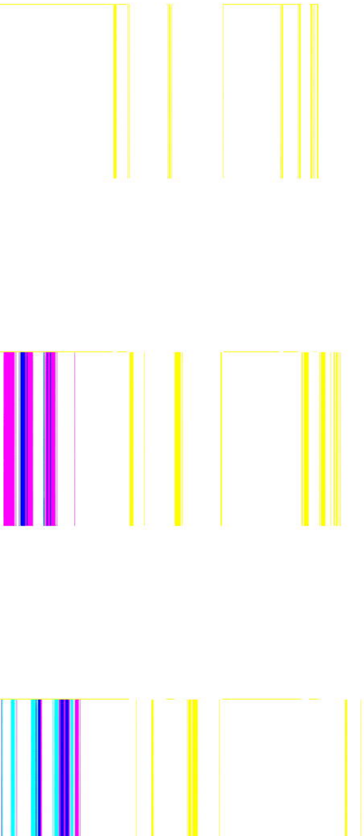

NOTES

Introduction. Deleuze's Scholasticism

1. Slavoj Žižek, *Organs without Bodies: On Deleuze and Consequences* (New York: Routledge, 2004). Gilles Deleuze, *The Logic of Sense*, trans. Mark Lester with Charles Stivale (New York: Columbia University Press, 1990); and Deleuze, *Difference and Repetition*, trans. Paul Patton (New York: Columbia University Press, 1994). While my readings privilege *The Logic of Sense* in certain respects, I adhere to the model of time outlined in *Difference and Repetition* beyond and in some sense against that presented in *The Logic of Sense*. This is detailed at the end of this introduction and in chapter 7.

2. I wish to thank Alan Schrift for sharing with me the program for the *agrégation* in philosophy during the years (1944–48) Deleuze studied at the Sorbonne, as well as the Sorbonne faculty record for the years 1945 to 1948 (it being unclear whether courses were offered there during the 1944–45 school year). Deleuze would have had the opportunity of studying with teachers such as Émile Bréhier (whom he cites positively in *The Logic of Sense*, and whose work on the incorporeal is taken up in what follows), Jean Laporte, Henri Gouhier, Maurice de Gandillac, and Martial Guéroult. Alan D. Schrift's consultation and his entries on Bréhier, Ferdinand Alquié, Étienne Gilson, and Jean Hyppolite in *Twentieth-Century French Philosophy: Key Themes and Thinkers* (Malden, MA: Blackwell, 2006) have been of particular help in tracking down Deleuze's potential exposure to ancient and Medieval thought during his period of university study. It is not clear whether Deleuze had sustained exposure to Medieval thought and, above all, to Medieval logic, though his first Spinoza book demonstrates that he certainly had more exposure than most of his immediate contemporaries, perhaps with the exception of thinkers such as Klossowski and Bataille. It is also possible that Alquié's *Le désir d'éternité* (Paris: Presses Universitaires de France, 1943) and its discussion of the "affective refusal of time" had some influence on Deleuze's formulation of the third synthesis of time. Giuseppe Bianco's entry on Alquié and Jean Hyppolite in *Aux sources de la pensée de Gilles Deleuze 1*, ed. Stéfan Leclercq (Mons, Belgium: Éditions Sils Maria, 2005), discusses Alquié's "dualism and separation between temporality and eternity" (94), an idea that is discussed at the end

of this introduction. It is also entirely possible that Deleuze could have attended Gilson's lectures at the Collège de France during his time at the Sorbonne. These connections merit further exploration; nevertheless what follows is not in any exacting sense an influence argument but more nearly a juxtaposition that aims to be useful in arguing for Deleuze's affinities with certain strains of thought he generally disassociates himself from (such as his teachers Alquié and to a certain extent Hyppolite). For more on Deleuze's formation, see François Dosse, *Gilles Deleuze and Félix Guattari: Intersecting Lives*, trans. Deborah Glassman (New York: Columbia University Press, 2010).

3. Deleuze evokes the problematic of divine names in *Expressionism in Philosophy: Spinoza*, trans. Martin Joughin (New York: Zone Books, 1992), esp. 44–67.

4. See especially Richard Cross, *Duns Scotus on God* (Aldershot, UK: Ashgate, 2005); Cross, *Physics of Duns Scotus: The Scientific Context of a Theological Vision* (Oxford: Oxford University Press, 1998); Giorgio Pini, *Categories and Logic in Duns Scotus: An Interpretation of Aristotle's Categories in the Late Thirteenth Century* (Leiden, The Netherlands: Brill, 2002); and Pini, "Univocity in Scotus's *Quaestiones super Metaphysicam*: The Solution to a Riddle," *Medioevo* 30 (2005), 69–110. A larger question I hope someday to pursue is the relative influence of Gilson's work on Deleuze and other thinkers of Deleuze's generation. In this context, see Gilson's important *Jean Duns Scot: Introduction à ses positions fondamentales* (Paris: Vrin, 1952). A helpful English excerpt from Gilson's work on Scotus can be found in *A Gilson Reader*, ed. Anton C. Pegis (Garden City, NY: Hanover House, 1957). For an excellent treatment of Deleuze and his relation to Scotus, see Nathan Widder, "John Duns Scotus," in *Deleuze's Philosophical Lineage*, ed. Graham Jones and Jon Roffe (Edinburgh: Edinburgh University Press, 2009). See also Daniel W. Smith, "The Doctrine of Univocity: Deleuze's Ontology of Immanence," in *Deleuze and Religion*, ed. Mary Bryden (London: Routledge, 2001); and Stéfan Leclercq, "Jean Duns Scot," in *Aux sources de la pensée de Gilles Deleuze 1*, ed. Stéfan Leclercq (Mons, Belgium: Éditions Sils Maria, 2005).

5. Primarily in *Expressionism in Philosophy: Spinoza*, trans. Martin Joughin (New York: Zone Books, 1992) and *Difference and Repetition*.

6. See Deleuze, "Seminar on Scholasticism and Spinoza," 14 January 1974, www.webdeleuze.com; and *Difference and Repetition*, 302–4.

7. See Adrian Johnston, *Žižek's Ontology: A Transcendental Materialist Theory of Subjectivity* (Evanston, IL: Northwestern University Press, 2008).

8. Notably many specialists on the Medieval material point out the proximity of Scotus and his predecessor Aquinas on some of the ontological issues according to which Deleuze would separate them, although these scholars then formulate other strong distinctions. See, for example, the works cited in n. 4 above and, especially relevant for what follows, Rudi te Velde, "Metaphysics and the Ques-

tion of Creation: Thomas Aquinas, Duns Scotus and Us," in *Belief and Metaphysics*, ed. Conor Cunningham and Peter M. Candler (London: SCM Press, 2007); and Giorgio Pini, "Scotus on Assertion and the Copula: A Comparison with Aquinas," in *Medieval Theories of Assertive and Non-Assertive Language*, ed. A. Maierù and L. Valente (Florence: Olschki, 2004). The former argues for Aquinas's ontology as ultimately superior to and more properly ontological than Scotus's.

9. Gilles Deleuze and Félix Guattari, *Anti-Oedipus: Capitalism and Schizophrenia*, trans. Mark Seem, Robert Hurley, and Helen R. Lane (Minneapolis: University of Minnesota Press, 1983); Deleuze and Guattari, *A Thousand Plateaus: Capitalism and Schizophrenia*, trans. Brian Massumi (Minneapolis: University of Minnesota Press, 1987); Deleuze and Guattari, *Kafka: Toward a Minor Literature*, trans. Dana Polan (Minneapolis: University of Minnesota Press, 1986); and Deleuze and Guattari, *What Is Philosophy?* trans. Hugh Tomlinson and Graham Burchell (New York: Columbia University Press, 1994).

10. Žižek, *Organs without Bodies*.

11. See Joe Hughes, *Deleuze and the Genesis of Representation* (London: Continuum, 2008); and A. Kiarina Kordela, "Dialectics and Structuralism as Valences," unpublished essay.

12. Such minor states are nonetheless quite distinct from the domain of "affect studies" and its concerns with negative emotions. At issue are states of being quite indifferent to the human, as opposed to human emotions. Questions of constructedness and agency are almost entirely beside the point.

13. Alain Badiou, *Deleuze: The Clamor of Being*, trans. Louise Burchill (Minneapolis: University of Minnesota Press, 2000), 46.

14. See Joshua Delpech-Ramey and Paul A. Harris, eds. "Spiritual Politics after Deleuze," special issue, *SubStance* 39:1 (2010); and selections from *Collapse: Philosophical Research and Development* 3 (2007), especially Robin Mackay's helpful "Editorial Introduction" (17–30), which gives a detailed overview and background framing of Deleuze's early essay (from 1946) "Mathesis, Science, and Philosophy," also included in the same volume (140–55). See also Joshua Delpech-Ramey, *The Hermetic Deleuze: Philosophy and Spiritual Ordeal* (Durham, NC: Duke University Press, forthcoming); and especially Christian Kerslake's *Deleuze and the Unconscious* (London: Continuum, 2007) and its compelling argument that Deleuze's model of the unconscious has more in common with the Jungian unconscious and with Bergson's concept of memory, as opposed to duration, than it does with Freud. This notion of a pure memory outside the parameters of duration is entirely in keeping with the discussion of eternity and the third synthesis of time in what follows.

15. Deleuze, *Difference and Repetition*, 115.

16. In this regard, I would concur with Tim Clark's insightful discussion of how "the inobservability of structure" is an "insistent problem" for Deleuze. See Clark, "Deleuze and Structuralism: Towards a Geometry of Sufficient Reason," in *Deleuze and Philosophy: The Difference Engineer*, ed. Keith Ansell Pearson (London: Routledge, 1997). Clark writes that "what is interesting about Deleuze's ungrounding of the structuralist model is that he does not immediately move to a dynamical systems model, nor does he simply reintroduce the ontological time of the turbulent flux. Rather, the model is overturned through the discovery of a *logical time* immanent in the space of the structure, in that coherent *logical space* in which structuralism grounds itself" (69, my emphasis).

17. See Deleuze, "Mathesis, Science, and Philosophy," where he writes: "Everyday life traces its path within the objectivity of the sensible; objects are outside of us, they owe us nothing, they are their own signification," (148).

18. See Mackay, "Editorial Introduction," 25.

19. For an extraordinary contemporary exploration of what constitutes this thingness of objects, see Jane Bennett, *Vibrant Matter: A Political Ecology of Things* (Durham, NC: Duke University Press, 2010). I would argue that the phenomenological tradition also takes up this question quite probingly, and sometimes in spite of its more overt human perceptive orientation. Sartre is discussed in what follows, but another good example is the discussion of rock-being in Martin Heidegger, *The Fundamental Concepts of Metaphysics: World, Finitude, Solitude*, trans. William McNeill and Nicholas Walker (Bloomington: Indiana University Press, 1995).

20. Quentin Meillassoux, *After Finitude: An Essay on the Necessity of Contingency*, trans. Ray Brassier (London: Continuum, 2008); Ray Brassier, *Nihil Unbound: Enlightenment and Extinction* (Basingstoke, UK: Palgrave Macmillan, 2007).

21. See blogs such as *Speculative Heresy* (http:/speculativeheresy.wordpress.com/), *Larval Subjects* (http:/larvalsubjects.wordpress.com), *Object-Oriented Philosophy* (http:/doctorzamalek2.wordpress.com/), *Networkologies* (http:/networkologies.wordpress.com/), *Speculations* (http:/www.publicpraxis.com/speculations/), *Another Heidegger Blog* (http:/anotherheideggerblog.blogspot.com/), *Naught Thought* (http:/naughtthought.wordpress.com/), and *Philosophy in a Time of Error* (http:/philosophyinatimeoferror.wordpress.com/). These blogs do not all engage equally with OOO, and some favor other "branches" of speculative realist thought. For straight OOO, see the blogs of its primary four practitioners.

22. Deleuze, "Mathesis, Science, and Philosophy," 146.

23. Ibid., 153.

24. Deleuze, *The Logic of Sense*, "Twenty-second Series—Porcelain and Volcano," 154–61, and appendix 5, "Zola and the Crack-Up," 321–33.

25. Giorgio Agamben, *Homo Sacer: Sovereign Power and Bare Life*, trans. Daniel Heller-Roazen (Stanford, CA: Stanford University Press, 1998). For a detailed consideration of Agamben's work on life in conjunction with Aristotelian thought and also Marx and contemporary biology, see the work of Melinda Cooper, especially "The Living and the Dead: Variations on *De Anima*," *Angelaki* 7:3 (2002), 81–104. Agamben himself considers Deleuze's "vitalism" alongside Aristotle and Foucault in "Absolute Immanence," in *Potentialities*, trans. Daniel Heller-Roazen (Stanford, CA: Stanford University Press, 1999) but gives too much exclusive emphasis, in my opinion, to Deleuze's final essay, "Immanence: A Life," in *Pure Immanence: Essays on a Life*, trans. Anne Boyman (New York: Zone Books, 2001).

26. Indeed, insofar as Foucault's *The Order of Things* might be seen as a polemic against an easy humanist vision of life and much more about systems of classification, so too Deleuze's work from this period falls under the same banner. See Michel Foucault, *The Order of Things: An Archaeology of the Human Sciences* (New York: Vintage Books, 1994).

27. Keith Ansell Pearson, *Germinal Life: The Difference and Repetition of Deleuze* (London: Routledge, 1999), 84.

28. See Eugene Thacker, *After Life* (Chicago: University of Chicago Press, 2010). The title of this introduction, "Deleuze's Scholasticism," is in fact a subtitle in Thacker's exceptional analysis of Deleuze and Medieval thought in *After Life*, and although I did not adopt it consciously from Thacker, I am sure it was in no small way due to the influence of Thacker's much more detailed study of the conjunction between Deleuze's work and medieval philosophy. I am also influenced by the model of Erin Felicia Labbie's *Lacan's Medievalism* (Minneapolis: University of Minnesota Press, 2006).

29. See the discussion in chapter 3 of Deleuze's distinction between and elevation of concepts over categories in his course lectures.

30. A few highlights from this work include Manuel DeLanda, *Intensive Science and Virtual Philosophy* (London: Continuum, 2005); Brian Massumi, *Parables for the Virtual: Movement, Affect, Sensation* (Durham, NC: Duke University Press, 2002); Steven Shaviro, *Without Criteria: Kant, Whitehead, Deleuze, and Aesthetics* (Cambridge, MA: MIT Press, 2009); Antonio R. Damasio, *Looking for Spinoza: Joy, Sorrow, and the Feeling Brain* (Orlando, FL: Harcourt, 2003); John Protevi, *Political Affect: Connecting the Social and the Somatic* (Minneapolis: University of Minnesota Press, 2009); Anne Sauvagnargues, *Deleuze: L'empirisme transcendental* (Paris: Presses Universitaires de France, 2009); and Simon Duffy, ed., *Virtual Mathematics: The Logic of Difference* (Manchester: Clinamen, 2006).

31. In addition to the works cited in the preceding note, two exemplary early discussions of the Deleuzian virtual are Brian Massumi, *A User's Guide to Capital-*

ism and Schizophrenia: Deviations from Deleuze and Guattari (Cambridge, MA: MIT Press, 1992); and Constantin Boundas, "Deleuze-Bergson: An Ontology of the Virtual," in *Deleuze: A Critical Reader*, ed. Paul Patton (Oxford: Blackwell, 1996).

32. Some years ago, when teaching a graduate seminar partially devoted to *Anti-Oedipus*, I resorted to bringing in each week a different acknowledgment by a major Deleuze scholar of the difficulty of defining the body without organs, as the students found this term in particular excessively frustrating. I am not attempting to reproduce such a compendium here.

33. For detailed discussions of the affirmative potential as well as the pitfalls of considering psychoanalysis a distinctly Jewish science, see Yosef Hayim Yerushalmi, *Freud's Moses: Judaism Terminable and Interminable* (New Haven, CT: Yale University Press, 1991); and Jacques Derrida, *Archive Fever: A Freudian Impression*, trans. Eric Prenowitz (Chicago: University of Chicago Press, 1996).

34. Exemplary criticisms by major Deleuze scholars include, of Žižek on Deleuze, Daniel W. Smith, "The Inverse Side of the Structure: Žižek on Deleuze and Lacan," *Criticism* 46:4 (Fall 2004), 635–50; and, of Hallward on Deleuze, Joshua Delpech-Ramey, "Without Art: Peter Hallward's *Out of This World: Deleuze and the Philosophy of Creation*," *Journal for Culture and Religious Theory* 8:3 (Fall 2007), 136–45. The literature on Badiou and Deleuze is too immense to cite here. Apart from chapter 5 and the concluding section of chapter 3, I do not address this relation in detail in this study, but it is one of the focal points of my forthcoming *At Odds with Badiou: Politics, Dialectics, and Religion from Sartre and Deleuze to Lacan and Agamben* (New York: Columbia University Press), especially the chapter "Deleuze, Badiou, and Royal Thought," which takes Badiou's claim that Deleuze is a royal thinker at face value but uses that at once to defend Deleuze and to emphasize his affinities with Badiou.

35. Deleuze, *Expressionism in Philosophy*, 63.

36. See Pini, "Univocity in Scotus's *Quaestiones super Metaphysicam*."

37. This is extrapolated and paraphrased from Deleuze's examples in his "Seminar on Scholasticism and Spinoza," discussed in detail in chapter 3. On the divine trace, see Thomas Aquinas, *Summa Theologica*, trans. Fathers of the English Dominican Province (Notre Dame, IN: Christian Classics, 1981), 1a q. 45, a 7.

38. See John Milbank, "The Soul of Reciprocity, Part Two: Reciprocity Granted," *Modern Theology* 17:4 (October 2001), 485–507; and Slavoj Žižek and John Milbank, *The Monstrosity of Christ: Paradox or Dialectic?*, ed. Creston Davis (Cambridge, MA: MIT Press, 2009). For Milbank's detailed discussion of questions of analogy and dialectic, see esp. 141–42, 173–216. My overall reading of Aquinas and dialectic is largely in accord with Milbank's, though his reading does not go into

as much detail on Deleuze specifically and also gets into the more mystical terrain of Eckhart, which I have avoided.

39. Deleuze, *Difference and Repetition*, 88–89.

40. This is where I take some issue with the primary thesis of Sean Bowden's exceptional new book on *The Logic of Sense*, namely that this work demonstrates the "ontological priority of events over substance." While this argument is certainly more valid for *The Logic of Sense* than for *Difference and Repetition*, it nonetheless does not fully reckon with the conundrum that, though Deleuze indeed gives a privileged place to events in *The Logic of Sense*—not one, however, that I have emphasized in this study—it is not clear, and to my mind seems unlikely, that their *emergence* is thus of the first order, for it appears on the contrary to be distinctly of the second, which again, for Deleuze, makes it superior. It is this reversal of the intuitive principles of hierarchy while maintaining a no less strict hierarchy that makes Deleuze both proximate to and ultimately distinct from the Scholastic thinkers in question here. This study does not engage further with Bowden's important thesis simply because it appeared as my text was already in final form and format. See Sean Bowden, *The Priority of Events: Deleuze's "Logic of Sense"* (Edinburgh: Edinburgh University Press, 2011).

41. Aquinas, *Summa Theologica*, 1a q. 10, a. 1. In the *Summa contra Gentiles*, trans. Fathers of the English Dominican Province (London: Washbourne, 1914–38), Aquinas puts it thus: "God, therefore, is without beginning and end, having His whole being at once. In this consists the nature of eternity" (I.15).

42. Peter Hallward, *Out of This World: Deleuze and the Philosophy of Creation* (London: Verso, 2006), 137. Hallward puts this in similar terms, here evoking Corbin and Spinoza, when he writes: "To put this in more explicitly theophanic terms: God expresses himself in the creatural, the creatural is nothing other than God, and the creatural offers an adequate path that leads to God. Yet to perceive God it is nonetheless necessary to follow this path, i.e. to move out past the creatural as such. What lives in the creature is not in the creature, precisely. . . . As Deleuze's contemporary Henry Corbin explains, absolute creativity (or God) 'cannot be an object (an objective given). . . .' Via Spinoza, Deleuze sets out from much the same point of departure" (57).

43. Ibid., 152–53.

44. Ideally there would be another term in this picture, which is the notion of emanation, or the question of "creation as emanation," to cite the title of a very helpful book by Thérèse Bonin about the origin of diversity in Albert the Great, Aquinas's teacher. See Thérèse Bonin, *Creation as Emanation: The Origin of Diversity in Albert the Great's "On the Causes and the Procession of the Universe"* (Notre Dame, IN: University of Notre Dame Press, 2001). It seems that emanation

may be closer to what Hallward is talking about by creation. See also Aquinas, *Summa Theologica*, 1a q. 44, a. 2, and *Summa Theologica*, 1a q. 45 in its entirety.

45. Aquinas, *Summa contra Gentiles*, II.17. He also writes in the third paragraph of chapter 17, "In creation, therefore, neither motion nor change exists."

46. Ibid.

47. Ibid., II.19.

48. Ibid.

49. Deleuze, *Difference and Repetition*, 183.

50. For Hallward's discussion of Deleuze and history, see *Out of This World*, 100–103. For an excellent discussion of this same topic alongside a detailed reading of the three syntheses of time, see Jay Lampert, *Deleuze and Guattari's Philosophy of History* (London: Continuum, 2006).

51. Aquinas, *Summa contra Gentiles*, II.19.

52. Aquinas, *Summa Theologica*, 1a q. 45, a 2.

53. Deleuze, *The Logic of Sense*, 1.

Chapter 1. Solid Dialectic in Sartre and Deleuze

1. Jacques Lacan, *The Four Fundamental Concepts of Psychoanalysis*, trans. Alan Sheridan (London: W. W. Norton, 1981), 95.

2. Jean-Paul Sartre, *Being and Nothingness*, trans. Hazel E. Barnes (New York: Washington Square, 1984), 61.

3. By way of argument against Husserl's notion of the transcendental ego, Sartre invokes Hegel to assert that consciousness of oneself—that produced, for example, by the feeling of shame—is only possible as reflected from the gaze of another; we do not start from the self and go outward to intuit a world as in Descartes and Husserl, but rather our world is defined in dialectical relation to an other. See the section titled "The Look" in *Being and Nothingness*, 340–400.

4. Fredric Jameson, *Sartre: The Origins of a Style* (New Haven, CT: Yale University Press, 1961), x.

5. This opposition is drawn out in the course of Sartre's study *The Transcendence of the Ego*, trans. Forrest Williams and Robert Kirkpatrick (New York: Farrar, Straus, and Giroux, 1957). For a helpful account of Sartre's early philosophical writings, see Dominick LaCapra, "Early Theoretical Studies: Art Is an Unreality," in *Jean-Paul Sartre*, ed. Harold Bloom (Philadelphia: Chelsea House, 2001).

6. Sartre, *Being and Nothingness*, 509.

7. See Maurice Merleau-Ponty, "The Intertwining—the Chiasm," in *The Visible and the Invisible*, trans. Alphonso Lingis (Evanston, IL: Northwestern University Press), 1968.

8. Jean-Paul Sartre, *The Wall*, trans. Lloyd Alexander (New York: New Directions, 1975). See especially the stories "The Wall" and "The Room."

9. Jameson, *Sartre*, 109.

10. See Maurice Merleau-Ponty, *Phenomenology of Perception*, trans. Colin Smith (London: Routledge, 2000), 57–62, 78–79.

11. Deleuze, *Difference and Repetition*, 59–60. For the same argument, see Deleuze, *The Logic of Sense*. There he writes that "Platonic dialectic is neither a dialectic of contradiction nor of contrariety, but a dialectic of rivalry (*amphisbetesis*), a dialectic of rivals and suitors" (254). Deleuze follows Bergson, whose theory of temporality, as outlined in *Matter and Memory*, trans. N. M. Paul and W. S. Palmer (New York: Zone Books, 1991), rests on the distinction between perception and recollection as attributes that differ in kind and not degree (67). See also Deleuze's *Bergsonism*, trans. Hugh Tomlinson and Barbara Habberjam (New York: Zone Books, 1991).

12. Deleuze, *The Logic of Sense*, 253–54.

13. For discussions of dualism and dialectic in Deleuze, see Fredric Jameson, "Marxism and Dualism in Deleuze" in *A Deleuzian Century?*, ed. Ian Buchanan (Durham, NC: Duke University Press, 1999; reprinted in *Valences of the Dialectic*); and Ian Buchanan, *Deleuzism: A Metacommentary* (Durham, NC: Duke University Press, 2000). Although they are formulated in very different terms, I am indebted to the essays collected in Fredric Jameson's *Valences of the Dialectic* (London: Verso, 2009). Indeed my very framework for reading Deleuze would not have been thinkable without my years of study with Professor Jameson and in particular the seminar on the dialectic that he gave in 1996. In the introductory essay to this collection, "Three Names of the Dialectic," Jameson writes: "[I]t now seems possible to abstract an emptier mechanism from the stages of Hegelian logic, one formalistic enough to claim application to an impressive variety of material and disciplinary, social and ideological, contents. In fact, that was exactly what structuralism achieved with the binary opposition, and this is perhaps the moment to celebrate that breakthrough, with which, in my opinion, and unbeknownst to the structuralists themselves, dialectical thought was able to reinvent itself in our time" (17). Although the rest of Jameson's book develops, at least implicitly, more pointed criticisms of such a formalism, of Aristotle, and—in a complicated fashion—of Deleuze, my project nonetheless might be framed as building on the positive implications of Jameson's statement above. It also develops his similarly double-edged claim, further in the same chapter, that "indeed, even the inaugural dead end of metaphysical dualism may well turn out to generate more productive developments than we have first suspected" (19).

14. I owe this turn of phrase to the study by mathematician G. Spenser Brown, *Laws of Form* (New York: Bantam Books, 1972).

15. Sartre, *Being and Nothingness*, 167.

16. Ibid.

17. Jameson, *Sartre*, 53–54.

18. Deleuze, *The Logic of Sense*, 5.

19. I owe this formulation to Rocco Gangle.

20. See Sartre's *Being and Nothingness*, 173.

21. Émile Bréhier, *La Théorie des incorporels dans l'ancien stoïcisme* (Paris: Vrin, 1970), 11–13, qtd. in Deleuze, *The Logic of Sense*, 5.

22. Sartre, *Being and Nothingness*, 167.

23. Ibid., 174. Sartre writes that "the past is given as a for-itself *become* in-itself. . . . In one sense then the past, which is at the same time for-itself and in-itself, *resembles* value or self" (174). By yet another chiasmatic logic, we might reverse the neat mapping of Chronos with in-itself and Aion with for-itself by returning to Sartre's reflections on Husserl in his *Transcendence of the Ego* from 1936. He outlines a four-part process of reflection that ends in Husserl's phenomenological reduction. First, the "I" exists, then it gains a special intuition, which leads it to an act of self-reflection, where the reflected consciousness "becomes the object of the reflecting consciousness without ceasing to affirm its own object (a chair, a mathematical truth, etc.)" (52–53). Without analyzing this example with the rigor it would demand, I would question whether the reflecting consciousness that falls into the space of phenomenological reduction can do so anywhere but in the present. Is this the blindness and insight of Sartrean and Husserlian consciousness, that the epiphanic perception of the for-itself and of the phenomenological reduction can only be perceived in a Chronos-like pure present? Does this give a new valence to Deleuze's general demotion of the present in *The Logic of Sense*? This is the claim in the discussion of *Difference and Repetition* in part 2 of this study and the more general claim of part 3.

24. Sartre, *Being and Nothingness*, 63–64.

25. Deleuze, *The Logic of Sense*, 23. Also see "Eating Well, or the Calculation of the Subject: An Interview with Jacques Derrida," in *Who Comes after the Subject*, ed. Eduardo Cadava, Peter Connor, and Jean-Luc Nancy (New York: Routledge, 1991).

26. This is not entirely uncharacteristic for Deleuze, who repeatedly echoes the necessity of beginning in the middle in his "On the Superiority of Anglo-American Literature," in Gilles Deleuze and Claire Parnet, *Dialogues*, trans. Hugh Tomlinson and Barbara Habberjam (New York: Columbia University Press, 1987).

27. Sartre, *Being and Nothingness*, 774.

28. Ibid., 777.

29. For an interesting and very different sort of phenomenology of the space of

writing, see Diana Fuss, *The Sense of an Interior: Four Writers and the Rooms That Shaped Them* (New York: Routledge, 2004).

30. Deleuze and Guattari, *A Thousand Plateaus*, 414–15.

31. This double or hybrid quality of the smiths is a virtue to the extent that the metal they work with has a fluidity that links it to all matter: "Metallurgy is the consciousness or thought of the matter-flow, and metal the correlate of this consciousness. . . . Not everything is metal, but metal is everywhere. Metal is the conductor of all matter" (ibid., 411). In the same passage, Deleuze and Guattari oppose metal to stone, linking metal alone to thought. It is my contention that there is also a thought of stone that is deeply resonant with Deleuzian ontology.

32. For a sustained attack on Sartre's gendered notions of holes and slime, see Christine Pierce, "Holes and Slime: Sexism in Sartre's Psychoanalysis" in *Immovable Laws, Irresistible Rights: Natural Law, Moral Rights, and Feminist Ethics* (Lawrence: University Press of Kansas, 2000).

33. The damning passage on slime and the feminine appears at the end of *Being and Nothingness*:

> At this instant I suddenly understand the snare of the slimy: it is a fluidity which holds me and which compromises me; I can not *slide* on this slime, all its suction cups hold me back; it can not slide over me, it clings to me like a leech. The sliding however is not simply denied as in the case of the solid; it is *degraded*. The slimy seems to lend itself to me, it invites me, for a body of slime at rest is not noticeably distinct from a body of very dense liquid. But it is a trap. The sliding is *sucked* in by the sliding substance, and it leaves its traces upon me. The slime is like a liquid seen in a nightmare, where all its properties are animated by a sort of life and turn back against me. Slime is the revenge of the In-itself. A sickly-sweet feminine revenge which will be symbolized on another level by the quality "sugary." This is why the sugar-like sweetness to the taste—an indelible sweetness, which remains indefinitely in the mouth even after swallowing—perfectly completes the essence of the slimy; it symbolizes the sugary death of the For-itself (like the wasp which sinks into the jam and drowns in it). (776–77)

34. See Luce Irigaray, "The 'Mechanics' of Fluids," in *This Sex Which Is Not One*, trans. Catherine Porter with Carolyn Burke (Ithaca, NY: Cornell University Press, 1985). For an analysis of a masculine fluid economy, see Alphonso Lingis, "Fluid Economy," in *Foreign Bodies* (New York: Routledge, 1994).

Chapter 2. Toward a Feminist Philosophy of Mind

1. Rosi Braidotti, "Toward a New Nomadism: Feminist Deleuzian Tracks; or, Metaphysics and Metabolism," in *Gilles Deleuze and the Theater of Philosophy*, ed. Constantin V. Boundas and Dorothea Olkowski (New York: Routledge, 1994). See also Rosi Braidotti, *Patterns of Dissonance* (New York: Routledge: 1991); and Braidotti, *Nomadic Subjects: Embodiment and Sexual Difference in Contemporary Feminist Theory* (New York: Columbia University Press, 1994).

2. For a superb treatment of these questions in eighteenth-century French philosophy and literature, see Natania Meeker, *Voluptuous Philosophy: Literary Materialism in the French Enlightenment* (New York: Fordham University Press, 2006). "Voluptuous" is a term that Klossowski evokes repeatedly in his study of Nietzsche. See discussion below.

3. Braidotti, "Toward a New Nomadism," 161.

4. Ibid., 163.

5. For a detailed reading of the body as an interplay of forces, especially as it relates to Nietzsche's active and reactive forces, and Deleuze's reading of this in his study of Nietzsche, see Dorothea Olkowski, "Nietzsche's Dice Throw: Tragedy, Nihilism, and the Body without Organs," in *Gilles Deleuze and the Theater of Philosophy*, ed. Constantin V. Boundas and Dorothea Olkowski (New York: Routledge, 1994), especially where she writes: "The body is not a medium and does not designate substance: it expresses the relationship between forces. The term 'body' does not simply refer, for Deleuze, to the psychophysiological bodies of human beings. Bodies may be chemical, biological, social, or political, and the distinction between these modes is not ontological" (120). In this study, I in fact attempt to think Deleuzian distinction as ontological.

6. Braidotti, "Toward a New Nomadism," 169.

7. Gillian Rose, *Feminism and Geography: The Limits of Geographical Knowledge* (Minneapolis: University of Minnesota Press, 1993), 146.

8. Gilles Deleuze, *Cinema 2: The Time-Image*, trans. Hugh Tomlinson and Robert Galeta (Minneapolis: University of Minnesota Press, 1989), 189.

9. Braidotti, "Toward a New Nomadism," 163.

10. Ibid., 165.

11. Deleuze, *Cinema 2: The Time-Image*, 205. On this topic, see also Gregory Flaxman, ed., *The Brain Is the Screen: Deleuze and the Philosophy of Cinema* (Minneapolis: University of Minnesota Press, 2000).

12. See Ian Buchanan and Claire Colebrook, eds., *Deleuze and Feminist Theory* (Edinburgh: Edinburgh University Press, 2000), in which this essay originally appeared.

13. Elizabeth Grosz, "Intensities and Flows," in *Volatile Bodies: Toward a*

Corporeal Feminism (Bloomington: Indiana University Press, 1994), 160. See also Grosz, "A Thousand Tiny Sexes: Feminism and Rhizomatics," which forms, along with Braidotti's essay, the section titled "Becoming-Woman," in *Gilles Deleuze and the Theatre of Philosophy*, ed. Constantin V. Boundas and Dorothea Olkowski (New York: Routledge, 1994). With slight variations, the two pieces by Grosz take up basically the same argument.

14. Here it is important to note that corporeal and incorporeal, embodiment and disembodiment, are not strictly oppositional. For more on the question of the incorporeal in Deleuze and Sartre (and its causal rather than oppositional relation to the corporeal), see my " 'To Cut Too Deeply and Not Enough': Violence and the Incorporeal," *Parallax* 9:1 (2003): 14–27.

15. Grosz, "Intensities and Flows," 164–65.

16. Gilles Deleuze, *Bergsonism*, trans. Barbara Habberjam and Hugh Tomlinson (New York: Zone Books, 1991), 25.

17. See Benedict de Spinoza, *Ethics*, trans. R. H. M. Elwes (New York: Dover, 1955), part 2, "On the Nature and Origin of the Mind," especially propositions 15, 16, and 17 (pp. 97–99). Spinoza writes, for example, that "although the external bodies, by which the human body has once been affected, be no longer in existence, the mind will nevertheless regard them as present, as often as this action of the body is repeated" proposition 17 (p. 99). Sartre makes a similar claim in *The Imaginary: A Phenomenological Psychology of the Imagination*, trans. Jonathan Webber (New York: Routledge, 2004).

18. Gilles Deleuze, *Expressionism in Philosophy: Spinoza*, trans. Martin Joughin (New York: Zone Books, 1992), 201–2. For helpful analyses of Deleuze's readings of Spinoza, see Michael Hardt, *Gilles Deleuze: An Apprenticeship in Philosophy* (Minneapolis: University of Minnesota Press), 1993, especially 56–111; and Moira Gatens, "Through a Spinozist Lens: Ethology, Difference, Power," in *Deleuze: A Critical Reader*, ed. Paul Patton (Oxford: Blackwell, 1996), 162–87.

19. Genevieve Lloyd, *Spinoza and the Ethics* (New York: Routledge, 1996), 125.

20. Such an expansive vision of Spinoza's notion of mind parallels and complements Moira Gaten's analysis, in *Imaginary Bodies: Ethics, Power and Corporeality* (New York: Routledge, 1996), of how Spinoza complicates "embodiment": "When the term 'embodiment' is used in the context of Spinoza's thought it should be understood to refer not simply to an individual body but to the *total* affective context of that body" (131). In the same fashion, mind would also refer to the total affective context.

21. Exemplary of this is the work of Judith Butler, who, like Braidotti and Grosz, also charts out the dense field of relations that comprise the mind-body duality. See especially *Bodies That Matter: On the Discursive Limits of "Sex"*

(New York: Routledge, 1993). I have not given more attention to Butler's work here because, unlike Braidotti and Grosz, her work is more in conversation with Derrida, Foucault, and Hegel than with Deleuze. See also Juliet Flower MacCannell and Laura Zakarin, eds., *Thinking Bodies* (Stanford, CA: Stanford University Press, 1994).

22. Grosz, "Intensities and Flows," 179.

23. Lloyd, *Spinoza and the Ethics*, 126–27.

24. A cautionary note is in order, as this radical potential for mind-body disjunction is not without its pitfalls. In *Technologies of the Gendered Body: Reading Cyborg Women* (Durham, NC: Duke University Press, 1996), Anne Balsamo illustrates how the potential for body alteration or disembodiment contained in the cyber or in virtual reality often works to reinscribe the most traditional of gender, racial, and sexual norms. As Balsamo writes, "[T]here is plenty of evidence to suggest that a reconstructed body does not guarantee a reconstructed cultural identity. Nor does 'freedom from the body,' imply that people will exercise the 'freedom to be' any other kind of body than the one they already enjoy or desire" (128). This critique notwithstanding, it seems there are positive disembodiment examples to be found, and I take up two of them at the end of this chapter. The critical difference between my examples and the cyborg/virtual reality ones is that the latter project disembodiment onto a generically ideal body, while the ones I will take up do not project disembodiment onto an ideal but negotiate it within the contours of the limited body at hand.

25. Pierre Klossowski, *Nietzsche and the Vicious Circle*, trans. Daniel W. Smith (Chicago: University of Chicago Press, 1997), 24. I have discussed this same phenomenon of sickness and its relation to the mind in a reading of different passages in Klossowski's study of Nietzsche in my "Klossowski or Thoughts-Becoming," in *Becomings: Explorations in Time, Memory, and Futures*, ed. Elizabeth Grosz (Ithaca, NY: Cornell University Press, 1999).

26. Deleuze takes up the importance of sickness in Nietzsche, but to a more limited extent than Klossowski. In *Nietzsche and Philosophy*, trans. Hugh Tomlinson (New York: Columbia University Press, 1983), he analyzes sickness in terms of power of reactive forces. I quote at length:

> What Nietzsche calls an active force is one which goes to the limit of its consequences. An active force separated from what it can do by reactive force thus becomes reactive. But does not this reactive force, in its own way, go to the limit of what it can do? . . . A reactive force can certainly be considered from different points of view. Illness, for example, separates me from what I can do, as reactive force it makes me reactive, it narrows my possibilities and condemns me to a diminished milieu to which I can do no

> more than adapt myself. But in another way, it reveals to me a new capacity, it endows me with a new will that I can make my own, going to the limit of a strange power. . . . Here we can recognise an ambivalence important to Nietzsche: all the forces whose reactive character he exposes are, a few lines or pages later, admitted to fascinate him, to be sublime because of the perspective they open up for us and because of the disturbing will to power to which they bear witness. (66)

In this passage, Deleuze overturns the hierarchy between active and reactive forces, arguing alongside Nietzsche that the reactive force of sickness can be its own form of activity and can inaugurate new and interesting states of being. Such a pronouncement is all the more interesting in light of Deleuze's own subsequent period of long convalescence and sickness before his death in 1995. One need only cite one of his latter works as a testament to the lucidity of thought produced under conditions of extreme physical hardship.

27. Ibid., 25.

28. It is not insignificant that Deleuze is one of the finest readers of Klossowski, and it is Deleuze to whom Klossowski dedicates his book on Nietzsche. It is Deleuze who describes the Klossowskian logic of opposition as a "disjunctive syntheses" and who cites Klossowski's *Nietzsche and the Vicious Circle* extensively in *Anti-Oedipus*. Above all, in his appendix to *The Logic of Sense* "Klossowski or Bodies-Language," Deleuze underscores the positive aspects of revocation. He refers to another context in which the mind and body work in disjunction, that of the pure body coupled with an impure mind and the superior disjunction of an impure body coupled with a pure mind:

> Does Klossowski simply mean that speaking prevents us from thinking about nasty things? No; the pure language which produces an impure silence is a *provocation* of the mind by the body; similarly, the impure language which produces a pure silence is a revocation of the body by the mind. . . . More precisely, what is revoked in the body? Klossowski's answer is that it is the integrity of the body, and that because of this the identity of the person is somewhat suspended and volatized. (291)

This is taken up in chapters 3 and 4.

29. Klossowski, *Nietzsche and the Vicious Circle*, 25.

30. This boundary-surpassing might take different forms when the mind-body disjunction occurs over an extended period of time and when it is consciously imposed. An example would be various practices associated with intake of food. In "The Problem of the Body in Deleuze and Guattari, Or, What Can a Body Do?," *Body and Society* 3:3 (September 1997), Ian Buchanan analyzes anorexia as an

interplay of forces or relations between food and the body. Although he discusses it in somewhat different terms than the mind-body disjunction, he describes an intensified state of being that results from a reactive relation to food: "If we are to relieve ourselves of the sometimes intolerable pressure that food places on us, we must confront food differently. But, since we cannot change what food does to us, we must change ourselves. This demands that we somehow find a new way of being, which effectively means a new way of becoming" (78–79). While Buchanan is careful to point out the negative effects of such an anorexic becoming, his analysis of the process underscores the delicacy and complexity of this gray zone of mind-body disjunction. While I have underscored the positive side of such a zone, it is clearly one of those liminal spaces that, with a slight twist, collapses into the negative and the destructive. This is not to say that positivities cannot be found even in this negative realm, but discussing them would entail a differently positioned and more nuanced analysis. A more contemporary example might be Christian Bale's comment about having dropped sixty pounds for his role in *The Machinist*: "I didn't set out to get as skinny as I did. It ended up being a very nice place to be mentally when you get that skinny." Quoted in *In Touch*, August 11, 2008, 57.

31. Klossowski, *Nietzsche and the Vicious Circle*, 30–31.

32. Such a state is, I think, captured by such films as *The Living End*, which depicts living with AIDS as the exuberant intensity of living with imminent sickness and mortality, and *Sick: The Life and Death of Bob Flanagan, Supermasochist*, which depicts the quest for extreme sadomasochistic experience alongside the succumbing to fatal cystic fibrosis.

Chapter 3. Klossowski and Orthodoxy

1. Georges Bataille, *Story of the Eye*, trans. Joachim Neugroschel (San Francisco: City Lights Books, 1987): 59–60.

2. In a rare acerbic moment, Deleuze comments in "On the Superiority of Anglo-American Literature" that "the little secret is generally reducible to a sad narcissistic and pious masturbation. . . . Georges Bataille is a very French author. He made the little secret the essence of literature, with a mother within, a priest beneath, an eye above" (47).

3. Pierre Klossowski, *"Roberte Ce Soir" and "The Revocation of the Edict of Nantes,"* trans. Austryn Wainhouse (New York: Marion Boyars, 1989), 49–50, translation modified. For a detailed analysis of Klossowski's hospitality trilogy, see Tracy McNulty's *The Hostess: Hospitality, Ethics, and the Expropriation of Identity* (Minneapolis: University of Minnesota Press, 2007); and my *The Delirium of Praise: Bataille, Blanchot, Deleuze, Foucault, Klossowski* (Baltimore: Johns Hopkins University Press, 2001).

4. Gilles Deleuze, "Klossowski or Bodies-Language," in *The Logic of Sense*, 281–82, translation slightly modified. See *Logique du sens* (Paris: Éditions de Minuit, 1969), 327.

5. Klossowski, *Roberte Ce Soir*, 97. The Latin is translated with some license. For a discussion of Klossowski's license in employing this term, a term itself generally equated with linguistic slippage or poetic license, see McNulty's *The Hostess: Hospitality, Ethics, and the Expropriation of Identity*, which provides a superb overview of Klossowski's hospitality trilogy with particular attention to the figure of the hostess and the excess she embodies: improper to law, to religion, and ultimately to the host himself, the hostess is in McNulty's reading at the core of the relation of hospitality and, beyond that, at the very heart of being.

6. Klossowski, *Roberte Ce Soir*, 119.

7. I make this argument in my *The Delirium of Praise* though here revise it somewhat, developing the theological hesitations I voice there. See esp. 109.

8. Deleuze, "Seminar on Scholasticism and Spinoza." 14 January 1974, www.webdeleuze.com

9. See Deleuze and Guattari, *Anti-Oedipus*; Jacques Lacan, *The Other Side of Psychoanalysis*, trans. Russell Grigg (New York: Norton, 2007); and Jean-François Lyotard, *Libidinal Economy*, trans. Iain Hamilton Grant (Bloomington: Indiana University Press, 1993).

10. I outline this argument and cite Lyotard's marvelous gloss of it in chapter 6 of *The Delirium of Praise*. In addition, chapter 5 of that work addresses the feminist potential of Roberte's participation in her attacks.

11. Pierre Klossowski, *La Monnaie vivante*, photographs by Pierre Zucca (Paris: Éditions Joëlle Eric Losfeld, 1994), 26, my translation.

12. Deleuze, "Seminar on Scholasticism and Spinoza."

13. Benedict de Spinoza, *A Theologico-Political Treatise*, trans. R. H. M. Elwes (New York: Dover, 1951), 27.

14. See Pierre Klossowski, *The Baphomet*, trans. Sophie Hawkes and Stephen Sartarelli (New York: Marsilio, 1988).

15. Deleuze, "Seminar on Scholasticism and Spinoza."

16. See Deleuze and Guattari, *A Thousand Plateaus*.

17. Deleuze, "Seminar on Scholasticism and Spinoza."

18. Roland Barthes, "Myth Today," in *Mythologies*, trans. Annette Lavers (New York: Hill and Wang, 1972): 109–59.

19. Deleuze, *Difference and Repetition*, 303. Giorgio Pini makes the important point that Scotus, especially in his *Questions on the Categories* and *Questions on the Sophistical Refutations*, adheres to the English tradition that, from the middle of the thirteenth century onward, asserted that being, when considered from the perspective of logic (the categories), is equivocal, whereas being considered from a

metaphysical lens is analogical. See Pini, "Univocity in Scotus's *Quaestiones super Metaphysicam*," 10, 18, 22–23. Pini's essay gives the full Latin citations for these works, which do not have full English translations, and an analysis of the shift toward univocity that we see in *Quaestiones super Metaphysicam* and late works.

20. Deleuze, *Difference and Repetition*, 303.

21. Ibid., 304.

22. John Milbank, "The Soul of Reciprocity, Part Two: Reciprocity Granted," *Modern Theology* 17:4 (October 2001): 505n2.

23. See Jean-Paul Sartre, *Critique of Dialectical Reason: Theory of Practical Ensembles*, trans. Alan Sheridan-Smith (London: NLB, 1976): "But it is man who invests things with his own *praxis*, his own future and his own knowledge. If he could encounter pure matter in experience, he would have to be either a god or a stone" (181–82).

24. See not only Alain Badiou, *Number and Numbers*, trans. Robin Mackay (London: Polity, 2008), but also the discussion in his *Logics of Worlds* of the current world order as being governed by a dual discourse of bodies and languages. Badiou critiques this world order, what he labels "democratic materialism," for being stuck in the two terms of "bodies" and "languages" and not attuned to the third term, which is the truth that surges forth as a rupture and exception from the first two. This is at odds with Badiou's more Klossowskian emphasis on the pure two (such as the love relation) in other writings. See Alain Badiou, *Logics of Worlds*, trans. Alberto Toscano (London: Continuum, 2009).

25. Alain Badiou, *The Century*, trans. Alberto Toscano (London: Polity, 2007), 59–60.

26. Alain Badiou, *Deleuze: The Clamor of Being*, trans. Louise Burchill (Minneapolis: University of Minnesota Press, 2000), 27.

27. Deleuze, *The Logic of Sense*, 29.

28. Badiou, *Deleuze: The Clamor of Being*, 28.

29. Ibid., 36.

30. The epithet "reactionary radicalism" is used provocatively, but in this instance "reactionary" refers to Badiou's specific embrace of terms under fire in much contemporary parlance (truth, universalism, the pure love of the heterosexual couple, and so forth) and his interest in extremely taboo topics, such as the way National Socialism might initially appear to resemble a truth process. Even Badiou's atheistic espousal of the Apostle Paul has a parallel with Octave's Sadean-inflected fascination with the Catholic Church. Yet both engage simultaneously in a radical reflection on the limits and potentialities of the dialectic. For more on this oxymoronic quality in Badiou and its relation to number, see my forthcoming *At Odds with Badiou: Politics, Dialectics, and Religion from Sartre and Deleuze to Lacan and Agamben* (New York: Columbia University Press).

Chapter 4. Cinema and the Tableau Vivant

1. Michel Foucault, "Theatrum Philosophicum," in *Language, Counter-Memory, Practice*, trans. Donald F. Bouchard and Sherry Simon (Ithaca, NY: Cornell University Press, 1977), 165.

2. Klossowski, *The Revocation of the Edict of Nantes*, 97–98.

3. Klossowski, *La Monnaie vivante* (Paris: Eric Losfeld, 1970), unpaginated [84].

4. Klossowski, *The Revocation of the Edict of Nantes*, 100.

5. Deleuze, *Cinema 2: The Time-Image*, 109.

6. Ibid., 104.

7. Damian Sutton's *Photography, Cinema, Memory: The Crystal Image of Time* (Minneapolis: University of Minnesota Press, 2009) takes up the relation of mobility and immobility in the cinema books with considerable subtlety, especially as this in turn relates to the photograph. He writes that "where Barthes saw immobility as a negative value, a semblance of death, using Deleuze we can see this as a seed for nonchronological time—the 'non-organic life which grips the world' " (60). Karen Beckman's *Crash: Cinema and the Politics of Speed and Stasis* (Durham, NC: Duke University Press, 2010), takes up some of the same questions, but without the focus on Deleuze.

8. Gilles Deleuze, *Cinema 1: The Movement-Image*, trans. Hugh Tomlinson and Barbara Habberjam (Minneapolis: University of Minnesota Press, 1986), 56.

9. The concluding chapters of this book attempt to push past this to think an immobility that is purely stuck and *not* in flux, yet not without its positive potential.

10. Jean-François Lyotard, "Acinema," in *The Lyotard Reader*, ed. Andrew Benjamin (Oxford: Blackwell, 1989), 177.

11. Ibid. For an exceptional study of agitation, animatedness, and other non-transcendent emotions, see Sianne Ngai, *Ugly Feelings* (Cambridge, MA: Harvard University Press, 2005).

12. Steven Shaviro, *The Cinematic Body* (Minneapolis: University of Minnesota Press, 1993), 230.

13. Ruiz's *Hypothèse du tableau volé* (1978) is based on the work of Klossowski and was done in collaboration with Klossowski. While loosely depicting the story of Klossowski's *The Baphomet*, it also contains elements from *The Revocation of the Edict of Nantes*, *Roberte Ce Soir*, and *Le Bain de Diane* (Paris: Jean-Jacques Pauvert, 1956; repr. Paris: Éditions de Minuit, 1980).

14. Gilles Deleuze, "Having an Idea in Cinema," in *Deleuze and Guattari: New Mappings in Politics, Philosophy, and Culture*, ed. Eleanor Kaufman and Kevin Jon Heller (Minneapolis: University of Minnesota Press, 1998), 16.

15. Ibid., 19.

16. For a similar analysis of Chris Marker's *La Jetée* involving a sequence of immobile images, see D. N. Rodowick, *Gilles Deleuze's Time Machine* (Durham, NC: Duke University Press, 1997), 4–5.

Chapter 5. Betraying Well (Žižek and Badiou)

1. Žižek, *Organs without Bodies*; and Badiou, *Deleuze: The Clamor of Being*, both hereafter cited in text.

2. Fredric Jameson, "Marxism and Dualism in Deleuze," in *A Deleuzian Century?*, ed. Ian Buchanan (Durham, NC: Duke University Press, 1999), reprinted as "Deleuze and Dualism," in Jameson, *Valences of the Dialectic*. In this work, see also Jameson's discussion of Deleuze and Derrida in the chapter "Hegel's Contemporary Critics," where he writes that they are "philosophers of Difference par excellence, whatever the spelling—yet with this fundamental 'difference' between them, namely that in the long run Deleuze is an ontologist" (114).

3. Slavoj Žižek, *The Puppet and the Dwarf: The Perverse Core of Christianity* (Cambridge, MA: MIT Press, 2003), 17.

4. The body without organs is one of the more elusive terms in Deleuze and Guattari's corpus, and its causal connection to desiring production is a difficult one to resolve. Insofar as the body without organs represents a limit state that is never quite reached, it might be seen as an effect rather than a cause of desiring production and, in this sense, more comparable to the incorporeal effect described in *The Logic of Sense* (Žižek's sterile Sense-Event) rather than the virtual enabler that Žižek makes it out to be. Such a reading of the body without organs is even more discernible in Deleuze and Guattari's *A Thousand Plateaus* (especially chapter 6, "How Do You Make Yourself a Body without Organs?") than it is in *Anti-Oedipus*.

5. See Michael Hardt and Antonio Negri, *Empire* (Cambridge, MA: Harvard University Press, 2000); and their *Multitude: War and Democracy in the Age of Empire* (New York: Penguin, 2004). Badiou does not broach Deleuze's politics as such in his study, though for Badiou the proper political procedure involves the proclamation of fidelity to a process of truth (certainly not a formulation Deleuze would adhere to). This fidelity to a truth process is what Badiou terms an "event," which is distinct from Deleuze's model of an event, the latter being much more explicitly incorporeal or virtual—though Badiou's event takes on its own form of virtuality in the difficulty of trying to locate or define it. Badiou's most extended example of what such an event would look like is his book-length analysis of the Apostle Paul's fidelity to the event of Christ's resurrection. See Alain Badiou, *Saint Paul: The Foundation of Universalism*, trans. Ray Brassier (Stanford, CA: Stan-

ford University Press, 2003). Badiou is also markedly critical of Hardt and Negri. See Alain Badiou, "Beyond Formalization: An Interview with Alain Badiou" *Angelaki* 8:2 (2003): 111–37. For Žižek's most sustained early response to Badiou, see Slavoj Žižek, *The Ticklish Subject: The Absent Centre of Political Ontology* (London: Verso, 1999).

6. Charles J. Stivale develops this term in his *The Two-Fold Thought of Deleuze and Guattari: Intersections and Animations* (New York: Guilford, 1998), but more in the service of discussing the thought-form of the collaborative works, whereas here I employ it to explore a doubleness from within.

7. Though Deleuze eschews the transcendental in favor of the immanent, Badiou locates Deleuze's adherence to the category of the virtual as itself a form of transcendence (46). The argument for the in-between, if not the mediating, function of castration is made by Deleuze himself in *The Logic of Sense*: "Castration, then, has a very special situation between that of which it is the result and that which it causes to begin. But it is not castration alone which is in the void, caught between the corporeal surface of sexuality and the metaphysical surface of thought. It is, in fact, the entire sexual surface which is intermediary between physical depth and metaphysical surface" (222). At other points in this discussion, Deleuze aligns castration as well as the phallus more with the realm of incorporeal surface effects. See esp. 206–9.

8. Seminar 6 on desire is one of the many unpublished seminars. For the unofficial translation, see *The Seminar of Jacques Lacan 1958–1959: Desire and Its Interpretation*, trans. Cormac Gallagher, from unedited manuscripts (available through Karnac Books, London, and online at www.lacaninireland.com/web/?page_id=123).

9. Bréhier, *La Théorie des incorporels dans l'ancien stoïcisme*, esp. 46.

10. Deleuze, *The Logic of Sense*, esp. 148–49, 221. The splendor of the incorporeal is not unlike what Lacan characterizes as the strange splendor of beauty in his discussion of Antigone in seminar 7. See Jacques Lacan, *The Ethics of Psychoanalysis*, trans. Dennis Porter (New York: W. W. Norton, 1992).

11. Deleuze, *The Logic of Sense*, 5. The question of the present is taken up in chapter 7 and in part 3.

12. Slavoj Žižek, *On Belief* (London: Routledge, 2001), 1.

13. Walter Benn Michaels, *The Shape of the Signifier: 1967 to the End of History* (Princeton, NJ: Princeton University Press, 2004).

Chapter 6. Lévi-Strauss and the Joy of Abstraction

1. Christopher Johnson, *Claude Lévi-Strauss: The Formative Years* (Cambridge: Cambridge University Press, 2003), 104–5.

2. Francis Korn, *Elementary Structure Reconsidered: Lévi-Strauss on Kinship* (Berkeley: University of California Press, 1973), 21.

3. Jonathan Culler, *Structuralist Poetics* (1975; London: Routledge, 2002), 50.

4. Claude Lévi-Strauss, "The Structural Study of Myth," in *Structural Anthropology*, trans. Claire Jacobson and Brooke Grundfest Schoepf (New York: Basic Books, 1963), 1:206–31. The idea that "since the monsters are overcome by men, we may thus say that the common feature of the third column is *denial of the autochtonous origin of man*" (215) seems of these mappings to be the least clear and well developed.

5. Gilles Deleuze, "How Do We Recognize Structuralism?," in *Desert Islands and Other Texts, 1953–1974*, trans. Michael Taormina, ed. David Lapoujade (New York: Semiotext(e), 2004), 178.

6. See Claude Lévi-Strauss, "Four Winnebago Myths," in *Structural Anthropology* vol. 2, trans. Monique Layton (New York: Basic Books, 1976), 198–210; see also Lévi-Strauss, *The Elementary Structures of Kinship*, trans. James Harle Bell and John Richard von Sturmer, ed. Rodney Needham (Boston: Beacon, 1969).

7. Claude Lévi-Strauss, "Selections from *Introduction to the Work of Marcel Mauss*," in *The Logic of the Gift: Toward an Ethic of Generosity*, ed. Alan D. Schrift (New York: Routledge, 1997), 54. He continues: "I am impelled to seek the reason, not from any wish to criticize, but out of a duty not to let the most fruitful aspect of his thinking be lost or vitiated. . . . There must be some crucial move, somewhere, that Mauss missed. . . . The only way to avoid the dilemma would have been to perceive that the primary, fundamental phenomenon is exchange itself, which gets split up into discrete operations in social life; the mistake was to take the discrete operations for the basic phenomenon" (54–55).

8. Claude Lévi-Strauss, "Structure and Form: Reflections on a Work by Vladimir Propp," in *Structural Anthropology*, vol. 2, 120–24; Vladimir Propp, *Morphology of the Folktale*, trans. Laurence Scott (Austin: University of Texas Press, 1968).

9. Lévi-Strauss, "Structure and Form," 119.

10. Ibid., 131.

11. In *The Political Unconscious: Narrative as a Socially Symbolic Act* (Ithaca: Cornell University Press, 1981), Fredric Jameson points to a dual problematic in Lévi-Strauss's reading of Propp, that on the one hand "Propp's 'functions' fail to attain an adequate level of abstraction" (120), but "[p]aradoxically, however, the other objection to be raised about Propp's method is the opposite one, namely that his analysis is *not yet meaningful enough*" (121). Yet Jameson goes on to attribute both opposing logics to the same impetus toward synchrony (which he then contrasts with the diachronous or historical element—see n. 14 below): "The two objections are thus essentially the same: both the insufficient formalization of the

model (its anthropomorphic traces) and the irreversibility it attributes to the functions are different aspects of the same basic error, namely to have written the primary narratives *in terms of another narrative*, rather than in terms of a synchronic system" (122).

12. Lévi-Strauss, "Structure and Form," 132–33.

13. Paul Ricoeur, "Le Symbolisme et l'explication structurale," *Cahiers internationaux de symbolisme* 4 (1964): 91. Jacques Derrida, *Of Grammatology*, trans. Gayatri Chakravorty Spivak (Baltimore: Johns Hopkins University Press, 1997), esp. 101–40; and Derrida, "Structure, Sign, and Play in the Discourse of the Human Sciences," in *Writing and Difference*, trans. Alan Bass (Chicago: University of Chicago Press, 1978), 278–93. For a reading of Ricoeur that to some extent mirrors Ricoeur's critical analysis of Lévi-Strauss with respect to history, see Jameson, *Valences of the Dialectic*, 475–612. It is interesting that Jameson discusses at some length questions of temporality and eternity in Augustine (where the three orders of time famously merge into one through consciousness) and links Ricoeur's humanism to these concerns. This is actually quite in keeping with my opposing focus on the link between Deleuzian temporality and Aquinas, as this alternate linkage marks an absolute reversal of the Augustinian humanist phenomenology described by Jameson in his lengthy concluding chapter. Indeed at issue here is something akin to a phenomenology of the inhuman structure.

14. To return to Jameson's analysis of Propp and Lévi-Strauss in *The Political Unconscious* (see n. 11 above), he does not simply dismiss this shared synchronic method in favor of a historical, diachronic one but instead insists that the former type of structural analysis (which also includes the work of A. J. Greimas) provides a first and necessary framework for making perceptible the narrative's historicity (which is signaled in Jameson's examples of *The Red and the Black* and *Wuthering Heights* by the antinomy between the "historical" and the "formalist" dimension, which itself allows for the visibility of the former). He writes: "Yet we would not have been able to detect this feature of the work—in which its historicity becomes accessible to us for the first time—had we not begun by respecting the working convention of first-level semiotics, namely that the text was at the start to be analyzed and laid out *as though* it were the replication of Propp's narrative line or 'deep structure' " (129, emphasis in original). While the argument of this chapter suggests an intermingling of diachrony and synchrony in the C-A-C versus A-C-A structure outlined below, it similarly appears that the joyous structure of the A-C-A would not be perceptible without the "first-level semiotics" of the C-A-C.

15. Karl Marx, *Capital: A Critique of Political Economy*, vol. 1, trans. Ben Fowkes (New York: Vintage Books, 1977).

16. For a very different consideration of the relation of "structure" to non-

reciprocity and entropy, see Michel Serres's incisive reading of La Fontaine's fable "The Wolf and the Lamb": "Knowledge in the Classical Age: La Fontaine and Descartes," in *Hermes: Literature, Science, Philosophy*, ed. Josué V. Harari and David F. Bell (Baltimore: Johns Hopkins University Press, 1982), 15–28. Serres highlights the relation of structure to minimal and maximal points as it might be traced to Plato and above all to Descartes, but even through Leibniz, and puts this under the sign of the wolf, the hunt, and the military arts. It seems that this line of analysis, while overlapping in certain respects with the terms and thinkers outlined here, resides in a parallel but noncoincident universe, for it is one in which the anthropomorphic subject still holds sway. Although not mentioned by Serres, Badiou's Platonism would serve as an exemplary last outpost of the trajectory outlined.

17. Deleuze, *The Logic of Sense*, 36–37.

18. Ibid., 38.

19. Ibid., 38–39, my emphasis, except for French quotations and "*proper name*."

20. Gilles Deleuze, *Proust and Signs*, trans. Richard Howard (New York: George Braziller, 1972). Deleuze opens with a discussion of jealousy's attentiveness to the reading of signs. He writes, "[T]he first law of love is subjective: subjectively, jealousy is deeper than love, it contains love's truth. This is because jealousy goes further in the apprehension and interpretation of signs" (9). For more on the question of Deleuze's reading of signs in Proust, see Ronald Bogue, *Deleuze on Literature* (New York: Routledge, 2003); and specifically on the sign of love, see Keith W. Faulkner, *The Force of Time: An Introduction to Deleuze through Proust* (Lanham, MD: University Press of America, 2008). Both of these books also touch on the themes of the next chapter, especially the distinction between masochism and sadism.

21. See Deleuze, *Proust and Signs*, where he discusses the convergence of "the series approach[ing] its own law" and "our capacity to love approach[ing] its own end" (68). This movement to higher distinction or organization and subsequent receding back to the lower level is notable in its affinity with Sartre's model of the serial structure that can turn into the more praxis-oriented group and then descend back into the serial (Deleuze's chapter is titled "Series and Group"), except that in Sartre there is a political hierarchy that favors the group. Deleuze's hierarchical model in the Proust book revolves around the question of art rather than seriality. See Sartre, *Critique of Dialectical Reason*.

22. Deleuze, *Proust and Signs*, 66.

23. Ibid., 72.

Chapter 7. Extreme Formality

1. Gilles Deleuze, *Spinoza: Practical Philosophy*, trans. Robert Hurley (San Francisco: City Lights Books, 1988); Michel Foucault, preface to Deleuze and Guattari, *Anti-Oedipus*, xv; Deleuze and Guattari, *What Is Philosophy?*; Deleuze, "Immanence: A Life," *Pure Immanence: Essays on a Life*, trans. Anne Boyman (New York: Zone Books, 2001).

2. Deleuze, *The Logic of Sense*, 149.

3. Lacan, *The Ethics of Psychoanalysis*, 314.

4. Ibid., 319.

5. See my extended discussion of this in "Why the Family Is Beautiful (Lacan against Badiou)," *Diacritics* 32:3–4 (2002), 135–51.

6. See Gilles Deleuze and Leopold von Sacher-Masoch, *Présentation de Sacher-Masoch* (Paris: Éditions de Minuit, 1967), which contains "Le froid et le cruel" by Deleuze and "Venus à la fourrure" by Sacher-Masoch. English translation: *Masochism*, trans. Jean McNeil (New York: George Braziller, 1971;. rpt. New York: Zone Books, 1989). The latter edition hereafter cited in text as CC.

7. Deleuze, *The Logic of Sense*, 63.

8. See Maurice Blanchot, *The Instant of My Death*, and Jacques Derrida, *Demeure: Fiction and Testimony*, trans. Elizabeth Rottenberg (Stanford, CA: Stanford University Press, 2000).

9. For a detailed discussion of Deleuze's relation to Masoch, see Edward P. Kazarian, "The Revolutionary Unconscious: Deleuze and Masoch," *SubStance* 39:2 (2010): 91–106.

10. Gilles Deleuze, "Michel Tournier and the World without Others," appendix to *The Logic of Sense*, 311. Hereafter cited in text as WwO. Originally published as "Une théorie d'Autrui (Autrui, Robinson et le pervers): Michel Tournier: *Vendredi ou les limbes du Pacifique*," *Critique* 241 (1967), 503–25.

11. See Quentin Meillassoux, *After Finitude: An Essay on the Necessity of Contingency*, trans. Ray Brassier (London: Continuum, 2008).

12. I tone down my condemnation of the Deleuzian possible in light of Ronald Bogue's excellent defense of it in Deleuze's later work and in relation to the arts as opposed to philosophy. Nonetheless, Bogue also locates the strong critique of the possible in Deleuze's 1967 essay on Tournier (and its link to the "a priori Other"). See Ronald Bogue, "The Art of the Possible," *Revue internationale de philosophie* 61: 241 (2007, n. 3), 273–86. I also wish to thank Professor Bogue for helpful comments he has made over the years, and for sending me some of his unpublished materials, which assisted in the composition of my introduction.

13. See Aquinas, *Summa Theologica*, 1a q. 10, a. 4, and *Summa contra Gentiles*, I.15, II.19. Interestingly, in another strange affinity with Aquinas—because

Deleuze, as discussed in the introduction, is always at pains to attack Aquinas's model of analogy, given his adherence to Scotus's model of univocity—he notes in "Coldness and Cruelty," a propos of the distinction between sadism and masochism, that "[t]he concurrence of sadism and masochism is fundamentally one of analogy only, their processes and formations are entirely different" (46). So here, analogy is not too terrible and in fact partakes of a logic of difference. For a damning discussion of Aquinas in the course lectures, see Deleuze, "Seminar on Scholasticism and Spinoza."

14. For a tour de force mapping of the workings of genesis in *Difference and Repetition* and *The Logic of Sense*, see Joe Hughes, *Deleuze and the Genesis of Representation* (London: Continuum, 2008). See also Levi Bryant on the static genesis and the structure-Other in *Difference and Givenness: Deleuze's Transcendental Empiricism and the Ontology of Immanence* (Evanston, IL: Northwestern University Press, 2008), esp. 220–62.

15. See Deleuze, *Proust and Signs*, and the discussion of that work in the preceding chapter.

16. Deleuze, *Difference and Repetition*, 115. Deleuze uses the same phrasing when he writes, "The extreme formality is there only for an excessive formlessness (Hölderlin's *Unförmliche*)" (91). ("L'extrême formalité n'est là que pour un informel excessif," *Différence et répétition* [Paris: Presses Universitaires de France, 1968], 122.) As John Marks writes with regard to judgment and cruelty:

> This means that the doctrine of judgement is only apparently more moderate than a system of "cruelty" according to which debt is measured in blood and inscribed directly on the body, since it condemns us to infinite restitution and servitude. Deleuze goes further to show how these four "disciples" [Nietzsche, D. H. Lawrence, Kafka, Artaud] elaborate a whole system of "cruelty" that is opposed to judgement, and which constitutes the basis for an ethics. The domination of the body in favour of consciousness leads to an impoverishment of our knowledge of the body. We do not fully explore the capacities of the body, and in the same way that the body surpasses the knowledge we have of it, so thought also surpasses the consciousness we have of it. Once we can begin to explore these new dimensions—the *unknown* of the body and the *unconscious* of thought—we are in the domain of ethics." (John Marks, "Ethics," in *The Deleuze Dictionary*, ed. Adrian Parr, rev. ed. (Edinburgh: Edinburgh University Press, 2010)

17. It is quite startling that the writings of the very early Deleuze (at age twenty-one in 1946) take up some of the same themes, in nascent form, that I am here associating with "anethics": the a priori Other and its undoing, sadism, things in themselves, the solitary, the perverse, and the aristocratic, not to mention Proust

and Sartre. See Gilles Deleuze, "Statements and Profiles," trans. and introduced by Keith W. Faulkner, *Angelaki* 8:3 (2003): 85–93; and especially Faulkner's excellent essay on the young Deleuze's "Description of a Woman" (1945) in conjunction with "Statements and Profiles," "Deleuze in Utero: Deleuze-Sartre and the Essence of Woman," *Angelaki* 7:3 (2002): 25–43.

18. Deleuze, *Difference and Repetition*, 88–89.

19. There are nonetheless points of confusion in the above passage such as the claim that the future and past "follow *a priori* from the order of time." How does one follow a priori? Is there then a second order of past and present that follows from a third synthesis of time?

20. Deleuze, *Difference and Repetition*, 111.

21. See especially Keith W. Faulkner's *Deleuze and the Three Syntheses of Time* (New York: Peter Lang, 2006), in which empty time is distinguished from eternity in the following fashion: "[U]nlike eternity, empty time retains events" (103). I am not entirely convinced that events indeed survive empty time, but it does seem quite plausible that they could be generated from empty time, in a fashion pertaining to the questions raised in n. 19 above. See also Jay Lampert, *Deleuze and Guattari's Philosophy of History* (London: Continuum, 2006), for an excellent and provocative discussion of the third synthesis of time.

22. Deleuze gives a similar gloss on the deep ontology of Freud's death instinct at a later point in "Coldness and Cruelty" when he writes that "Thanatos *is*; it is an absolute. And yet the 'no' does not exist in the unconscious because destruction is always presented as the other side of a construction" (116). My brief analysis of Deleuze's not entirely negative relation to Freud does not do justice to the complexity of this relation. For more on this topic, see Keith Ansell Pearson, *Germinal Life: The Difference and Repetition of Deleuze* (London: Routledge, 1999), esp. 104–21; and Christian Kerslake, *Deleuze and the Unconscious* (London: Continuum, 2007). My reading of Deleuze on Freud is more positive than that of Pearson or Kerslake, and this is perhaps because in highlighting the above notion of a positive space for the yes that is not exactly the unconscious but instead some version of the death instinct, it is more akin to Kerslake's claim that Deleuze's "unconscious" is really more like a pure form of Bergsonian memory than something that works according to a Freudian structure of repression. Though it must be noted that Freud's *Beyond the Pleasure Principle*, trans. James Strachey (New York: W. W. Norton, 1961), itself departs from the economic repressive model of Freud's work from the 1910s, hence its interest for Deleuze in this pre–*Anti-Oedipus* moment.

23. Faulkner notes in *Deleuze and the Three Syntheses of Time* that "the practical law itself signifies nothing other than the empty form of time" (106) and observes that Deleuze reads Kant's second critique through the lens of Freud's death instinct, which is also linked to the body without organs. For a succinct

overview of Deleuze's reading of Kant's three critiques with respect to the problem of genesis, see Deleuze, "The Idea of Genesis in Kant's Esthetics," in *Desert Islands and Other Texts.*

24. Deleuze writes in *Difference and Repetition* that "the thinker is necessarily solitary and solipsistic" (282) and evokes solitude with respect to sadism in "Coldness and Cruelty" (19). In a very different fashion, Mario Perniola's *Sex Appeal of the Inorganic*, trans. Massimo Verdicchio (London: Continuum, 2004), also distinguishes between masochism and sadism in that for Perniola sadism embraces the "neutral and impersonal sexuality of the thing that feels" (43), whereas masochism is at odds with this.

25. This is another way in which I would take issue with Peter Hallward's focus on creativity as the motor force behind Deleuze's thought in *Out of This World.* See discussion in introduction. Moreover, structure in my reading also retains the potential to be beyond or outside of relationality, something precluded by Sean Bowden's excellent but more analytically inspired analysis of the pivotal role of structure in *The Logic of Sense* read alongside "How Do We Recognize Structuralism?" See Bowden, *The Priority of Events*, esp. 152–84.

26. Deleuze writes in *Difference and Repetition* that "the dark precursor is not a friend" (145).

Chapter 8. French Thought and the Space of American Literature

1. Alexis de Tocqueville, *Democracy in America*, 2 vols., trans. Henry Reeve (New Rochelle, NY: Arlington House, 1966), 1:1.

2. Ibid., 2:1.

3. Ibid., 2:1–6.

4. Ibid., 2:2.

5. Ibid., 2:3.

6. Jean-Pierre Fichou, *La Civilisation américaine*, 3rd ed. (Paris: Presses Universitaires de France, 1979), 46, my translation.

7. Jean Baudrillard, *America*, trans. Chris Turner (London: Verso, 1988), 39.

8. Ibid., 5. Baudrillard says much the same thing when he writes, "I ask of the Americans only that they be Americans. I do not ask them to be intelligent, sensible, original, I ask them only to populate a space incommensurate with my own, to be for me the highest astral point, the finest orbital space" (27–28).

9. Ibid., 54–55.

10. For a more comprehensive assessment of the connection between America and French intellectuals, see Jean-Philippe Mathy, *Extrême Occident: French Intellectuals and America* (Chicago: University of Chicago Press, 1993), especially chapter 5, "Poetics of Space: The Body of America" (163–206) and chapter 6,

"(Running) Out of History," (207–50), which deals extensively with Baudrillard's *America*. While my analysis is greatly indebted to Mathy's study, it takes up the same relation from a less general perspective and singles out the specific configuration of movement/immobility and exterior/interior space.

11. Deleuze, "On the Superiority of Anglo-American Literature," in Deleuze and Parnet, *Dialogues*, 36–37, my emphasis.

12. Myra Jehlen makes a similar revalorization in *American Incarnation: The Individual, the Nation, and the Continent* (Cambridge, MA: Harvard University Press, 1986) when she writes that "rather than ask why Americans lack a 'sense of history,' we can now as well ask why Europeans have the particular sense of it that they do" (7). Jehlen displays a strikingly Deleuzian sensibility when she considers the dialectic as a function of time and posits a more spatialized America as "outside of time" and thus not caught up in the either-or of the dialectic but rather in the both-and of "nonantagonistic opposition" (12). Finally, she also gestures to a connection between physical and mental space: "For it is precisely because the concept of America is rooted in the physical finite that it can become metaphysical" (9).

13. Deleuze and Parent, *Dialogues*, 37–38, my emphasis.

14. Many of these linkages between mind, movement, and matter were expressed well before Deleuze by yet another Frenchman, Henri Bergson. See especially Bergson's *Matter and Memory*, as well as Deleuze's *Bergsonism*. As mentioned in chapter 2, for an in-depth study of Deleuze's philosophical proximity to Bergson, see Hardt, *Gilles Deleuze: An Apprenticeship in Philosophy*, 1–25; and Boundas, "Deleuze-Bergson," 81–106.

15. Jack Kerouac, *On the Road* (New York: Penguin Books, 1976), 82.

16. Ibid., 120–21.

17. Ibid., 102.

18. Ibid., 138.

19. Vladimir Nabokov, *Lolita* (New York: Vintage International, 1955), 152.

20. Ibid., 175–76.

21. One need only cite the collection of essays on Auster published in French that grew out of an entire colloquium devoted to Auster in France. See Annick Duperray, ed., *L'oeuvre de Paul Auster: Approches et lectures plurielles* (Arles: Actes Sud; [Marseilles]: Université de Provence-IRMA [GRENA], 1995). See especially the section on *The New York Trilogy*, 75–149.

22. Paul Auster, *The Music of Chance* (New York: Penguin Books, 1990), 1.

23. Ibid., 6.

24. Ibid., 12. As Tim Woods glosses the same passage (in "*The Music of Chance*: Aleatorical (Dis)harmonies Within 'The City of the World' " in *Beyond the Red Notebook: Essays on Paul Auster*, ed. Dennis Barone (Philadelphia: University of

Pennsylvania Press, 1995), 143–161), "This disembodiment, a release of self-consciousness, is also a shift from the material world into the immaterial world, or the space of incorporality" (147).

25. Auster, *The Music of Chance*, 109–10.

26. Ibid., 125.

27. Deleuze and Guattari, *A Thousand Plateaus*, 280–81.

28. Paul Auster, *Ghosts*, in *The New York Trilogy* (New York: Penguin Books, 1990), 171–72.

Chapter 9. Bartleby, the Immobile

1. Herman Melville, "Bartleby, the Scrivener," in *Billy Budd and Other Stories* (New York: Penguin Classics, 1986).

2. Considered here are Deleuze's "Bartleby; or, The Formula," in *Essays Critical and Clinical*, trans. Daniel W. Smith and Michael A. Greco (Minneapolis: University of Minnesota Press, 1997); Jacques Rancière, "Deleuze, Bartleby, and the Literary Formula," in *The Flesh of Words: The Politics of Writing*, trans. Charlotte Mandell (Stanford, CA: Stanford University Press, 2004); and Giorgio Agamben, "Bartleby, or On Contingency," in *Potentialities*, trans. Daniel Heller-Roazen (Stanford, CA: Stanford University Press, 1999).

3. See especially the work of Antonio Negri, in particular Michael Hardt and Antonio Negri, *Labor of Dionysus: A Critique of the State-Form* (Minneapolis: University of Minnesota Press, 1994); and the essays by Agamben, Lazzarato, and Virno in *Radical Thought in Italy: A Potential Politics*, ed. Michael Hardt and Paolo Virno (Minneapolis: University of Minnesota Press, 1996). See also Jean-Luc Nancy, *The Inoperative Community*, trans. Peter Connor, Lisa Garbus Michael Holland, and Simona Sawhney (Minneapolis: University of Minnesota Press, 1991); Maurice Blanchot, *The Unavowable Community*, trans. Pierre Joris (Barrytown, NY: Station Hill, 1988); and Giorgio Agamben, *The Coming Community*, trans. Michael Hardt (Minneapolis: University of Minnesota Press, 1993).

4. Deleuze, "Bartleby; or, The Formula," 73.

5. Ibid., 76.

6. Ibid., 85.

7. Rancière, "Deleuze, Bartleby, and the Literary Formula," 161.

8. Ibid., 164.

9. Ibid.,155.

10. Deleuze, "Bartleby; or, The Formula,"84.

11. Deleuze, *Cinema 1: The Movement-Image*, 184–86.

12. See my discussion of Deleuze, Badiou, hierarchy, and the question of the political in *At Odds with Badiou*. I argue that Deleuze and Badiou both employ

hierarchy and are in certain senses royal or "aristocratic" thinkers. This is not leveled as a criticism of either Deleuze or Badiou but more nearly an implicit siding with Badiou in his criticisms in *Metapolitics* of Rancière's model of equality. See Alain Badiou, *Metapolitics*, trans. Jason Barker (London: Verso, 2005), 107–23.

13. Quoted in Rancière, "Deleuze, Bartleby, and the Literary Formula," 161.

14. Ibid., 162.

15. Ibid.

16. Rancière claims that Deleuze's *Proust and Signs* represents an "entire effort . . . to expel the animal/mineral metaphor from Proust's work to construct a . . . coherent figure of the vegetative work as manifestation of an *anti-physis* for which Charlus's body, surcharged with signs, serves as blazon" (ibid., 152). In fact Deleuze registers considerable unease at the vegetative image of the three trees in Proust's *Within a Budding Grove*, the vegetative being something that is more resistant to explanation than the madeleine. See Deleuze, *Proust and Signs*, 56.

17. Rancière, "Deleuze, Bartleby, and the Literary Formula," 161–62.

18. Melville, "Bartleby," 27–28.

19. Agamben, "Bartleby, or On Contingency," 255.

20. Indeed, the oscillation between the potential to be or to not be might be considered the central abiding theme of all of Agamben's oeuvre. For more on this, see my "The Saturday of Messianic Time (Agamben and Badiou on the Apostle Paul)," *South Atlantic Quarterly* 107:1 (2008): 37–54.

21. Playfully symptomatic of this contagion is Branka Arsić's *Passive Constitutions; or, 7½ Times Bartleby* (Stanford, CA: Stanford University Press, 2007), in which the seven and a half chapters are entitled "Bartleby or Error," "Bartleby or Melancholy," "Bartleby or Stupidity," "Bartleby or the Junkie," "Bartleby or the Impersonal," "Bartleby or the Celibatory Machine," Bartleby or the Witness," and "Bartleby or the Cloud."

Chapter 10. In the Middle of Things

1. Gilles Deleuze, *The Fold: Leibniz and the Baroque*, trans. Tom Conley (Minneapolis: University of Minnesota Press, 1993), 29.

2. Ibid., 119.

3. Baudrillard, *America*, 23.

4. Ibid., 6, 7.

5. Andrew Marvell, "To His Coy Mistress," in *The Complete Poems*, ed. Elizabeth Story Donno (Middlesex, UK: Penguin Books, 1972), 51.

6. Baudrillard, *America*, 79.

Chapter 11. Midnight, or the Inertia of Being

1. Deleuze, *The Logic of Sense*, 222. This relation of the deaths corresponds to the two notions of Other—the structure-Other and the a priori Other—outlined in chapter 7, though Deleuze does not draw out this parallel explicitly.

2. Deleuze and Parnet, "On the Superiority of Anglo-American Literature," in *Dialogues*, 37.

3. Maurice Blanchot, *The Space of Literature*, trans. Ann Smock (Lincoln: University of Nebraska Press, 1982), 30–33, my emphasis.

4. Ibid., 22.

5. Ibid., 37.

6. Ibid., 46.

7. Ibid., 93. Interestingly, Deleuze links cyclical time to the present-inflected Chronos in *The Logic of Sense*: "Thus the time of the present is always a limited but infinite time; infinite because cyclical, animating a physical eternal return as the return of the Same, and a moral eternal wisdom as the wisdom of the Cause" (61). Whereas Deleuze gives this a subtle pejorative twist by linking it to the Same and the Cause, it is strikingly proximate to Badiou's model of temporality ("limited but infinite"). See my discussion of Deleuze and Badiou in *At Odds with Badiou*.

8. Blanchot, *The Space of Literature*, 116.

9. Deleuze, *The Logic of Sense*, 63.

10. Blanchot, *The Space of Literature*, 109–10.

11. Though *The Space of Literature* certainly represents a reaction to the engaged humanism of Sartre's "What Is Literature?," it is not nearly as at odds with Sartre's philosophical studies, or with his early short stories collected in *The Wall*, as it might seem. See *What Is Literature? and Other Essays*, trans. Bernard Frechtman (Cambridge, MA: Harvard University Press, 1988); and *The Wall*, discussed in chapter 1.

12. Maurice Blanchot, *When the Time Comes*, trans. Lydia Davis (Barrytown, NY: Station Hill, 1985), 21. The narrator indeed refers openly to his extraordinary immobility: "my steps were the steps of immobility"(4), and "there could be nothing of me there but this endless immobility" (6).

13. For a discussion of the immobility or potential mobility of natural objects from a legal standpoint, see Christopher D. Stone, *Should Trees Have Standing? and Other Essays on Law, Morals, and the Environment* (Dobbs Ferry, NY: Oceana, 1996).

14. See Deleuze, *Essays Critical and Clinical.*

15. Deleuze, *Cinema 1: The Movement-Image*, 185.

16. Thomas Carl Wall, *Radical Passivity: Levinas, Blanchot, and Agamben* (Albany: State University of New York Press, 1999), 88.

17. Wall writes, "That death does not complete the movement of dying disturbs the often too facilely understood notion of human finitude: the equation of death with rest and peace. Far from setting a limit to dying, death magnifies its incompletion, placing it, as it were, under glass. Like the time of writing and of the image, it never achieves the present moment" (ibid., 95).

18. Ibid., 79–80.

19. Ibid., 83–84.

20. Mouloud Mammeri, *La Colline oubliée* (Paris: Plon, 1952), 26, my translation.

21. See Mildred Mortimer, *Mouloud Mammeri, écrivain algérien* (Sherbrooke, Québec: Naaman, 1982), 14.

22. Maurice Blanchot, *The Writing of the Disaster*, trans. Ann Smock (Lincoln: University of Nebraska Press, 1995), 4.

23. Such an oblique portrayal of the disaster, in this case the Algerian War, through an eerie defamiliarization of the everyday, is the achievement of Mohammed Dib's *Who Remembers the Sea*, trans. Louis Tremaine (Boulder, CO: Lynne Rienner, 1985).

24. Ann Smock, "Translator's Remarks," in Blanchot, *The Writing of the Disaster*, ix.

25. Wall, *Radical Passivity*, 95.

26. See Richard Dedekind, "Continuity and Irrational Numbers," in *Essays on the Theory of Numbers*, trans. Wooster Woodruff Beman (Chicago: Open Court, 1909).

27. For a meditation on unbecoming, see John Paul Ricco, *The Logic of the Lure* (Chicago: University of Chicago Press, 2002).

28. See Sartre, *Being and Nothingness*, and Sartre, *Critique of Dialectical Reason*. For a redemptive discussion of the in-itself and the practico-inert as concepts that enable a theory of the inhuman and the incorporeal avant la lettre, see my "To Cut Too Deeply and Not Enough."

29. Ann Smock, *What Is There to Say?* (Lincoln: University of Nebraska Press, 2003), viii–ix.

30. Ibid., 84.

31. Christopher Diffee, "Postponing Politics in Hawthorne's *Scarlet Letter*," *MLN* 111:5 (1996), 835–871 quote on 837.

32. Ibid., 840.

33. Ibid., 839.

Chapter 12. Living Virtually in a Cluttered House

1. Gaston Bachelard, *The Poetics of Space*, trans. Maria Jolas (Boston: Beacon, 1969), 8.

2. Ibid., 9–10.

3. Ibid., 16.

4. Deleuze, *The Logic of Sense*, 1.

5. The question of vantage point, orientation, and the relation between phenomenology and sexual and racial orientation is provocatively taken up in Sarah Ahmed's *Queer Phenomenology: Objects, Orientations, Others* (Durham, NC: Duke University Press, 2006). Insofar as "queer" might refer to a spatial perception that is "off center" or "slantwise" (65–66), it is an apt term for what is at stake here. This is all the more pronounced in Eve Kosofsky Sedgwick's ruminations on "queer" as being the mark of something that is perceived differently in childhood (see "Queer and Now" in *Tendencies* [Durham, NC: Duke University Press, 1993], esp. 3). While Ahmed's analysis employs phenomenology strictly to better understand human relationships, I think the more radical approach, something that Deleuze distills from the phenomenologists he reads, is to use phenomenology to broach what it might mean to be a rock.

6. Deleuze, *The Fold: Leibniz and the Baroque*, 29.

7. Ibid., 29.

8. Ibid., 119.

9. Ibid.,11–12.

10. Bernard Cache in *Earth Moves: The Furnishing of Territories*, trans. Anne Boyman (Cambridge, MA: MIT Press, 1995) presents the body/soul relation in a spatial framework similar to what will be discussed presently: "Body and soul are thus constructed in the same manner, at the intersection of a cluster of radii of curvature. Both are then simply effects of convergence that are constituted in space, on either side of the surface of the world that envelops them. It follows that the body is no less ideal than the mind, despite the claims of those who would like to see it as something material or tangible" (120).

11. Deleuze's most focused discussion of Leibniz and incompossibility can be found in *The Fold: Leibniz and the Baroque*, "Incompossibility, Individuality, Liberty," 59–75, and in *The Logic of Sense*, "Sixteenth Series of the Static Ontological Genesis," 109–117.

12. Lacan, *The Four Fundamental Concepts of Psychoanalysis*, 85.

13. Deleuze, *The Fold: Leibniz and the Baroque*, 49. Deleuze also defines inflection as that place where the tangent crosses the curve (14) or "the pure Event of the line or of the point, the Virtual, ideality par excellence" (18). It is important to note that Deleuze makes a distinction between differen*t*iation and differen*c*ia-

tion. See *Difference and Repetition*, esp. chapter 4, "Ideas and the Synthesis of Difference."

14. For further architectural applications and developments of Deleuze's concept of the fold, see Greg Lynn, ed., *Folding in Architecture*, (London: Architectural Design, 1993). See also the special issue "The Virtual House" in *ANY* 19/20 (1997).

15. Cache, *Earth Moves*, 34.

16. Ibid., 36.

17. As Cache states, "[T]he slippage we had noted at the site of the point of inflection in many baroque motifs would seek to expose this singularity. The whole question would then be to make the barely perceptible perceptible, without altering its nature" (38).

18. In this regard, inflection can be compared to Husserl's notion of the *phenomenological reduction*, which is performed by a bracketing or " 'parenthesizing' of the Objective world" so that new avenues of perception are opened. See Edmund Husserl, *Cartesian Meditations*, trans. Dorion Cairns (Dordrecht, The Netherlands: Kluwer Academic, 1991), 20.

19. Cache, *Earth Moves*, 36.

20. Ibid., 48.

21. Ibid. Fredric Jameson views Deleuze as essentially a modernist philosopher—something I would claim holds for most of his so-called French postmodern generation—and such an assessment goes hand in hand with the analyses presented here. See *Valences of the Dialectic*, 113.

22. Such a methodological assumption is to my mind the underlying flaw in the work of Pierre Bourdieu.

23. Vincent P. Pecora, *Households of the Soul* (Baltimore: Johns Hopkins University Press, 1997), xi.

24. Ibid., 13.

25. Ibid., 28–30.

26. Ibid., 27.

27. Marcel Proust, *Time Regained*, vol. 6 of *In Search of Lost Time*, trans. Andreas Mayor and Terence Kilmartin, rev. D. J. Enright (New York: Modern Library, 1993), 287.

28. Another evocative object for Marcel is the stiff napkin he is given with the refreshments he is served while waiting in the Guermantes library. The napkin reminds him of a stiff towel he had used to wipe his face at another significant moment of his life, his arrival at Balbec:

> and this napkin now, in the library of the Prince de Guermantes's house, unfolded for me—concealed within its smooth surfaces and its folds—the

> plumage of an ocean green and blue like the tail of a peacock. And what I found myself enjoying was not merely these colours but a whole instant of my life on whose summit they rested, an instant which had been no doubt an aspiration towards them and which some feeling of fatigue or sadness had perhaps prevented me from enjoying at Balbec but which now, freed from what is necessarily imperfect in external perception, pure and disembodied, caused me to swell with happiness (259).

Like the two-story house, the napkin, itself replete with folds, unfolds a new perception that affords Marcel no small measure of joy. On yet another level, which is beyond the scope of this study, a more refined critique of Proustian temporality and its relation to objects such as the napkin or the madeleine is in order. These objects, capable of provoking an array of different sensory modes of recollection, serve primarily as catalysts and conduits into the past. This structure, alluring though it is, does not in my opinion fundamentally alter received concepts of linear time. In this sense, it is the diametric opposite of the example that opens Deleuze's *The Logic of Sense*. For Proust, the object is in the present, and the memory it evokes is in the past; Deleuze, alongside phenomenologists such as Beauvoir, Merleau-Ponty, and Sartre, conceptualizes far more radical possibilities of the simultaneous coexistence of an object in two (or more) distinct temporal registers. To put it in the terms of *Difference and Repetition*, Proust does not get beyond the second synthesis of time (memory).

29. Denis Wood and Robert J. Beck, with Ingrid Wood, Randall Wood, and Chandler Wood, *Home Rules* (Baltimore: Johns Hopkins University Press, 1994), 223.

30. See Maurice Merleau-Ponty, "The Intertwining—the Chiasm" in *The Visible and the Invisible*, 130–55. Merleau-Ponty highlights the impossibility of determining which hand does the touching and which is the one touched.

31. For a strong argument against the primacy of vision in literary-philosophical works such as these, see Martin Jay, *The Denigration of Vision in Twentieth-Century French Thought* (Berkeley: University of California Press, 1993).

32. Wood and Beck, *Home Rules*, 304.

33. Ibid., 305.

34. Ibid., 304.

35. Maurice Blanchot, *Aminadab* (Paris: Gallimard, 1942). In an otherwise critical review of this novel, Sartre offers singular praise for the executioner episode. See "*Aminadab;* ou, du fantastique considéré comme un langage," in *Situations I* (Paris: Gallimard, 1947), 113–32 (see p. 125). Additionally, in *The Poetics of Space*, Bachelard provides a brief analysis of the "radically simple" inner room in Blanchot's novel *Death Sentence* (228–29).

BIBLIOGRAPHY

Agamben, Giorgio. *The Coming Community*. Trans. Michael Hardt. Minneapolis: University of Minnesota Press, 1993.

———. *Homo Sacer: Sovereign Power and Bare Life*. Trans. Daniel Heller-Roazen. Stanford, CA: Stanford University Press, 1998.

———. *Potentialities*. Trans. Daniel Heller-Roazen. Stanford, CA: Stanford University Press, 1999.

Ahmed, Sarah. *Queer Phenomenology: Objects, Orientations, Others*. Durham, NC: Duke University Press, 2006.

Alquié, Ferdinand. *Le Désir d'éternité*. Paris: Presses Universitaires de France, 1943.

Aquinas, Thomas. *Summa contra Gentiles*. 5 vols. Trans. Fathers of the English Dominican Province. London: Washbourne, 1914–38.

———. *Summa Theologica*. 5 vols. Trans. Fathers of the English Dominican Province. Notre Dame, IN: Christian Classics, 1981.

Aristotle. *The Basic Works of Aristotle*. Ed. Richard McKeon. New York: The Modern Library, 2001.

Arsić, Branka. *Passive Constitutions; or, 7½ Times Bartleby*. Stanford, CA: Stanford University Press, 2007.

Auster, Paul. *The Music of Chance*. New York: Penguin Books, 1990.

———. *The New York Trilogy*. New York: Penguin Books, 1990.

Bachelard, Gaston. *The Poetics of Space*. Trans. Maria Jolas. Boston: Beacon, 1969.

Badiou, Alain. "Beyond Formalization: An Interview with Alain Badiou." *Angelaki* 8:2 (2003): 111–37.

———. *The Century*. Trans. Alberto Toscano. London: Polity, 2007.

———. *Deleuze: The Clamor of Being*. Trans. Louise Burchill. Minneapolis: University of Minnesota Press, 2000.

———. *Logics of Worlds*. Trans. Alberto Toscano. London: Continuum, 2009.

———. *Metapolitics*. Trans. Jason Barker. London: Verso, 2005.

———. *Number and Numbers*. Trans. Robin Mackay. London: Polity, 2008.

———. *Saint Paul: The Foundation of Universalism*. Trans. Ray Brassier. Stanford, CA: Stanford University Press, 2003.

Balsamo, Anne. *Technologies of the Gendered Body: Reading Cyborg Women.* Durham, NC: Duke University Press, 1996.
Barthes, Roland. *Mythologies.* Trans. Annette Lavers. New York: Hill and Wang, 1972.
Bataille, Georges. *Story of the Eye.* Trans. Joachim Neugroschel. San Francisco: City Lights Books, 1987.
Baudrillard, Jean. *America.* Trans. Chris Turner. London: Verso, 1988.
Beckman, Karen. *Crash: Cinema and the Politics of Speed and Stasis.* Durham, NC: Duke University Press, 2010.
Bennett, Jane. *Vibrant Matter: A Political Ecology of Things.* Durham, NC: Duke University Press, 2010.
Bergson, Henri. *Matter and Memory.* Trans. N. M. Paul and W. S. Palmer. New York: Zone Books, 1991.
Bianco, Giuseppe. "Jean Hyppolite et Ferdinand Alquié." In *Aux sources de la pensée de Gilles Deleuze 1*, ed. Stéfan Leclercq. Mons, Belgium: Éditions Sils Maria, 2005.
Blanchot, Maurice. *Aminadab.* Paris: Gallimard, 1942.
———. *Death Sentence.* Trans. Lydia Davis. Barrytown, NY: Station Hill, 1978.
———. *The Instant of My Death.* And Jacques Derrida, *Demeure: Fiction and Testimony.* Trans. Elizabeth Rottenberg. Stanford, CA: Stanford University Press, 2000.
———. *The Space of Literature.* Trans. Ann Smock. Lincoln: University of Nebraska Press, 1982.
———. *The Unavowable Community.* Trans. Pierre Joris. Barrytown, NY: Station Hill, 1988.
———. *When the Time Comes.* Trans. Lydia Davis. Barrytown, NY: Station Hill, 1985.
———. *The Writing of the Disaster.* Trans. Ann Smock. Lincoln: University of Nebraska Press, 1995.
Bogue, Ronald. "The Art of the Possible." *Revue internationale de philosophie* 61:241 (2007, no. 3): 273–86.
———. *Deleuze on Literature.* New York: Routledge, 2003.
Bonin, Thérèse. *Creation as Emanation: The Origin of Diversity in Albert the Great's "On the Causes and the Procession of the Universe."* Notre Dame, IN: University of Notre Dame Press, 2001.
Boundas, Constantin V. *Deleuze: A Critical Reader*, ed. Paul Patton. Oxford: Blackwell, 1996.
———. "Deleuze-Bergson: An Ontology of the Virtual." In *Deleuze: A Critical Reader*, ed. Paul Patton. Oxford: Blackwell, 1996.

Bowden, Sean. *The Priority of Events: Deleuze's "Logic of Sense."* Edinburgh: Edinburgh University Press, 2011.

Braidotti, Rosi. *Nomadic Subjects: Embodiment and Sexual Difference in Contemporary Feminist Theory*. New York: Columbia University Press, 1994.

———. *Patterns of Dissonance*. Cambridge: Routledge, 1991.

———. "Toward a New Nomadism: Feminist Deleuzian Tracks; or, Metaphysics and Metabolism." In *Gilles Deleuze and the Theater of Philosophy*, ed. Dorothea Olkowski and Constantin V. Boundas. New York: Routledge, 1994.

Brassier, Ray. *Nihil Unbound: Enlightenment and Extinction*. Basingstoke, UK: Palgrave Macmillan, 2007.

Bréhier, Émile. *La Théorie des incorporels dans l'ancien stoïcisme*. Paris: Vrin, 1970.

Brown, G. Spenser. *Laws of Form*. New York: Bantam, 1972.

Bryant, Levi. *Difference and Givenness: Deleuze's Transcendental Empiricism and the Ontology of Immanence*. Evanston, IL: Northwestern University Press, 2008.

Buchanan, Ian. *Deleuzism: A Metacommentary*. Durham, NC: Duke University Press, 2000.

———. "The Problem of the Body in Deleuze and Guattari, Or, What Can a Body Do?" *Body and Society* 3:3 (September 1997).

Buchanan, Ian, and Claire Colebrook, eds. *Deleuze and Feminist Theory*. Edinburgh: Edinburgh University Press, 2000.

Butler, Judith. *Bodies That Matter: On the Discursive Limits of "Sex."* New York: Routledge, 1993.

Cache, Bernard. *Earth Moves: The Furnishing of Territories*. Trans. Anne Boyman. Cambridge, MA: MIT Press, 1995.

Clark, Tim. "Deleuze and Structuralism: Towards a Geometry of Sufficient Reason." In *Deleuze and Philosophy: The Difference Engineer*, ed. Keith Ansell Pearson. London: Routledge, 1997.

Cooper, Melinda. "The Living and the Dead: Variations on *De Anima*." *Angelaki* 7:3 (2002): 81–104.

Cross, Richard. *Duns Scotus on God*. Aldershot, UK: Ashgate, 2005.

———. *Physics of Duns Scotus: The Scientific Context of a Theological Vision*. Oxford: Oxford University Press, 1998.

Culler, Jonathan. *Structuralist Poetics*. 1975; New York: Routledge, 2002.

Damasio, Antonio R. *Looking for Spinoza: Joy, Sorrow, and the Feeling Brain*. Orlando, FL: Harcourt, 2003.

Dedekind, Richard. "Continuity and Irrational Numbers." In *Essays on the Theory of Numbers*, trans. Wooster Woodruff Beman. Chicago: Open Court, 1909.

DeLanda, Manuel. *Intensive Science and Virtual Philosophy*. London: Continuum, 2005.

Deleuze, Gilles. *Bergsonism*. Trans. Barbara Habberjam and Hugh Tomlinson. New York: Zone Books, 1991.

———. *Cinema 1: The Movement-Image*. Trans. Barbara Habberjam and Hugh Tomlinson. Minneapolis: University of Minnesota Press, 1986.

———. *Cinema 2: The Time-Image*. Trans. Robert Galeta and Hugh Tomlinson. Minneapolis: University of Minnesota Press, 1989.

———. *Desert Islands and Other Texts, 1953–1974*. Trans. Michael Taormina. Ed. David Lapoujade. Los Angeles: Semiotext(e), 2004.

———. *Deux régimes de fous: Textes et entretiens, 1975–1995*. Paris: Éditions de Minuit, 2003.

———. *Difference and Repetition*. Trans. Paul Patton. New York: Columbia University Press, 1994.

———. *Différence et répétition*. Paris: Presses Universitaires de France, 1968.

———. *Essays Critical and Clinical*. Trans. Daniel W. Smith and Michael A. Greco. London: Verso, 1998.

———. *Expressionism in Philosophy: Spinoza*. Trans. Martin Joughin. New York: Zone Books, 1992.

———. *The Fold: Leibniz and the Baroque*. Trans. Tom Conley. Minneapolis: University of Minnesota Press, 1993.

———. "Having an Idea in Cinema." In *Deleuze and Guattari: New Mappings in Politics, Philosophy, and Culture*, ed. Eleanor Kaufman and Kevin Jon Heller. Minneapolis: University of Minnesota Press, 1998.

———. "Immanence: A Life." In *Pure Immanence: Essays on a Life*, trans. Anne Boyman. New York: Zone Books, 2001.

———. *The Logic of Sense*. Trans. Mark Lester with Charles Stivale. New York: Columbia University Press, 1990.

———. *Logique du sens*. Paris: Éditions de Minuit, 1969.

———. "Mathesis, Science and Philosophy." *Collapse: Philosophical Research and Development* 3 (2007): 141–55.

———. *Nietzsche and Philosophy*. Trans. Hugh Tomlinson. New York: Columbia University Press, 1983.

———. *Proust and Signs*. Trans. Richard Howard. New York: George Braziller, 1972.

———. "Seminar on Scholasticism and Spinoza." 14 January 1974. www.webdeleuze.com.

———. *Spinoza: Practical Philosophy*. Trans. Robert Hurley. San Francisco: City Lights Books, 1988.

———. "Statements and Profiles." Trans. and introduced by Keith W. Faulkner. *Angelaki* 8:3 (2003): 85–93.

———. "Une Théorie d'autrui (Autrui, Robinson et le pervers): Michel Tournier: *Vendredi ou les limbes du pacifique*." *Critique* 241 (1967): 503–25.

Deleuze, Gilles, and Félix Guattari. *Anti-Oedipus: Capitalism and Schizophrenia*. Trans. Mark Seem, Robert Hurley, and Helen R. Lane. Minneapolis: University of Minnesota Press, 1983.

———. *Kafka: Toward a Minor Literature*. Trans. Dana Polan. Minneapolis: University of Minnesota Press, 1986.

———. *A Thousand Plateaus: Capitalism and Schizophrenia*. Trans. Brian Massumi. Minneapolis: University of Minnesota Press, 1987.

———. *What Is Philosophy?* Trans. Hugh Tomlinson and Graham Burchell. New York: Columbia University Press, 1994.

Deleuze, Gilles, and Claire Parnet. *Dialogues*. Trans. Hugh Tomlinson and Barbara Habberjam. New York: Columbia University Press, 1987.

Deleuze, Gilles, and Leopold von Sacher-Masoch. *Masochism*. Trans. Jean McNeil. New York: Zone Books, 1989.

———. *Présentation de Sacher-Masoch*. Paris: Éditions de Minuit, 1967.

Delpech-Ramey, Joshua. *The Hermetic Deleuze: Philosophy and Spiritual Ordeal*. Durham, NC: Duke University Press, forthcoming.

———. "Without Art: Peter Hallward's *Out of This World: Deleuze and the Philosophy of Creation*." *Journal for Culture and Religious Theory* 8:3 (Fall 2007): 136–45.

Delpech-Ramey, Joshua, and Paul A. Harris, eds. "Spiritual Politics after Deleuze." Special issue, *SubStance* 39:1 (2010).

Derrida, Jacques. *Archive Fever: A Freudian Impression*. Trans. Eric Prenowitz. Chicago: University of Chicago Press, 1996.

———. *Demeure: Fiction and Testimony*. And Maurice Blanchot, *The Instant of My Death*. Trans. Elizabeth Rottenberg. Stanford, CA: Stanford University Press, 2000.

———. "Eating Well; or, the Calculation of the Subject: An Interview with Jacques Derrida." In *Who Comes after the Subject*, ed. Peter Connor, Eduardo Cadava, and Jean-Luc Nancy. New York: Routledge, 1991.

———. *Of Grammatology*. Trans. Gayatri Chakravorty Spivak. Baltimore: Johns Hopkins University Press, 1997.

———. *Writing and Difference*. Trans. Alan Bass. Chicago: University of Chicago Press, 1978.

Dib, Mohammed. *Who Remembers the Sea*. Trans. Louis Tremaine. Boulder, CO: Lynne Rienner, 1985.

Diffee, Christopher. "Postponing Politics in Hawthorne's *Scarlet Letter.*" *MLN* 111:5 (1996): 835–871.

Dosse, François. *Gilles Deleuze and Félix Guattari: Intersecting Lives.* Trans. Deborah Glassman. New York: Columbia University Press, 2010.

Duffy, Simon, ed. *Virtual Mathematics: The Logic of Difference.* Manchester: Clinamen, 2006.

Duperray, Annick. *L'Oeuvre de Paul Auster: Approches et lectures plurielles.*: Arles: Actes Sud; Marseille: Université de Provence-IRMA (GRENA), 1995.

Faulkner, Keith W. *Deleuze and the Three Syntheses of Time.* New York: Peter Lang, 2006.

———. "Deleuze in Utero: Deleuze-Sartre and the Essence of Woman." *Angelaki* 7:3 (2002): 25–43.

———. *The Force of Time: An Introduction to Deleuze through Proust.* Lanham, MD: University Press of America, 2008.

Fichou, Jean-Pierre. *La Civilisation américaine.* 3rd ed. Paris: Presses Universitaires de France, 1979.

Flaxman, Gregory, ed. *The Brain Is the Screen: Deleuze and the Philosophy of Cinema.* Minneapolis: University of Minnesota Press, 2000.

Foucault, Michel. *Language, Counter-Memory, Practice.* Trans. Sherry Simon and Donald F. Bouchard. Ithaca, NY: Cornell University Press, 1977.

———. *The Order of Things: An Archaeology of the Human Sciences.* New York: Vintage Books, 1994.

Freud, Sigmund. *Beyond the Pleasure Principle.* Trans. James Strachey. New York: W. W. Norton, 1961.

Fuss, Diana. *The Sense of an Interior: Four Writers and the Rooms That Shaped Them.* New York: Routledge, 2004.

Gatens, Moira. *Imaginary Bodies: Ethics, Power, and Corporeality.* New York: Routledge, 1996.

———. "Through a Spinozist Lens: Ethology, Difference, Power." In *Deleuze: A Critical Reader*, ed. Paul Patton. Oxford: Blackwell, 1996.

Gilson, Étienne. *Jean Duns Scot: Introduction à ses positions fondamentales.* Paris: Vrin, 1952.

———. "John Duns Scotus." In *A Gilson Reader*, ed. Anton C. Pegis. Garden City, NY: Hanover House, 1957.

Grosz, Elizabeth, ed. *Becomings: Explorations in Time, Memory, and Futures.* Ithaca, NY: Cornell University Press, 1999.

———. "Intensities and Flows." In *Volatile Bodies: Toward a Corporeal Feminism.* Bloomington: Indiana University Press, 1994.

——— "A Thousand Tiny Sexes: Feminism and Rhizomatics." In *Gilles Deleuze and the Theater of Philosophy*, ed. Dorothea Olkowski and Constantin V. Boundas. New York: Routledge, 1994.

Hallward, Peter. *Out of This World: Deleuze and the Philosophy of Creation*. London: Verso, 2006.

Hardt, Michael. *Gilles Deleuze: An Apprenticeship in Philosophy*. Minneapolis: University of Minnesota Press, 1993.

Hardt, Michael, and Antonio Negri. *Empire*. Cambridge, MA: Harvard University Press, 2000.

———. *Labor of Dionysus: A Critique of the State-Form*. Minneapolis: University of Minnesota Press, 1994.

———. *Multitude: War and Democracy in the Age of Empire*. New York: Penguin, 2004.

Hardt, Michael, and Paolo Virno, eds. *Radical Thought in Italy: A Potential Politics*. Minneapolis: University of Minnesota Press, 1996.

Heidegger, Martin. *The Fundamental Concepts of Metaphysics: World, Finitude, Solitude*. Trans. William McNeill and Nicholas Walker. Bloomington: Indiana University Press, 1995.

Hughes, Joe. *Deleuze and the Genesis of Representation*. London: Continuum, 2008.

Husserl, Edmund. *Cartesian Meditations*. Trans. Dorion Cairns. Dordrecht, The Netherlands: Kluwer Academic, 1991.

Irigaray, Luce. *The Sex Which Is Not One*. Trans. Catherine Porter with Carolyn Burke. Ithaca, NY: Cornell University Press, 1985.

Jameson, Fredric. "Marxism and Dualism in Deleuze." In *A Deleuzian Century?*, ed. Ian Buchanan. Durham, NC: Duke University Press, 1999. Reprinted in Jameson, *Valences of the Dialectic*.

———. *The Political Unconscious: Narrative as a Socially Symbolic Act*. Ithaca, NY: Cornell University Press, 1981.

———. *Sartre: The Origins of a Style*. New Haven, CT: Yale University Press, 1961.

———. *Valences of the Dialectic*. London: Verso, 2009.

Jay, Martin. *Downcast Eyes: The Denigration of Vision in Twentieth-Century French Thought*. Berkeley: University of California Press, 1993.

Jehlen, Myra. *American Incarnation: The Individual, the Nation, and the Continent*. Cambridge, MA: Harvard University Press, 1986.

Johnson, Christopher. *Claude Lévi-Strauss: The Formative Years*. Cambridge: Cambridge University Press, 2003.

Johnston, Adrian. *Žižek's Ontology: A Transcendental Materialist Theory of Subjectivity*. Evanston, IL: Northwestern University Press, 2008.

Kaufman, Eleanor. *At Odds with Badiou: Politics, Dialectics, and Religion from Sartre and Deleuze to Lacan and Agamben*. New York: Columbia University Press, forthcoming.

———. *The Delirium of Praise: Bataille, Blanchot, Deleuze, Foucault, Klossowski*. Baltimore: Johns Hopkins University Press, 2001.

———. "The Saturday of Messianic Time (Agamben and Badiou on the Apostle Paul)." *South Atlantic Quarterly* 107:1 (2008): 37–54.

———. " 'To Cut Too Deeply and Not Enough': Violence and the Incorporeal." In *Theology and the Political: The New Debates*, ed. John Milbank, Creston Davis, and Slavoj Žižek. Durham, NC: Duke University Press, 2005. Originally published in *Parallax* 9:1 (2003): 14–27.

———. "Why the Family Is Beautiful (Lacan against Badiou)." *Diacritics* 32:3–4 (2002): 135–51.

Kaufman, Eleanor, and Kevin Jon Heller, eds. *Deleuze and Guattari: New Mappings in Politics, Philosophy, and Culture*. Minneapolis: University of Minnesota Press, 1998.

Kazarian, Edward P. "The Revolutionary Unconscious: Deleuze and Masoch." *SubStance* 39:2 (2010): 91–106.

Kerouac, Jack. *On the Road*. New York: Penguin Books, 1976.

Kerslake, Christian. *Deleuze and the Unconscious*. London: Continuum, 2007.

Klossowski, Pierre. *The Baphomet*. Trans. Sophie Hawkes and Stephen Sartarelli. New York: Marsilio, 1988.

———. *La Monnaie vivante*. Photographs by Pierre Zucca. Paris: Eric Losfeld, 1970.

———. *La Monnaie vivante*. Paris: Éditions Joëlle Losfeld, 1994.

———. *Le Bain de Diane*. Paris: Jean-Jacques Pauvert, 1956. Reprint, Paris: Éditions de Minuit, 1980.

———. *Nietzsche and the Vicious Circle*. Trans. Daniel W. Smith. Chicago: University of Chicago Press, 1997.

———. *"Roberte Ce Soir" and "The Revocation of the Edict of Nantes."* Trans. Austryn Wainhouse. New York: Marion Boyars, 1989.

Kordela, A. Kiarina. "Dialectics and Structuralism as Valences." Unpublished essay.

Korn, Francis. *Elementary Structure Reconsidered: Lévi-Strauss on Kinship*. Berkeley: University of California Press, 1973.

Labbie, Erin Felicia. *Lacan's Medievalism*. Minneapolis: University of Minnesota Press, 2006.

Lacan, Jacques. *The Ethics of Psychoanalysis* (Seminar 7). Trans. Dennis Porter. New York: W. W. Norton, 1992.

———. *The Four Fundamental Concepts of Psycho-analysis* (Seminar 11). Trans. Alan Sheridan. London: W. W. Norton, 1981.

———. *The Other Side of Psychoanalysis* (Seminar 17). Trans. Russell Grigg. New York: W. W. Norton, 2007.

LaCapra, Dominick. "Early Theoretical Studies: Art Is an Unreality." In *Jean-Paul Sartre*, ed. Harold Bloom. Philadelphia: Chelsea House, 2001.

Lampert, Jay. *Deleuze and Guattari's Philosophy of History*. London: Continuum, 2006.

Leclercq, Stéfan. "Jean Duns Scot." In *Aux sources de la pensée de Gilles Deleuze 1*, ed. Stéfan Leclercq. Mons, Belgium: Sils Maria, 2005.

Lévi-Strauss, Claude. *The Elementary Structures of Kinship*. Trans. James Harle Bell and John Richard von Sturmer. Ed. Rodney Needham. Boston: Beacon, 1969.

———. *Structural Anthropology*. Trans. Monique Layton. New York: Basic Books, 1963.

———. *Structural Anthropology*. Vol. 2. Trans. Monique Layton. New York: Basic Books, 1976.

———. "Selections from Introduction to the Work of Marcel Mauss." In *The Logic of the Gift: Toward an Ethic of Generosity*, ed. Alan D. Schrift. New York: Routledge, 1997.

Lingis, Alphonso. *Foreign Bodies*. New York: Routledge, 1994.

Lloyd, Genevieve. *Spinoza and the Ethics*. New York: Routledge, 1996.

Lynn, Greg, ed. *Folding in Architecture*. London: Architectural Design, 1993.

Lyotard, Jean-François. "Acinema." In *The Lyotard Reader*, ed. Andrew Benjamin. Oxford: Blackwell, 1989.

———. *Libidinal Economy*. Trans. Iain Hamilton Grant. Bloomington: Indiana University Press, 1993.

MacCannell, Juliet Flower, and Laura Zakarin, eds. *Thinking Bodies*. Stanford, CA: Stanford University Press, 1994.

Mackay, Robin. "Editorial Introduction." *Collapse: Philosophical Research and Development* 3 (2007): 4–38.

Mammeri, Mouloud. *La Colline oubliée*. Paris: Plon, 1952.

Marks, John. "Ethics." In *The Deleuze Dictionary*, rev. ed., ed. Adrian Parr. Edinburgh: Edinburgh University Press, 2010.

Marvell, Andrew. *The Complete Poems*. Ed. Elizabeth Story Donno. Middlesex, UK: Penguin Books, 1972.

Massumi, Brian. *Parables for the Virtual: Movement, Affect, Sensation*. Durham, NC: Duke University Press, 2002.

———. *A User's Guide to Capitalism and Schizophrenia: Deviations from Deleuze and Guattari*. Cambridge, MA: MIT Press, 1992.

Marx, Karl. *Capital: A Critique of Political Economy* Vol. 1. Trans. Ben Fowkes. New York: Vintage Books, 1977.

Mathy, Jean-Philippe. *Extrême-Occident: French Intellectuals and America*. Chicago: University of Chicago Press, 1993.

McNulty, Tracy. *The Hostess: Hospitality, Ethics, and the Expropriation of Identity*. Minneapolis: University of Minnesota Press, 2007.

Meeker, Natania. *Voluptuous Philosophy: Literary Materialism in the French Enlightenment*. New York: Fordham University Press, 2006.

Meillassoux, Quentin. *After Finitude: An Essay on the Necessity of Contingency*. Trans. Ray Brassier. London: Continuum, 2008.

Melville, Herman. "Bartleby, the Scrivener." In *Billy Budd and Other Stories*. New York: Penguin Classics, 1986.

Merleau-Ponty, Maurice. *Phenomenology of Perception*. Trans. Colin Smith. London: Routledge, 2000.

———. *The Visible and the Invisible*. Trans. Alphonso Lingis. Evanston, IL: Northwestern University Press, 1968.

Michaels, Walter Benn. *The Shape of the Signifier: 1967 to the End of History*. Princeton, NJ: Princeton University Press, 2004.

Milbank, John. "The Soul of Reciprocity Part Two: Reciprocity Granted." *Modern Theology* 17:4 (October 2001): 485–507.

Mortimer, Mildred. *Mouloud Mammeri, écrivain algérien*. Sherbrooke, Québec: Naaman, 1982.

Nabokov, Vladimir. *Lolita*. New York: Vintage International, 1955.

Nancy, Jean-Luc. *The Inoperative Community*. Trans. Lisa Garbus, Michael Holland, Peter Connor, and Simona Sawhney. Minneapolis: University of Minnesota Press, 1991.

Ngai, Sianne. *Ugly Feelings*. Cambridge, MA: Harvard University Press, 2005.

Olkowski, Dorothea. "Nietzsche's Dice Throw: Tragedy, Nihilism, and the Body without Organs." In *Gilles Deleuze and the Theater of Philosophy*, ed. Constantin V. Boundas and Dorothea Olkowski. New York: Routledge, 1994.

Olkowski, Dorothea, and Constantin V. Boundas, eds. *Gilles Deleuze and the Theater of Philosophy*. New York: Routledge, 1994.

Pearson, Keith Ansell. *Germinal Life: The Difference and Repetition of Deleuze*. London: Routledge, 1999.

Pecora, Vincent P. *Households of the Soul*. Baltimore: Johns Hopkins University Press, 1997.

Perniola, Mario. *Sex Appeal of the Inorganic*. Trans. Massimo Verdicchio. London: Continuum, 2004.

Pierce, Christine. "Holes and Slime: Sexism in Sartre's Psychoanalysis." In *Immovable Laws, Irresistible Rights: Natural Law, Moral Rights, and Feminist Ethics*. Lawrence: University Press of Kansas, 2000.

Pini, Giorgio. *Categories and Logic in Duns Scotus: An Interpretation of Aris-*

totle's Categories in the Late Thirteenth Century. Leiden, The Netherlands: Brill, 2002.

———. "Scotus on Assertion and the Copula: A Comparison with Aquinas." In *Medieval Theories of Assertive and Non-Assertive Language*, ed. L. Valente and A. Maierù. Florence: Olschki, 2004.

———. "Univocity in Scotus's *Quaestiones super Metaphysicam*: The Solution to a Riddle." *Medioevo* 30 (2005): 69–110.

Propp, Vladimir. *Morphology of the Folktale*. Trans. Laurence Scott. Austin: University of Texas Press, 1968.

Protevi, John. *Political Affect: Connecting the Social and the Somatic*. Minneapolis: University of Minnesota Press, 2009.

Proust, Marcel. *Time Regained*. Vol. 6 of *In Search of Lost Time*. Trans. Terence Kilmartin and Andreas Mayor, rev. D. J. Enright. New York: Modern Library, 1993.

Rancière, Jacques. *The Flesh of Words: The Politics of Writing*. Trans. Charlotte Mandell. Stanford, CA: Stanford University Press, 2004.

Ricco, John Paul. *The Logic of the Lure*. Chicago: University of Chicago Press, 2002.

Ricoeur, Paul. "Le Symbolisme et l'explication structurale." *Cahiers internationaux de symbolisme* 4 (1964): 81–96.

Rodowick, D. N. *Gilles Deleuze's Time Machine*. Durham, NC: Duke University Press, 1997.

Rose, Gillian. *Feminism and Geography: The Limits of Geographical Knowledge*. Minneapolis: University of Minnesota Press, 1993.

Ruiz, Raúl, director. *Hypothèse du tableau volé* [The hypothesis of the stolen painting]. 1979.

Sartre, Jean-Paul. "*Aminadab*; ou, du fantastique considéré comme un langage." In *Situations I*. Paris: Gallimard, 1947.

———. *Being and Nothingness*. Trans. Hazel E. Barnes. New York: Washington Square, 1984.

———. *Critique of Dialectical Reason: Theory of Practical Ensembles*. Trans. Alan Sheridan-Smith. London: NLB, 1976.

———. *The Imaginary: A Phenomenological Psychology of the Imagination*. Trans. Jonathan Webber. New York: Routledge, 2004.

———. *The Transcendence of the Ego*. Trans. Forrest Williams and Robert Kirkpatrick. New York: Farrar, Straus, and Giroux, 1957.

———. *The Wall*. Trans. Lloyd Alexander. New York: New Directions, 1975.

———. *What Is Literature? and Other Essays*. Trans. Bernard Frechtman. Cambridge, MA: Harvard University Press, 1988.

Sauvagnargues, Anne. *Deleuze: L'Empirisme transcendental*. Paris: Presses Universitaires de France, 2009.

Schrift, Alan D. *Twentieth-Century French Philosophy: Key Themes and Thinkers*. Malden, MA: Blackwell, 2006.

Scotus, John Duns. *God and Creatures: The Quodlibetal Questions*. Trans. Felix Alluntis and Allan B. Wolter. Princeton, NJ: Princeton University Press, 1975.

———. *Philosophical Writings: A Selection*. Trans. Allan Wolter. New York: Nelson, 1962.

———. *A treatise on God as first principle; a revised Latin text of the* De primo principio *translated into English along with two related questions from an early commentary on the Sentences*. Trans. Allan B. Wolter. Chicago: Forum Books, 1966.

Sedgwick, Eve Kosofsky. *Tendencies*. Durham, NC: Duke University Press, 1993.

Serres, Michel. "Knowledge in the Classical Age: La Fontaine and Descartes." In *Hermes: Literature, Science, Philosophy*, ed. David F. Bell and Josué V. Harari. Baltimore: Johns Hopkins University Press, 1982.

Shaviro, Steven. *The Cinematic Body*. Minneapolis: University of Minnesota Press, 1993.

———. *Without Criteria: Kant, Whitehead, Deleuze, and Aesthetics*. Cambridge, MA: MIT Press, 2009.

Smith, Daniel W. "The Doctrine of Univocity: Deleuze's Ontology of Immanence." In *Deleuze and Religion*, ed. Mary Bryden. London: Routledge, 2001.

———. "The Inverse Side of the Structure: Žižek on Deleuze and Lacan." *Criticism* 46:4 (Fall 2004): 635–50.

Smock, Ann. *What Is There to Say?* Lincoln: University of Nebraska Press, 2003.

Spinoza, Benedict de. *Ethics*. Trans. R. H. M. Elwes. New York: Dover, 1955.

———. *A Theologico-Political Treatise*. Trans. R. H. M. Elwes. New York: Dover, 1951.

Stivale, Charles J. *The Two-Fold Thought of Deleuze and Guattari: Intersections and Animations*. New York: Guilford, 1998.

Stone, Christopher D. *Should Trees Have Standing? and Other Essays on Law, Morals, and the Environment*. Dobbs Ferry, NY: Oceana, 1996.

Sutton, Damian. *Photography, Cinema, Memory: The Crystal Image of Time*. Minneapolis: University of Minnesota Press, 2009.

Thacker, Eugene. *After Life*. Chicago: University of Chicago Press, 2010.

Tocqueville, Alexis de. *Democracy in America*. 2 vols. Trans. Henry Reeve. New Rochelle, NY: Arlington House, 1966.

"The Virtual House." *ANY* 19/20 (1997).

Velde, Rudi te. "Metaphysics and the Question of Creation: Thomas Aquinas, Duns Scotus and Us." In *Belief and Metaphysics*, ed. Conor Cunningham and Peter M. Candler. London: SCM Press, 2007.

Wall, Thomas Carl. *Radical Passivity: Levinas, Blanchot, and Agamben.* Albany: State University of New York Press, 1999.

Widder, Nathan. "John Duns Scotus." In *Deleuze's Philosophical Lineage*, ed. Jon Roffe and Graham Jones. Edinburgh: Edinburgh University Press, 2009.

Wood, Dennis, and Robert J. Beck, with Ingrid Wood, Randall Wood, and Chandler Wood. *Home Rules.* Baltimore: Johns Hopkins University Press, 1994.

Woods, Tim. "*The Music of Chance*: Aleatorical (Dis)Harmonies within 'The City of the World.'" In *Beyond the Red Notebook: Essays on Paul Auster*, ed. Dennis Barone. Philadelphia: University of Pennsylvania Press, 1995.

Yerushalmi, Yosef Hayim. *Freud's Moses: Judaism Terminable and Interminable.* New Haven, CT: Yale University Press, 1991.

Žižek, Slavoj. *On Belief.* London: Routledge, 2001.

———. *Organs without Bodies: On Deleuze and Consequences.* New York: Routledge, 2004.

———. *The Puppet and the Dwarf: The Perverse Core of Christianity.* Cambridge, MA: MIT Press, 2003.

———. *The Ticklish Subject: The Absent Centre of Political Ontology.* London: Verso, 1999.

Žižek, Slavoj, and John Milbank. *The Monstrosity of Christ: Paradox or Dialectic?*, ed. Creston Davis. Cambridge, MA: MIT Press, 2009.

INDEX